CENTRAL EUROPE TOWARDS MONETARY UNION: MACROECONOMIC UNDERPINNINGS AND FINANCIAL REPUTATION

Central Europe towards Monetary Union: Macroeconomic Underpinnings and Financial Reputation

edited by

Ronald MacDonald

and

Rod Cross

Department of Economics,
International Centre for Macroeconomic Modelling,
University of Strathclyde, Glasgow,
United Kingdom

KLUWER ACADEMIC PUBLISHERS
BOSTON / DORDRECHT / LONDON

A C.I.P. Catalogue record for this book is available from the Library of Congress.

ISBN 0-7923-7967-5

Published by Kluwer Academic Publishers,
P.O. Box 17, 3300 AA Dordrecht, The Netherlands.

Sold and distributed in North, Central and South America
by Kluwer Academic Publishers,
101 Philip Drive, Norwell, MA 02061, U.S.A.

In all other countries, sold and distributed
by Kluwer Academic Publishers,
P.O. Box 322, 3300 AH Dordrecht, The Netherlands.

Printed on acid-free paper

Printed in the Netherlands.

TABLE OF CONTENTS

List of Contributors vii

Chapter 1 Introduction
Ronald MacDonald and Rod Cross 1

Chapter 2 Macroeconomic Policy and Institutions During the Transition to European Union Membership
William Branson, Jorge Braga Macedo and Jürgen von Hagen 5

Chapter 3 Real Exchange Rate Behaviour and Resource Allocation in the Visegrád Four
C. Paul Hallwood and Ronald MacDonald 31

Chapter 4 Monetary Control on the Path to EU and EMU Membership
Rod Cross 59

Chapter 5 Impact of Capital Inflows into the Czech Republic and Policy Responses
Miroslav Hrncir 71

Chapter 6 Reforms and Development of the Banking Systems in Transition Economies
Eva Várhegyi 89

Chapter 7 Financial Fragility, or What Went Right and What Could Go Wrong in Central European Banking
Christian Weller and Jürgen von Hagen 121

Chapter 8 Bond Markets in Advanced Transition: a Synopsis of the Visegrád Bond Markets
Katinka Barysch, Friedrich Heinemann and Max Steiger 149

Chapter 9 Market Structure, Return Dynamics and Efficiency of the Visegrád Stock Markets
Jürgen Kähler 247

Index 277

LIST OF CONTRIBUTORS

Ronald MacDonald
University of Strathclyde

Rod Cross
University of Strathclyde

William Branson
Princeton University, CEPR and NBER

Jorge Braga De Macedo
Nova University at Lisbon, CEPR and NBER

Jürgen von Hagen
University of Bonn and CEPR

C. Paul Hallwood
University of Connecticut

Miroslav Hrncir
Czech National Bank

Eva Várhegyi
Center for International Private Enterprise

Christian Weller
University of Bonn

Katinka Barysch
Centre for European Economic Research

Friedrich Heinemann
Centre for European Economic Research

Max Steiger
Centre for European Economic Research

Jürgen Kähler
Universität Erlangen-Nürnberg

Chapter 1

INTRODUCTION*

Ronald MacDonald
Department of Economics and International Centre for Macroeconomic Modelling, University of Strathclyde

Rod Cross
Department of Economics and International Centre for Macroeconomic Modelling, University of Strathclyde

* This volume grew out of a research project, "The Implications of Financial Innovation and Deregulation for Economies in Transition", which was financed by the European Commission under research grant 94-0715-R. The editors and contributors are grateful to the European Commission for the funding of this project. The views expressed in this volume are those of the authors, and do not represent the views of the Commission.

A key objective of the Central European Economies (CEEs) on their transition path from planned to more market-oriented economies has been membership of the European Union (EU). The start of Economic and Monetary Union (EMU) in 1999 has added membership of the EMU to the agenda for the CEEs. EU membership was a key theme at the inter-governmental meeting of Czechoslovakia, Hungary and Poland in Visègrad as these countries embarked on transition. Early in 1993 the Czech Republic and Slovakia separated, so there are now four Visègrad countries. The task of preparing for EU and EMU membership is the key theme underlying the papers in this volume. The Czech Republic, Hungary and Poland have been fast-tracked for EU membership along with Cyprus, Estonia and Slovenia, with 2003 being the earliest feasible date for admission. Slovakia, because of concerns expressed about its political structures, is on the list of CEEs earmarked for a later round of negotiations regarding EU membership.

R. MacDonald and R. Cross (eds.), Central Europe Towards Monetary Union: Macroeconomic Underpinnings and Financial Reputation, 1–4.

There are many issues to be resolved before the Visègrad countries are admitted into the EU. This volume focuses on the issues relating to macroeconomic policies and financial sector structures. The macroeconomic policy papers focus on the macroeconomic policy mix, fiscal policies and institutional structures, monetary policies, exchange rate policies and capital flows. The financial sector papers cover the banking sector and equity and bond markets. Some of the papers address these issues from the vantage point reached after a decade of transition, others confine themselves to some of the key features of major upheavals in the earlier years of transition.

In Chapter 2 William Branson, Jorge Braga de Macedo and Jürgen von Hagen analyse the appropriate macroeconomic policy mix for the Visègrad economies. After detailing the institutional procedures underlying the formulation of fiscal policy, they recommend an assignment of a Pre-Pegging Exchange Rate Regime (PPERR), aimed at nominal exchange rate devaluation, which in turn should achieve a real exchange rate devaluation to achieve external balance on the trajectory to EU membership; and a Multi-Annual Fiscal Adjustment Strategy (MAFAS) assigned to maintain internal balance.

Chapter 3, by Paul Hallwood and Ronald MacDonald, analyses the path of the real exchange rate during the transition process. They focus on the role played by the increase in importance of market-led resource allocation for the behaviour of real exchange rates, and use econometric tests to determine if there are significant differences between the time series properties of the exchange rates in the Visègrad economies and those in more advanced market economies.

Monetary policy issues are addressed by Rod Cross in Chapter 4. This contribution discusses the general issues underlying monetary control in the Visègrad economies. Inflation rates in these economies have some way to fall in order to satisfy EMU entry requirements. The relevance of monetarist precepts and the natural rate of unemployment hypothesis are discussed along with the role of expectations, foreign exchange market intervention and monetary targets in determining the effects of disinflation on the real economies of the Visègrad countries.

The impact of capital inflows into the transition economies is considered in Chapter 5. Miroslav Hrncir focuses on the experience of the Czech Republic prior to the 1997 crisis. The capital inflows partly reflected the foreign direct investment to be expected in a transition economy, but external borrowing by Czech entities played a major role alongside short-term inflows attracted by the then fixed exchange rate and substantial interest rate differential. Hrncir assesses the effectiveness of the sterilisation measures undertaken and the lessons for regulatory and structural policies, and for the exchange rate regime.

In Chapter 6, Èva Várhegyi provides an overview of the task of transforming the Visègrad banking systems from mono-banking to a system concordant with EU banking directives. The weaknesses inherited from the central planning era, such as non-performing loans to state-owned enterprises, made privatisation and measures to encourage competition more difficult. The restructuring measures pursued in the Visègrad countries are compared, and the progress in satisfying EU directives is assessed.

After the Czech Republic was forced to abandon its fixed exchange rate regime in May 1997, many commentators expected the CEEs to suffer banking crises similar to those that occurred subsequently in Russia and South East Asia. In Chapter 7, Christian Weller and Jürgen von Hagen analyse why this did not happen. They argue that a juxtaposition of factors peculiar to the early stages of transition, particularly the relatively small degree of lending to the private sector and the underdeveloped asset markets, helped save the CEE banking sectors from major financial crises. They warn that these blessings in disguise will disappear as the CEEs move towards EU accession, and warn that improvements in bank regulation and supervision are vital to avoid exposure to such crises in the future.

The development of bond markets in the Visègrad economies is discussed in Chapter 8. Katinka Barysch, Friedrich Heinemann and Max Steiger provide a comprehensive account of the institutional and legal frameworks underlying the primary and secondary bond markets and their integration with international capital markets. They highlight low liquidity, incompleteness in the term structure of interest rates and the absence of derivative markets as areas where much ground needs to be made up before EU accession.

This volume concludes in Chapter 9 with Jürgen Kähler's assessment of the structure, rate of return dynamics and efficiency of the Visègrad stock markets. Using the London stock markets as a benchmark, Kähler argues that the Budapest, Prague and Warsaw, but not the Bratislava, markets have made major progress in terms of organisational efficiency and regulation. The markets in question lack the depth and sophistication of mature markets like London, but show the signs of mature, emerging stock markets.

The chapters presented in this volume grew out of papers presented at a series of workshops in Stary Smòkovec, Budapest and Glasgow: the editors are grateful to the organisers of these workshops for the excellent hospitality. The contributors to these chapters owe a major debt of gratitude to the following workshop participants, from whose first-hand knowledge the contributors benefited greatly: Jarek Bauc (University of Lodz); Rita Bozzai (Financial Research Limited, Budapest); Antoni Chawluk (University of Oxford); Pal Gaspar (Financial Research Institute, Budapest); Zora Kominkova (Slovak National Bank); Roman Matousek (Czech National Bank); Josef Mervart (Czech National Bank); Victoria Muckova (Slovak National Bank); Marion Nemec (Slovak National Bank); Jarek Neneman (University of Lodz); Jerzy Prsuki (University of Lodz) and Andrej Raczko (University of Lodz).

Chapter 2

MACROECONOMIC POLICY AND INSTITUTIONS DURING THE TRANSITION TO EUROPEAN UNION MEMBERSHIP*

William H. Branson
Princeton University, CEPR and NBER

Jorge Braga Macedo
Nova University at Lisbon, CEPR and NBER

Jürgen von Hagen
Bonn University and CEPR

ABSTRACT

A framework is developed for macroeconomic policy analysis in four countries of Central Europe (CE) in transition to EU membership (Czech Republic, Hungary, Poland, and Slovakia). A Multi-Annual Fiscal Adjustment Strategy (MAFAS) and a Pre-Pegging Exchange Rate Regime (PPERR) appropriate for maintaining internal and external balance are described and evidence on budgetary procedures is presented, in comparison with those prevailing in EU member states.

The comparison suggests that the four CE countries are better fit for fiscal stabilization than Greece, Spain and Portugal were in the 1970s. Nevertheless, there is still much room for institutional improvement. A stronger commitment mechanism to fiscal targets at the preparatory stage would improve fiscal performance in all four countries. The adoption of a kind of convergence program would also be made easier if some group procedures can be adopted among them.

* A longer version appeared as NBER Working Paper no. 6555, May 1998 and will be published in the 25th anniversary volume of WIIW, Vienna. We thank participants of ACE project conferences at the University of Manheim, in Stary Smokovec, Slovakia, and at the University of Strathclyde. for their comments and Jeff Frankel and Paul de Grauwe for their discussion at the 1995 NBER and 1997 European Summer Institutes respectively. The second author is President of the OECD Development Centre, but the opinions expressed remain personal.

R. MacDonald and R. Cross (eds.), Central Europe Towards Monetary Union: Macroeconomic Underpinnings and Financial Reputation, 5–29.

1. INTRODUCTION

A common orientation for macroeconomic policy and institutions can be found in the countries of Central Europe (CE) aiming at membership in the European Union (EU). Policy-making institutions in the Czech Republic, Hungary, Poland and Slovakia will eventually conform to those of the EU. The criteria for joining the single currency set forth in the Treaty on European Union will also imply the eventual convergence of their macroeconomic performance. The process of development of a market economy lasts several decades, and the fulfillment of the criteria is not part of the forthcoming enlargement negotiations. Nevertheless, world financial markets already monitor the change in the economic regime of CE countries towards nominal stability. Indeed, this occurs both in member and associated states. The reason for this scrutiny is that the regime change requires that the national medium term strategy is credible and that the macroeconomic framework is understood not just internationally but also by citizens and social partners within the country.

Whether or not the reform strategy is understood at home and abroad depends on how policy-making institutions interact with the specifics of the economy and society. The absence of a tax system which is efficient, equitable and simple to run is seen as a major microeconomic and macroeconomic obstacle to growth, as well as to social consensus. The same is true, more broadly, of the absence of a transparent legal environment, which deters domestic and foreign investment. These examples show how institutions may determine whether popular support for reforms is sustained during the transition or instead a "stop and go" reform pattern will emerge, delaying adjustment and ultimately threatening national cohesion. That being said, we confine our analysis of institutions to budgetary procedures in four countries in an advanced stage of transition.

Evaluating the macroeconomic policies and performance of an economy in transition is a difficult task. In earlier work, Branson and Macedo (1995) developed a framework for that purpose. Here we present more detailed evidence on Czech, Polish, Hungarian, and Slovak budgetary procedures and we extend the framework.

The first problem Branson and Macedo faced in developing an analytical framework is that, before the beginning of the transition, these economies had very large governments and public enterprise sectors, making it difficult to distinguish monetary from fiscal policy. In a centrally planned economy, there is no private sector, so there is no separate public sector and no public sector deficit or debt. Without a private sector, there is no one for a public sector to have a deficit with. Then monetary policy is simply the provision of finance for investment in the plan. Essentially fiscal and monetary policies are the same thing. The four CE countries were somewhat more advanced, than other transition economies in having some market institutions at the beginning of transition.

As the economies move through the transition, privatization creates a private sector and the distinction between public and private sectors acquires macroeconomic significance. Fiscal policy gradually emerges as the concepts of public expenditure, tax revenues, government budget, and public debt become operational. With the creation of a central bank, and the withdrawal of the central bank from automatic financing of the budget deficit, monetary policy emerges as the provision of credit to the private sector. During the transition, the countries are expected to introduce market-oriented policy-making institutions in which the distinction between fiscal and monetary policy is clear, and the use of these policies in maintaining internal and external balance can be analyzed in the usual fashion.

Fortunately, at least for economic analysis, these national economies, as all others, face an external constraint along the entire transition path. Their foreign debt cannot become so large that international financial markets perceive that they cannot service it. Their export earnings must be sufficient to finance imports and debt service as the economy becomes increasingly marketized. Therefore, the approach we take to the analysis of macroeconomic policy is first to look for signs of external balance, and then to look to internal balance as the economy is increasingly decontrolled. Signs of internal imbalance, either excessive budget deficits or unacceptably high inflation, are taken as indicators that a currently satisfactory external situation could become unsatisfactory in the future, as the internal imbalance spills over to the external sector.

The second problem is how to evaluate macroeconomic policies and, possibly, recommend policy changes, without a quantitative macroeconomic model. Development of a quantitative model is precluded both because the structure of the CE economies is changing rapidly, and because of the lack of sufficient data. To deal with this problem, they developed as a macroeconomic framework the model of external and internal balance with high capital mobility and a fixed real exchange rate that assigns fiscal policy to internal balance and monetary policy to external balance. The focus is on the development of a Multi-Annual Fiscal Adjustment Strategy (MAFAS) and a Pre-Pegging Exchange Rate Regime (PPERR) as instruments for stabilization.

In their approach to external balance, the CE economies could adopt a PPERR that entails essentially no active nominal devaluation aimed at real devaluation as the country converges toward union membership. In their approach to internal balance, the CE countries could adopt a MAFAS. Both of these policy paths could bring the economies to the point of accession to the EU along as smooth a convergence path as possible. In general, PPERR and MAFAS would be forms of credible policy that stabilize the economy as it enters the world market.

The PPERR avoids the "inconsistent trio" of fixed exchange rate, free capital movements, and independent monetary policy by freeing monetary policy to be targeted on external balance, represented by a suitable reserve position. The MAFAS then sets fiscal policy to maintain internal balance, as represented by a low rate of inflation. The arithmetic of debt sustainability can be used to determine the appropriate primary deficit that is consistent with a non-growing ratio of debt to output. Thus the fiscal adjustment can be consistent with low inflation and a non-growing debt ratio.

The institutional environment is an important prerequisite for a successful transition to EU membership. Since 1994, the Transition Report of the European Bank for Reconstruction and Development includes indicators of regime change featuring the development of market institutions. Branson and Macedo (1995) reported "success criteria" ranging from "politics" to "market institutions and business mentality", including 17 "other criteria", such as geographical situation, market size, stability of law, workforce's level of education, international credit standing, quality of the environment, etc. The ranking presented then was Czech Republic, Hungary and Slovenia at the top of the region, closely followed by Poland. Slovakia was somewhat behind, mostly due to a low score on the "politics" dimension. The "other" criteria include "monetary conditions" and "tax advantages" as well as "functioning of state administration" but no mention was made of tax reform, budgetary procedures or the macroeconomic policy mix.

Yet the credibility of the transition also requires policy-making institutions in the monetary and fiscal fields which do not exist under central planning. The requirements are more exacting and more country-specific than the independence of the central bank in matters of monetary policy that was envisioned in the 1992 EU Treaty. Certainly, monetary financing of budget deficits was curtailed during stabilization in former Czechoslovakia, and continues to be forbidden in the Czech Republic and Slovakia, but the situation is less promising in Hungary and Poland.

We deal with the difficulties of emerging fiscal and monetary policy by discussing the institutional arrangements for credible fiscal policy-making in Section 2. The section evaluates the progress of the four CE countries in attaining an institutional framework conducive to stable public finances. We deal with the absence of quantitative models in Section 3 by presenting a framework for evaluation of a macroeconomic transition path and applying it to the four CE countries. Both sections draw on our previous work. Section 4 concludes.

2. BUDGETING PROCESS AND CREDIBLE MAFAS

2.1 The Role of Budget Processes in Economic Transition

A basic problem in all transition economies is to achieve effective control over the government budget. Since the transition is from a state of central planning and strong involvement of the government in the production sector, achieving control over the budget is connected with the problem of reducing and restructuring government expenditures and strengthening the government's system of tax revenues. This means that fiscal reform necessarily involves major distributional conflict. These conflicts jeopardize reform programs, as the fight between differing groups within society over the allocation of the reform's costs and benefits leads to postponement and to solutions of reciprocity, i.e., political outcomes that hold some good for everyone, but an inefficient outcome for society.

Institutional structures can help avoid such inefficiencies. Of course, institutions do not make the distributional conflicts disappear. However, by defining the rules of the game they structure the ways in which the opposing parties can present and defend their claims. Institutional rules divide decision-making processes into individual steps and determine which steps are taken when they assign roles and responsibilities to the various actors, and, by regulating the flow of information, they distribute strategic influence and create or destroy opportunities for collusion. A basic claim of political economy is that institutional rules have systematic effects on the outcome of the decision making processes they govern.

The budget process is the set of institutional rules relevant in the context of budgetary policies and, therefore, in the context of fiscal reform. Formally, the budget is a list of revenues and expenses conveying what the government expects and is authorized to do during a certain time period. The budget process, in the broadest sense, is a system of rules, both formal and informal, governing the decision making process that leads to the formulation of a budget by the executive, its passage through the legislature, and its implementation. Political economy views the budget process as a mechanism through which political interest groups "bargain over conflicting goals, make side-payments, and try to motivate one another to accomplish their objectives" [Wildavsky (1975, p. 4)]. Constitutional theory holds that the budget process should be the principal and effective locus of conflict resolution between competing claims on public resources, to assure the stability, consistency, and efficiency of the government's financial policy. Informal decision-making and agreements outside the budget process, "non-decisions" (i.e. the lack of nodes of deliberate decisions in the process), and the use of off-budget funds are all sources constitutional failure of the budget process. They promote irresponsibility and obscurity of government financial policies [von Hagen and Harden, (1994)].

The importance of individual elements of the budget process, such as veto powers or committee structures, for fiscal performance has long been studied empirically in the context of American state governments. Only recently an emerging literature considers the impact of the budget process on the fiscal performance of national governments on an international scale. In contrast to the American literature, this new approach is based on comprehensive characterizations of the budget process, summarized in numerical indices describing the quality of a process. Thus, von Hagen (1992) and von Hagen and Harden (1994), (1996) show that the stark differences in fiscal performance among the EU governments can be explained to a large extent by differences in budgetary institutions. They identify decentralization of the budget process, i.e. the degree to which geographical, sectoral or other special interests dominate over the common interest of the government in budgetary decisions, as the main cause of weak fiscal discipline. Specifically, they show that countries with a low degree of centralization of the budget process have systematically higher ratios of public spending, and deficits and debts, to GDP than countries with large degrees of centralization. Similarly, Alesina et al (1996) show that countries with a high degree of centralization of the budget process in Latin America have lower deficits and debts. Results also suggest that Latin American countries with a centralized budget process are able to achieve a higher degree of macroeconomic stabilization and are less prone to credit-rationing. An appropriate budget process is thus an important prerequisite of a successful fiscal regime, and reform of the budget process can be an important part of a fiscal reform aiming at fiscal stabilization. The papers gathered in Poterba and von Hagen (1999), featuring references to the 1997 World Development Report, confirm this.

2.2 Political Economy Considerations

A general characteristic of modem public finances is that government activities, including tax benefits, tend to be targeted at specific groups while being paid for by the general taxpayer [Buchanan and Tullock (1961), Olson (1965)]. The incongruence between those who benefit and those who pay has important implications. Policy makers representing spending agencies or groups benefiting from particular public activities take into account the full benefit from expanding the programs they are concerned with, but recognize only that part of the costs that falls on their constituencies. As a result, policy makers systematically over-estimate the net marginal benefit of increasing public spending and, hence, use their political influence to increase spending beyond the level that would equate social marginal costs and benefits. For example, a member of parliament representing a local electoral district will appreciate the full value of road improvements for the local economy. But since his district pays only a small portion of the central government's tax revenues, he will ask for more road improvements when the central government pays for them than when they have to be paid for by local taxes. As all policy makers have reasons to behave in the same way, the result is excessive spending. Even if current spending is divided efficiently between current and future taxes, this leads to excessive deficits and debts, too. This the common pool problem of government budgeting [Ostrom et al (1993)].

The common pool problem can be shown to generate both excessive spending and excessive deficits and debt [Poterba and von Hagen (1999)]. Obviously, it is a result of a coordination failure among the participants of budgetary decisions: as in other common pool problems, the issue is that the individual decision maker does not recognize the externality his (individually) optimal decision exerts on the others. Specifically, the individual decision maker bidding for more public monies does not take into account the resulting increase in the burden falling on (current and future) tax payers who are not members of his constituency.

The basic claim of the political economy of budgeting is that this coordination failure can be overcome by appropriate design of the budget process. To achieve this, the budget process must promote decision making with a view towards the common interest of the government rather than the individual interests of politicians representing interest groups. Thus, a budget process with a high degree of centralization helps to internalize the relevant externalities and reduces the spending and deficit biases resulting from the common pool problem. As in other common-pool problems, leadership and bargaining are the principal mechanisms that can be employed for this purpose.

The budget processes of EU states can generally be divided into four main steps: a preparatory stage within the executive, a legislative stage in parliament, an implementation stage again within the executive, and an ex post control stage involving courts of auditors or similar institutions. Here, we are mainly concerned with the first three stages. For each one of these, institutional mechanisms can be identified that mitigate the common pool problem.

During the preparatory stage, the budget process can be interpreted as a game between the various ministers forming the government. Ministers heading spending departments represent special interests within the executive. In contrast, the prime minister and the finance minister can be assumed to put more emphasis on the collective interest of the government as a group. There are two principal mechanisms to achieve this. One is collective bargaining among the spending ministers at the outset of the process to set the main parameters of the budget (i.e. its total size, departmental allocations and the size of the deficit). The other is to give the finance minister and the prime minister a role of strategic dominance over the spending ministers. Since the prime minister and the finance minister pursue the collective interest of the group rather than individual or sectoral interests, vesting them with special powers reduces the influence of special interests in budgetary decisions. Hallerberg and von Hagen (1997) argue that the choice between these two approaches is ultimately a function of the structure of government. Multi-party coalition governments will find it easier to adopt a bargaining approach rather than vesting the finance minister - who must necessarily be a member of one of the coalition parties - with special powers. The reason is that this would raise legitimate fears that the finance minister would use his powers to favor the members of his own party. To increase the stability of the bargaining approach, coalition governments often write their fiscal strategy into the coalition agreement to protect it against reneging. In contrast, single-party governments tend to prefer the strategic dominance approach, because it is more flexible than a negotiated coalition agreement. This pattern of choices can be observed among EU governments.

At the parliamentary stage, the degree of centralization depends largely on the agenda setting power of the executive over the legislature. Agenda setting power is stronger in unicameral systems, where the executive faces only one opponent, than in bi-cameral systems. In bi-cameral systems, the executive's agenda-setting power is effectively strengthened if the budgetary powers of the upper house are limited, such as in France, Germany or the US. Agenda-setting power depends on the scope of amendments that parliament can make to the government's budget proposal. It also hinges on the government's ability to impose a voting procedure on parliament, such as a vote of confidence or the possibility to force parliament to vote over large sections of the budget simultaneously.

At the implementation stage, the critical variable is the degree to which the budget law effectively binds government actions. The more scope there is for deviations from the budget act, and the more frequent supplementary budgets are, the less binding is the budget act. Furthermore, strengthening the finance minister's control over the budget implementation, e.g. by subjecting spending departments to quarterly cash limits, limits the scope of strategic behavior in the implementation. A final dimension concerns the informativeness of the budget documents. The less informative they are, the more the government can hide its true intentions from the scrutiny of the parliamentary committees and the ex-post control organs, leading to a greater scope of deviations from the budget act. Von Hagen and Harden

(1996) construct indices characterizing budget processes of European governments in these dimensions. A large value on their index of centralization indicates a high degree of centralization. According to the political economy of budgeting, this should be paired with smaller deficits than a small value of the index. That prediction is borne out by data from twelve EU member countries.

If appropriate design of the government budget process can be an important element of a fiscal strategy aiming and fiscal stabilization, then reform of the budget process becomes critical in a macroeconomic reform strategy. We now turn to an analysis of the budget processes in the four CE countries.

2.3 Budget Processes in the Four CE Countries

Budgetary institutions in the CE countries are obviously still very young. Even where all the necessary laws exist, they have been in operation only for a short time, so that a common understanding of the rules of all participants in the process, which is often more important in practice than the letter of the law, is still only emerging. Nevertheless, a first assessment of the young institutions is possible.

For this purpose, our research is based on a questionnaire answered by local experts from government and the central banks. The answers of the respondents are used to characterize the budget processes using a list of items reported in Table 1. They are grouped in four dimensions: the degrees of centralization of each stage in the budget process, and the informativeness of the budget.

Table 1. Dimensions of Budget Characterizations

Preparatory Stage	Parliamentary Stage	Implementation Stage	Informativeness
Existence of numerical constraints for budget	Formal limits on amendments	blocking power of finance minister	scope of off-budget funds
commitment power of numerical constraints	amendments required to leave deficit unchanged	existence of cash limits on departments	separation of budget documents
structure of budget negotiations	budgetary powers of upper house	requirement of disbursement approval	transparency of budget documents
agenda setting power of finance minister	Government power to choose voting procedure	carryover of funds to next year	link to national accounts
procedure for conflict resolution	Government power to call vote of confidence	scope of budgetary transfers	government loans reported
	Sequence of votes	difficult to obtain supplementary budget	

Source: von Hagen (1992)

Budget preparation in the four countries evolves in the executive branch of government. It starts with the formulation of budgetary targets for total spending and revenues. These targets are proposed by the prime or finance ministers and adopted by the Cabinet. In Poland and the Czech Republic, other members of cabinet can make counter proposals. In Hungary and Slovakia, fiscal targets are also part of the government's coalition agreement. Only in Slovakia they are not fully derived from general macroeconomic forecasts. Budget negotiations are conducted bilaterally between the finance minister and the spending ministers; remaining conflicts from these bilateral negotiations are resolved in cabinet meetings (Czech Republic, Poland and Hungary) or in senior cabinet committees (Slovakia and Hungary). The latter tends to provide a greater check on reciprocity than the former and, hence, promotes fiscal discipline.

Among the four countries, only Poland has a bi-cameral parliament. The upper house examines and amends the budget under the same rules as the lower house. However, its budget can be overruled by an absolute majority vote in the lower house. Only in the CR are parliamentary amendments formally restricted in that they cannot change the overall balance of the budget. In Slovakia, however, an amendment requires the consent of the executive. In Poland and Slovakia, the government's position is strengthened by the rule that its proposal will be implemented if parliament does not pass a budget bill on time. In Poland, the president can dissolve parliament if a budget has not been passed on time. In the other two countries, the previous budget will be prorated into the next year in that case. The Polish parliament holds an initial vote on the government's proposal which, if the proposal is rejected, forces the government to resign. The Polish president under the current constitution has a right to veto the budget bill within 30 days after its passage through parliament; this right will be eliminated according to the draft of the new constitution.

There are strong similarities in the implementation stages. Spending departments are required to seek approval before they can spend funds and are subject to cash limits to control the flow of funds. In Slovakia, Poland, and Hungary, the finance minister can block expenditures during implementation. Budgetary transfers are possible within chapters of the budget; but transfers between chapters can be authorized by the finance ministers in Hungary and Slovakia. The Czech finance minister can authorize substantive changes in the budget in exceptional cases without legislative approval. Carry-over of funds into the next fiscal year requires legislative approval in the Czech Republic and in Hungary. In Slovakia, a limited portion of the budget can be carried over without explicit approval, while, in Poland, investment expenditures can be carried over with no limits, reserves cannot be carried over at all, and the carry-over of other funds requires authorization in cabinet.

National budgets are presented in a unified document except in Hungary. The budget document provides a breakdown by functional classifications except in Poland, by administrative responsibility, by sources of revenue, and a classification of capital and current expenditures. A link to national accounting is provided in Poland and in Slovakia. Social security and other transfer programs are not included in the government budget.

To translate these qualitative characterizations into a numerical scale, we follow the methodology of von Hagen (1992). Scores ranging from zero to four are given for each individual item. The scores are then normalized such that the maximum score in each dimension is 16. The overall index is the harmonic mean of these four sub-indices. Table 2 reports the scores of the four countries according to each item and on the overall index.

Table 2. Index of Centralization for Four Budget Processes

Item	Czech Republic	Poland	Slovak Republic	Hungary
Executive Stage	6.7	7.3	10.7	11.3
Parliamentary Stage	8	5	5.5	7
Implementation Stage	11.2	10.0	11.0	11.9
Informativeness	10.4	12.0	14.4	7.2
Index	8.9	8.1	9.8	9.1

On the overall index, the differences among the four countries are small compared to the differences among the EU countries, where the index ranges from 5 to 15. But differences in the individual items are interesting. Centralization at the preparatory stage is weak in the Czech Republic and Poland compared to Hungary and Slovakia. These differences are mainly due to a greater scope for compromise among ail members of cabinet - a greater scope for reciprocity - in the former countries and the link between fiscal targets and coalition agreements prevailing in the latter two. Centralization at the legislative stage is stronger in the Czech Republic, the only country with formal limits on amendments, and Hungary, where the government seems to have more control over voting procedures relating to the budget. The relatively small importance of off-budget funds contributes to Slovakia's high rank on informativeness, while in Hungary, informativeness is lower partly because of the importance of off-budget activities of the government.

The role of these indices is to facilitate cross-country comparison of institutional environments and to derive predictions about the relative fiscal performance about the countries considered. Two strong caveats apply to the latter function. First, all four countries are still in the process of transition and have started this process from different fiscal positions. This is particularly true for the Czech Republic and Slovakia. According the OECD Economic Surveys produced in 1996, the splitting of the federation in 1993 created windfall gains for the Czech government and windfall losses for the

Slovak government, making a comparison of fiscal performance in terms of deficit and spending ratios difficult.

Second, the institutions characterized by our indices are themselves still young. In contrast to the EU and Latin American experiences described in earlier studies, we cannot rely much on "established practices". The relatively strong design of the budget process in Slovakia, for example, may be a reflection of the fiscal crisis experienced after the splitting of the federation, while the relatively weak design of the Czech process may reflect a bit of complacency on the part of the government in view of the relatively comfortable fiscal outcome of 1993 and 1994.

With these caveats in mind, fiscal outcomes are consistent with the rankings of our indices: Hungary and Slovakia show smaller deficits than Poland and the Czech Republic. For a more careful interpretation, however, it is perhaps more adequate to consider the changes in deficits rather than the levels. Here, the two countries ranking best on the index of centralization (Slovakia and Hungary) achieved significant improvements since 1993. In contrast, Poland showed no sign of deficit improvement, while the Czech fiscal balance worsened over this period. The Slovak and the Hungarian improvements came with falling ratios of government expenditures to GDP, which points to the sustainability of the improvements. Poland's spending ratio fell only very slightly. The decline in the Czech central government spending was matched by an even stronger decline in revenues, painting a less promising picture of future fiscal developments. This evidence suggests that the stronger design of the budget processes in Slovakia and Hungary were helpful for these governments to achieve fiscal consolidation.

2.4 International Comparisons

It is interesting to use the institutional indices for a comparison between our four countries and the current members of the EU. In that group, Poland is closest to Spain (index = 7.8) and the Czech Republic falls between Spain and Portugal (index = 8.1). Austria (index = 10.2) is closer to Slovakia and Hungary. Greece has an index value of 5.4. Centralization at the preparatory stage is best comparable to the Netherlands (9.8), Portugal (9.8) stronger than in Italy (5.1) and Spain (5.3), but much weaker than in Denmark (12.2) or Austria (13.2). Centralization at the legislative stage is comparable to Denmark (8) in the Czech case, but, due to the lack of amendment controls, only to Italy (5) or Ireland (5) in the other cases. In contrast, centralization at the implementation stage is relatively high, comparable to Austria (11.4) and Denmark (9.6). Similarly, the four countries score relatively well regarding the informativeness of the budget, where the Netherlands (14.4) and Denmark (10.6) have comparable index values.

Improvement in procedures from the viewpoint of future taxpayers have been slow, in part because budgetary institutions in EU states have remained virtually unchanged for decades. In the early 1980s improvements did occur in Denmark, for largely domestic reasons. The other case of improvement is Portugal, where a MAFAS was gradually set in place in the late 1980s and then implemented in 1992, as an accompanying policy to membership in the European Monetary System.

Considering the recent experience of the Southern European countries with multi-party democracy, the transition to a more market-oriented regime and fiscal outcomes is particularly interesting for CE countries as institutional change and macroeconomic performance interact. Greece, Spain and Portugal all experienced rapidly rising government expenditures and deficits following their liberalizations. Defining two years of non-increasing government spending ratios as successful fiscal stabilization, it took Greece until 1985 to achieve stabilization, Spain equally to 1985, though starting at a later date, and Portugal, which started yet later, until 1983. Deficit stabilization was reached by all three countries in 1985. Thus, consistent with the ranking on our institutional index, Portugal took the shortest, and Greece the longest time to fiscal stabilization. The three Southern European cases are described in Bliss and Macedo (1990).

The adoption of a kind of convergence program is easier if some group procedures can be adopted. The attempt to merge multilateral surveillance with excessive deficit procedures in the run up to the single currency is certainly a welcome step among member states. The time it took and the interference with other areas of institutional reform suggests the limits of external pressure [Macedo (1999)].

3. THE MACRO EVALUATION FRAMEWORK

3.1 Policy Assignment

Another basic problem in all transition economies is analyzing macroeconomic policy without a quantitative model. This problem has come up in the course of the evaluation of World Bank structural adjustment programs [Branson et al (1996)]. There a framework that combines a model of policy assignment and debt sustainability criteria was developed to deal with the problem. A version of this framework, adapted for the particular circumstances of the CE countries, seems useful for analyzing their macro policies with reference to something like a convergence program. This would encompass a PPERR, a MAFAS and a catalog of structural measures designed to remove the macroeconomic and microeconomic obstacles to growth.

The convergence program presumably has realistic objectives for internal balance, represented by GDP growth and inflation; external balance, represented by foreign exchange reserves; and the current account (and thereby growth of debt). The program sets the instruments for fiscal policy, monetary policy, and the exchange rate that are expected simultaneously to bring the economy at least close to the objectives. No issue of policy assignment arises at this stage. However, during the course of the program, it is almost certain that some unpredictable disturbance will appear, and policy will have to adjust. But if time and information are in short supply, it can be essential to know in advance which instrument should take the lead in adjustment, depending on which target variable has gone off course.

The reason is that some pairings of instruments to targets will lead to convergence back toward the joint objectives, but other pairings will lead away. The first pairings are stable policy assignments; the second are unstable. The basis for a stable policy assignment is the principle of effective market classification, which says that each instrument should be assigned to the target variable that is relatively most sensitive to that instrument [Mundell (1962)]. This is essentially the application of the principle of comparative advantage to policy choice.

Mundell analyzed the problem of assignment when there are two targets and two instruments. The government budget surplus represents fiscal policy and the interest rate represents monetary policy. These are used as instruments to reach internal and external balance. The targets are measured by non-inflationary aggregate demand and balance of payments equilibrium respectively. In that case stability is ensured by assigning fiscal policy to internal balance and monetary policy to external balance. He also showed that the opposite assignment is unstable.

An example of an unstable assignment which is relevant to fast reformers in CE is a monetary policy reaction to the investment boom which would follow if the transition to EU membership is perceived to be successful. Figure 1, reproduced from Branson and Macedo (1995), illustrates the situation. The economy is represented at point T_0 after the transition begins but before the investment boom. An investment boom would shift both equilibrium curves out (or up; it is the same thing since both are downward sloping). The budget or monetary policy would have to tighten both for internal and external balance. The target for policy would move to point T_1 in the figure.

Figure 1. Policy reaction to an Investment Boom

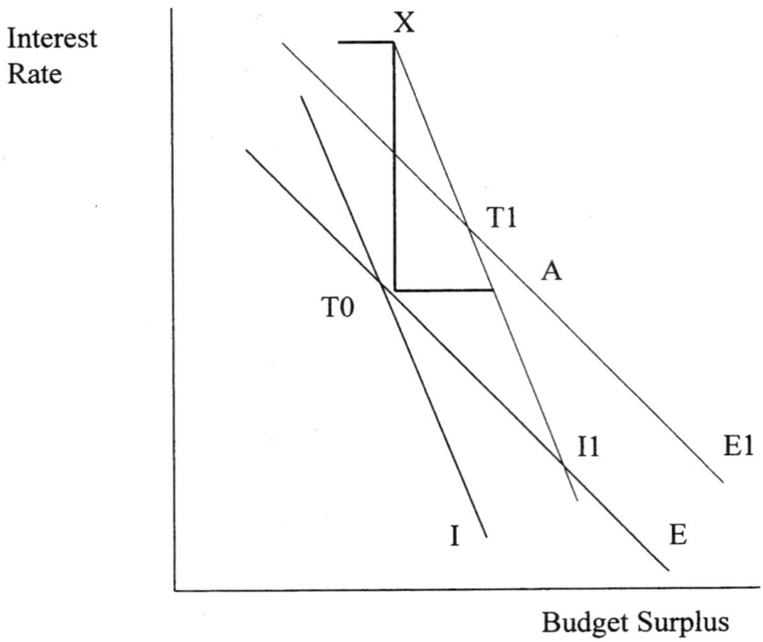

An initial fiscal policy reaction would take the economy to point A, close to T_1, requiring small further policy adjustments to get right on target. If fiscal policy does not adjust sufficiently, monetary policy is left to hold down aggregate demand. An initial monetary policy reaction would take the economy toward a point such as *X*, onto internal balance, but with a balance of payments surplus. The unstable assignment moves the economy away from the joint target. Once again the stable assignment is fiscal policy to maintain internal balance and monetary policy to maintain external balance.

3.2 Application to the CE Countries

In the application to the CE countries, our macro evaluation framework extends the assignment model to three targets and three instruments. It uses the principle of effective market classification to assign fiscal policy to internal balance, the real exchange rate to the current account, and the interest rate to external balance in terms of foreign exchange reserves.

We generally assume that an unacceptably high level of aggregate demand (or high rate of inflation) indicates the need for reduction in the primary (or non-interest) budget deficit, or increase in the surplus. This can be interpreted as reducing inflation by reducing aggregate demand, or it can be interpreted as reducing the need for inflation tax financing of the deficit. As in the two by two example just described, we assume that the level of aggregate demand A depends on the primary budget deficit p and the real interest rate r:

$$A = A(p,r);\ A_p > 0;\ A_r < 0. \tag{1}$$

The corresponding adjustment equation for the primary deficit can be written as:

$$dp = -\delta[A(p,r) - A^*] \tag{2}$$

Here the primary deficit is assumed to adjust to the difference between aggregate demand and its target value A^*.

There are two objectives for external balance: appropriate levels of the current account balance and foreign exchange reserves. The path of the real exchange rate e is tied to the current account objective, which is a suitable level of the primary current account balance C. Then the domestic rate of inflation gives the path of the nominal exchange rate consistent with the path of the real rate that attains the current account objective. The current account adjustment equation is given by:

$$de = -\lambda[C(e,Z) - C^*];\ C_e > O. \tag{3}$$

Here C^* is the target for the primary current account balance and Z are other variables affecting the primary current account.

Most countries have some degree of international capital mobility, so that if their real interest rates get too far below international rates, there will be a capital outflow and loss of reserves. This implies that maintenance of external balance in terms of the level of foreign exchange reserves requires keeping real interest rates high enough relative to international rates that the relevant investors are willing to keep their deposits and other investments in the country. This relationship is expressed in the capital mobility term K in equation (4):

$$dF - dR = K[r - r^* - de - rp(p)];\ K' > 0;\ rp' > 0. \tag{4}$$

Here dF is the total capital account, the change in national net foreign assets, dR is the change in net foreign exchange reserves, and K is the net private capital inflow. F, R, and K are all measured in foreign exchange. Following Branson and Jaffee (1991), K is a function of the interest differential adjusted for expected real depreciation and a risk premium, where r is the domestic real interest rate, r^* is the international real interest rate and de is now the expected rate of depreciation of the real exchange rate. The risk premium rp embodies the market's estimate of the risk in holding local currency assets, the monopoly power of local financial intermediaries, and other aspects of financial structure capital markets. It includes departures from uncovered interest parity and changes in the real exchange rate rather than the decomposition between political and currency risk used e.g. by Frankel and MacArthur (1988). The risk premium is assumed to be an increasing function of the primary budget deficit p. The degree of capital mobility is expressed in the size of the positive derivative of the capital mobility term K.

The corresponding adjustment equation for the real interest rate is given by:

$$dr = -\beta[K - K^*], \tag{5}$$

where K is specified as in equation (4) and K^* is the target for the private capital account. Given dF, this implies the target for reserve movements.

The three adjustment equations can be linearized around the equilibrium values of e, p and r (denoted respectively by $\widetilde{e}$, $\widetilde{p}$ and $\widetilde{r}$) and presented in matrix form as in equation (6):

$$\begin{pmatrix} de \\ dp \\ dr \end{pmatrix} = \begin{bmatrix} \lambda_{Ce} & 0 & 0 \\ 0 & -\delta A_p & -\delta A_r \\ 0 & -\beta K' rp' & -\beta K' \end{bmatrix} \begin{pmatrix} e - \widetilde{e} \\ p - \widetilde{p} \\ r - \widetilde{r} \end{pmatrix} \tag{6}$$

This system is recursive for simplicity. It would be easy to include p or r in the Z vector which affects the primary current account in equation (3). Given that the matrix is bloc-diagonal, the stability conditions are a negative trace and a positive determinant of the two by two system in the lower bloc of the matrix in equation (6). This is the system behind the example, in Figure 1. It is clear from our sign assumptions that the trace of the matrix is negative and the sign of the determinant of the two by two system is positive.

Coming back to Figure 1, it can be seen as implying a real exchange rate which keeps the current account at its desired level. To the extent that the investment boom falls exclusively on domestic goods, the equilibrium real exchange rate would not change in the adjustment process. In general however the real exchange rate will have to change. If equation (3) above is violated, and the required change in e does not happen, the two by two policy assignment can no longer ensure stable adjustment to the new three by three equilibrium.

3.3 Domestic and Foreign Debt Sustainability

The policy assignments discussed above include a target value for the current account and a policy setting for the primary budget deficit. These are respectively the rates of change of the country's foreign debt and the government's public debt, introducing the intertemporal dimension into the discussion. The intertemporal consistency of the application of the macro framework can be checked by looking at the arithmetic of foreign or public debt sustainability [Cohen (1985)].

The country's budget constraint in real terms can be written as a formula for the growth of the ratio of foreign debt to exports:

$$df = (r^* - n^*)f + c(e), \tag{7}$$

where f is the ratio of foreign debt to exports, df is its arithmetic (not percentage) annual increase, r^* is the international real interest rate from equation (4), n^* is the growth rate of exports, and c is the primary current account deficit as a fraction of exports (with c' positive).

In the case of the public debt, the government's budget constraint in real terms is:

$$db = (r - n)b + p - s, \tag{8}$$

where b is the ratio of public debt to GDP, db is its arithmetic annual increase, r is the real interest rate, n is the growth rate of real GDP, p is now the primary budget deficit as a fraction of GDP, and s is the ratio of seigniorage to GDP. Seigniorage here includes both the "inflation tax" and real growth in demand for base money as the economy grows. The seigniorage term in the debt dynamics equation (8) is

$$s = (dq + n) / v, \tag{9}$$

where dq is the inflation rate, and v is the velocity of base money.

The intertemporal model gives the equilibrium values for e, p and r in the assignment model presented in equation (6) above. To solve the intertemporal model, first use (9) to determine s. Then (7) is one equation in the policy variables r and p, given the objective of $db = 0$. Equation (4) can be solved for the tradeoff between the two policy variables r and p, given dF - dR. Equation (7) can be solved for the value of the real exchange rate e which creates a primary current account surplus that sets $df = 0$, recursive to the first two equations.

Generally, the current values of the variables on the right side of equations (7) and (8) are known, so they can be used to calculate the paths of the debt ratios, or the components of an IMF program, on the assumption that the paths of these variables remain unchanged. However, these variables are all endogenous, and their paths will change over time. In the absence of a quantitative model, it is difficult to predict how their paths will change, so we need to use the assignment model for policy to proceed incrementally. The directions for policy change indicated by the debt dynamics approach are the same as those indicated by the policy assignment model. If inflation threatens internal balance, reduce the primary budget deficit. If the current account deficit is too large, devalue in real terms. If foreign exchange reserves are too low, or falling too fast, tighten monetary policy; that is, shift from money finance toward debt finance of the existing budget deficit. These three relationships give the direction of policy actions and the expected outcomes.

3.4 A Policy Matrix Applied to CE Countries

The CE countries provide especially interesting conditions for application of the macroeconomic framework. Their commitment to eventual adherence to the EU gives them clear terminal conditions, including either a fixed nominal exchange rate or joining a single currency. Thus while an early devaluation in order to establish external balance may be necessary, at some point along the path they will adopt the PPERR, limiting the movement of the exchange rate, what the EU Treaty calls observation of "normal fluctuation margins". The introduction of PPERR also requires a successful move to full currency convertibility.

The CE countries are developing countries with changing structures, so the MAFAS and PPERR must be flexible enough to accommodate structural change. The countries are also in a sense competing with each other not to fall behind on the path to accession, to fall into the next round of potential entrants from the south or further east. So getting to the point where MAFAS and PPERR can be credibly adopted has some urgency.

We have two objectives in applying the framework to the CE countries. The first is to see to what extent movements of target variables and instruments correspond as expected since the beginning of the transition. This could be taken either as a test of how well the framework fits, or of how far along they are in the transition. Branson and Macedo (1995) show that the correspondence between movements in net exports of goods and non-factor services and the real effective exchange rate is reasonable in all cases, and that between the inflation rate and the budget deficit is not bad. All of the countries still have substantial capital controls and are in the early stages of financial reform and development. Only Hungary showed the expected correspondence between movements in the real interest differential and foreign exchange reserves; none is revealed yet for the other countries.

The second objective of the application is to assess how far along in the transition to EU membership the CE countries are. We want to get some idea of which countries are close to the point at which they can adopt MAFAS and PPERR, and which may require front-loaded structural adjustment, in the form of deficit reduction procedures or real devaluation, before adopting MAFAS and PPERR.

In applying the framework to the CE countries, we first focus on external balance. The countries still have a substantial public sector yet to be privatized; the definition of the public debt is unclear, and data are not available; the coverage of the public sector deficit is uncertain. In addition, in some cases there is still a degree of price control that makes the concept of internal balance unclear. On the other hand, the concept of external balance and the external constraint are clear. Thus we first ask if the economy is in external balance, both in terms of the current stock of foreign debt, and in terms of the current flow in the current account deficit. Then we ask if the fiscal position seems consistent with internal balance, taking a large fiscal deficit as an indicator that a current state of external balance may be threatened in the future.

For external balance, we check whether net exports of goods and non-factor services, as the flow measure, corresponds to the real effective exchange rate as expected. In particular, does the trend in net exports suggest the need for a real devaluation prior to adopting a PPERR? In assessing the trend in net exports we also look at the dynamics of foreign debt. Up to 1994, Hungary shows the most rapid increase in the ratio, with the debt rising by almost half of export revenue in a year. Poland also has a rising ratio. Slovakia is near zero, and the Czech ratio is falling. If the current ratio of foreign debt to exports is not increasing, then the country is likely to be able to sustain the debt path in the absence of structural change with negative consequences for the current account.

As a measure of internal balance we look to the inflation rate, with the budget deficit as the corresponding policy instrument. The aggregate budget deficit is a necessary, but not sufficient indicator for internal balance, for institutional, measurement and structural reasons.

Fiscal consolidation will involve major structural changes in the budget. Aside from further improvements in the tax system, measures are likely to be taken on the expenditure side. An example is the very high level of publicly-provided pensions, with liberal provisions for retirement. In several of the CE countries, the flow of public pension payments is well above 10 percent of GDP. If we use a discount rate of 10 percent to capitalize this stream, pension debt is 100 percent of GDP. Thus something structural is likely to be done about pensions, as well as many other fiscal issues. Thus fiscal consolidation may require some form of social contract to be effective, and it will change the future fiscal position.

In a situation in which the public-private distinction is still emerging, there are conceptual and practical problems in measuring the public deficit, and even worse, the public debt. These reflect the initial absence of a private sector, discussed in the introduction. There is a substantial overlap between monetary and fiscal policy, as much of credit creation finances public sector activity early in the transition. Thus in the early stages net domestic credit creation may be the best measure of fiscal policy, rather than the budget deficit. Unfortunately, data on credit creation are only available since the beginning of the transition for the CE countries, so it is difficult to make any comparisons across the beginning. As the private sector and central bank develop, the focus will shift to the budget deficit as the measure of fiscal policy. Branson and Macedo (1995) tracked both credit creation and the budget deficit as fiscal measures. It would be good to have a measure of the weight of the private sector in the economy as a way of weighting the two measures.

Normally in doing an analysis of macroeconomic policy we would use a version of equation (8) to study public debt sustainability. However, the lack of clear distinction between private and public sectors and the lack of data make this impossible now. The existence of substantial arrears among public enterprises, the financial system, and the government, with gross debt probably much greater than net debt, make assignment of debt to sectors conceptually difficult, even if we had the data. The existence of unmeasured future claims on the government, such as the pension problem, mentioned earlier, add to the conceptual difficulty. Perhaps the CE governments have a good opportunity for the introduction of a system of generational accounting as their budget processes emerge. See an evaluation of Portugal's MAFAS using this method in Auerbach et al (1999).

The macro framework as applied to the CE countries is summarized in the policy matrix of Figure 2. There across the top we ask is external balance sustainable, and have the answers "Yes" and "No" defining the two columns. Down the side we ask is internal balance sustainable, with the answers defining the two rows. We put external balance across the top to signify that we have a clearer view of that than of internal balance. The main importance of the internal balance indicators are to suggest that countries in the lower off-diagonal box are likely to slide to the right if internal balance is not achieved. It also seems likely that it is easier to move down in the matrix, with internal balance threatened by inefficient budgetary considerations and political pressures than it is to move up. This points to the need for institutional reform, already discussed in Section 2.

Figure 2. Policy Matrix

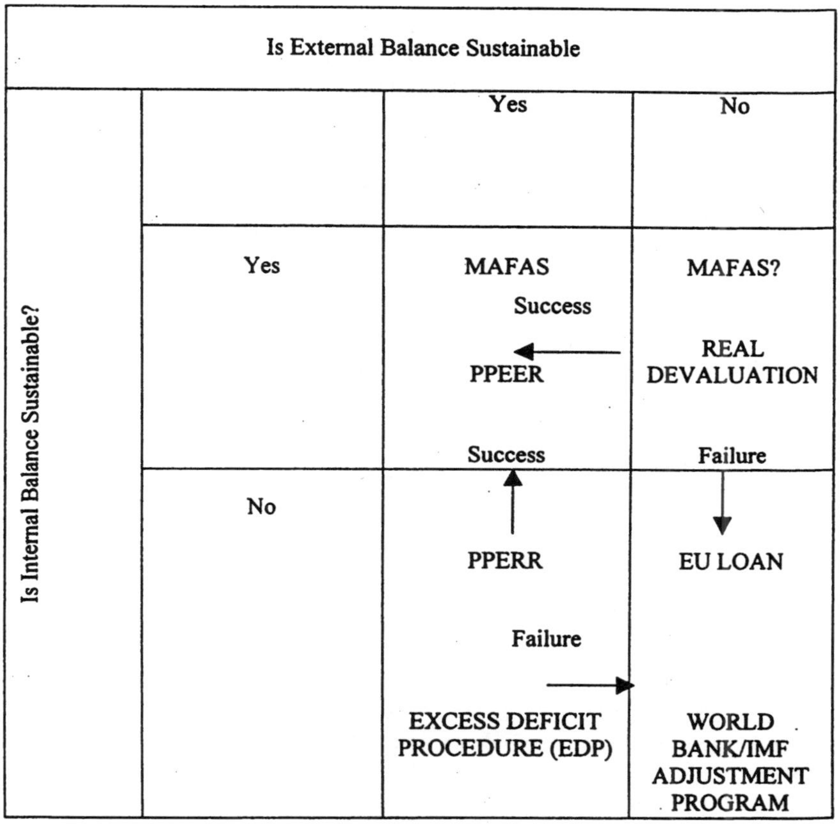

Countries in the upper diagonal box are already on or close to a convergence trajectory toward accession to the EU in terms of both external and internal balance, and are in a position to adopt MAFAS and PPERR. Countries in the lower diagonal box are out of balance on both dimensions, and are candidates for an EU loan or an IMF/World Bank structural adjustment program to get close enough to the trajectory to consider MAFAS and PPERR.

Countries on the off-diagonal boxes in the policy matrix are in balance on one front but out of balance on the other, with some discrete adjustment needed to get close to the convergence trajectory. Countries in the upper off-diagonal box may require a discrete real devaluation to restore external balance before adopting PPERR. They may want to adopt a form of MAFAS that creates the resource freedom to ensure that the devaluation has the intended effect. Countries in the lower diagonal box may require a front-loaded application of a kind of "excessive deficit procedure" (as called for by the Union Treaty for member states) as part of their MAFAS. Their PPERR may allow for some real appreciation as the excessive deficit procedure takes hold. Successful adjustment in either off-diagonal box moves the country to the upper diagonal box, close enough to the convergence trajectory to sustain MAFAS and PPERR. Failed adjustment leads to the lower diagonal box and the need for an adjustment program with outside assistance and conditionality.

The four countries are close to sustainability. The Czech Republic could consider both MAFAS and PPERR. Slovakia seems to be moving towards the upper diagonal box, but it still is probably too soon to adopt MAFAS and PPERR. Hungary has moved from the lower diagonal box, in need of improvement on both external and internal balance, to the upper diagonal box and has been considering MAFAS and PPERR. Poland seemed on the border between the left and right boxes in the bottom row, but, due to strong growth, has been moving up and could consider MAFAS as well as PPERR.

4. CONCLUSION

The four CE countries are in the middle of the current EU group in terms of the institutional index in Section 2. Although a prediction of this kind is obviously highly uncertain, this would suggest that they are institutionally better fit for fiscal consolidation and, hence, for EU membership than Greece, Spain and Portugal were in the 1970s. Nevertheless, there is still much room for institutional improvement. A stronger commitment mechanism to fiscal targets at the preparatory stage would improve fiscal performance in all four countries. In the Czech Republic and Poland, reforms of the budget process may be useful to address the relative weakness of the preparatory stage. In Poland, Slovakia and Hungary, the relatively weak position of the government compared to the legislature is probably the weakest point in the current process.

The four countries are close to sustainability in the policy matrix of Section 3. The Czech Republic could consider both MAFAS and PPERR. Slovakia seems to be moving towards the upper diagonal box, but it still is probably too soon to adopt MAFAS and PPERR. Hungary has moved from the lower diagonal box, in need of improvement on both external and internal balance, to the upper diagonal box and has been considering MAFAS and PPERR. Poland seemed on the border between the left and right boxes in the bottom row, but, due to strong growth, has been moving up and could consider MAFAS as well as PPERR.

In sum, the CE four are closer to EU procedures and performances, on both macroeconomic, structural and institutional grounds, than other EU associated states and even than some member states were in the recent past. The fact that they established CEFTA (which Slovenia since joined) also helps set them apart from other EU associates in the region. At the same time it makes the adoption of a kind of convergence program easier if some group procedures can be adopted. But, in spite of the progress already achieved, the adaptation is likely to trail the forthcoming enlargement negotiations of the EU.

REFERENCES

Alesina, Alberto, Ricardo Hausmann, Ernesto Stein (1995), *Budget Processes and Fiscal Discipline in Latin American Countries*, Inter-American Development Bank.

Auerbach, Alan, Larry Kotlikoff, Jorge Braga de Macedo, José Braz and Jan Walliser (1999), "Generational Accounting in Portugal", in Alan Auerbach, Larry Kotlikoff and Willi Leiblitz, *Generational Accounting Around the World*, Chicago University Press, pp. 471-488.

Bliss, Christopher and Jorge Braga de Macedo, editors (1990), *Unity with Diversity in the European Economy: The Community's Southern Frontier*, Cambridge, Cambridge University Press.

Branson, William H. and Jorge Braga de Macedo (1995), "Macroeconomic Policy in Central Europe", CEPR Discussion Paper.

Branson, William H. and Dwight M. Jaffee (1991), "The Globalization of Information and Capital Mobility", in Joshua Ronan and Joshua Livnat eds., *Accounting and Financial Globalization*, (Westport CT: Qurom Books).

Branson, William H. et al. (1996), *World Bank Support for Structural and Sectoral Adjustment: the Second OED Overview*, Washington, D.C.

Cohen, Daniel (1985), "How to Evaluate the Solvency of an Indebted Country", *Economic Policy*, Vol. 1, No. l.

Macedo, Jorge Braga, (1993) "Portugal's European integration: the limits of external pressure", Nova Economics Working Paper No. 369, December.

Frankel, Jeffrey and Alan MacArthur (1988) "Political vs. Currency premia in International Real Interest Differentials", *European Economic Review*, 32.

Hallerberg, Mark, and Jürgen von Hagen (1997) "Electoral Institutions, Cabinet Negotiations and Government Deficits in the EU", CEPR Discussion Paper.

Mundell, Robert A. (1962) "The Appropriate Use of Monetary and Fiscal Policy under Fixed Exchange Rates", *IMF Staff Papers* (Washington, DC: IMF).

Poterba, James and Jürgen von Hagen (1999) *Fiscal Institutions and Fiscal Performance*, University of Chicago Press.

Von Hagen, Jürgen (1992) *Budgeting Procedures and Fiscal Performance in the EC*, European Commission DG 11, Economic Papers 96, Luxembourg.

Von Hagen, Jürgen and Ian Harden (1994) "National Budget Processes and Fiscal Performance", in *European Economy Reports and Studies*, 3, 1994, 311-418.

Von Hagen, Jürgen and Ian Harden (1996) "Budget Processes and Commitment to Fiscal Discipline", IMF Working Paper.

Wildavsky, Aaron (1975) "Budgeting. A Comparative Analysis".

Chapter 3

REAL EXCHANGE RATE BEHAVIOUR AND RESOURCE ALLOCATION IN THE VISEGRAD FOUR

C. Paul Hallwood
Department of Economics, University of Connecticut

Ronald MacDonald
Department of Economics, University of Strathclyde

Abstract. In this chapter we present a simple micro-macro-economic model to analyze the behavior of equilibrium real exchange rates in transitional economies. The model highlights that such real exchange rates will be driven by the sensitivity of resource allocation and the distribution of consumption to changes in relative prices, and on the nature of shocks to the equilibrium level of unemployment. For an economy experiencing a successful transition process, it is argued that the real exchange rate should be mean reverting. Evidence that the real exchange rates of Hungary and Poland have exhibited some mean reversion since the inception of the transition period is reported.

Determining how well economic transition is going is a question that has exercised economists and politicians since the earliest days after the fall of Communism in central and Eastern Europe. Early studies found little evidence that structural change had gone very far (see, for example, Berg and Blanchard, 1994, Borensztein, Demkas and Ostry, 1993, Calvo and Coricelli, 1993, Blanchard, Commander and Coricelli, 1994). On the other hand, three more recent studies by Halpern and Wyplosz (1997), Krajnyak and Zettelmayer (1998) and Begg, Halpern and Wyplosz (1999), find that in many transition economies (TEs), even from the earliest days, successful transition was well underway.

R. MacDonald and R. Cross (eds.), Central Europe Towards Monetary Union: Macroeconomic Underpinnings and Financial Reputation, 31–58.

The common criterion in the latter three papers is that a trending appreciation in the *equilibrium* real exchange rate (as proxied by the dollar wage) signals that a transition is going well. This criterion makes sense for, according the famous Balassa-Samuelson theorem the real exchange rate of a country with faster productivity growth should appreciate relative to a reference currency such as the US dollar. Thus, as it is widely thought that TEs started off with very badly allocated resources, a transition that was going well would allocate resources more efficiently, so spurring productivity growth and appreciation in the equilibrium real exchange rate. That is the theory. The difficult part is to estimate the *equilibrium* real exchange rate with sufficient statistical precision to give confidence in the estimates. There is no need here to describe the ingenuity used in the above papers to obtain these estimates. However, it should be noted that those estimates that are obtained are of such low statistical significance as to leave unanswered the question as to whether the *equilibrium* real exchange rates were in the decade after the fall of Communism trending or not. Thus, we are left still searching for a statistically viable criterion by which to measure the success of transitional reforms in central and Eastern Europe.

Descriptive, as opposed to the above noted quantitative, approaches are taken by six experts in Brown (1999). However, authoritative as these assessments are, one is still left wonder as to how well the transitions are going, for the six experts choose six different criteria and by no means come to a common conclusion. Some of them arguing that the transition is now over in some TEs, others arguing that it still has a long way to go.

Our own approach to assessing how well transition is going is quantitative, and it is based on the argument that successful transition from planned to market economy should be assessed with reference to the extent to which markets, rather than central planners, are allocating resources. This point of view agrees with that of Svejnar (1999) who argues that the transition is over when "central planning and direct government intervention is replaced by an efficiently functioning market system" (page 77). We fill out this criterion by choosing the real exchange rate as the market price of interest. In particular, we investigate whether real exchange rates in TEs behave much as they do in market economies.

In open economies the real exchange rate plays a crucial role in resource allocation, and this is especially true in TEs which are in the process of introducing rational price-structures to replace the distorted price-systems of central planning. Below we discuss at the theoretical level how a TE's equilibrium real exchange rate may be shocked by the application of sequenced transitional policies, such as liberalization of a country's traded goods sector prior to its non-traded goods sector - which approximates the actual sequence in many TEs. A novel feature of our approach, which extends related work by Branson and De Macedo (1995), Halpern and Wyplosz (1997), Krajnyak and Zettelmayer (1998) and Begg, Halpern and Wyplosz (1999), and exploited in our econometric modeling, is that macroeconomic and relative price equilibrium are inter-dependent. More specifically, the equilibrium real exchange rate is seen as being determined by equilibrium relative prices, rather than just simultaneous internal and external balance in macroeconomic equilibrium. In theory it is possible for an economy to be in macroeconomic equilibrium - i.e. operating at full employment with stable prices - while the level of the real exchange rate is indeterminate. This would be the case of a centrally planned economy which was, in effect, ignoring relative price signals in resource allocation, or of a TE where relative prices were yet to play a major role in resource allocation. However, as relative prices become incrementally more important in the allocation of resources, it becomes possible to talk about the 'set of equilibrium relative prices', which we proxy with the equilibrium real exchange rate.

What is important about this is for assessing how well the transitions are going is that the evolving equilibrium real exchange rate creates a 'centre of gravity' to which we expect actual, or observed, relative prices to gravitate. In a statistical sense, therefore, we expect that when relative prices have become important in a country's resource allocation, the real exchange rate will be mean reverting. But when relative prices are not yet much involved in resource allocation - as when reform policies have either not had enough time to work, or, have been inadequately applied, the real exchange rate need not be mean reverting, indeed, it may follow a random walk. The time series properties of the real exchange rates of the Visegrad countries are examined below.

The paper proceeds as follows: in section 1 the nature of sequenced economic reform in TEs stylized; section 2 outlines a simple microeconomic-macroeconomic model of the equilibrium real exchange rate and develops from it a testable hypothesis for the application of time series techniques; section 3 describes a data set which is used in section 4 to analyze the time-series properties of real exchange rates in the Visegrad economies. The paper closes with a concluding section.

1. GRADUALISM IN ECONOMIC REFORMS

Economic reform began before the 1989 Revolutions in Poland and Hungary and in 1991 in what was Czechoslovakia. There was a presumption even among strong pro-market advocates that 'big bang' reforms should be properly delivered into an appropriate 'technical' universe of market-orientated institutions and legal frameworks. As these could not be simply called into existence 'big bang' never occurred. As we agree with Genberg (1991) that such was the scope of second best problems that no economically sensible ordered sequence could have been designed, the actual sequencing of reforms in TEs was bound to be somewhat indeterminate. Thus, across the Visegrad four, while there is a semblance of ordering, it did not follow any strict blue print.

The main features of the processes of economic liberalization include the extent to which prices are allowed to affect resource allocation, the extent to which soft budget constrains have been retained, and the degree to which foreign trade and the capital account have been liberalized. The gradual adoption by enterprises of the hard budget constraint is important for an economy in transition because enterprises operating under it are driven to optimize both output and input use - their resource allocation decisions responding to price signals.

Current account convertibility was introduced gradually through the 1980s in Hungary, in 1990 in Poland, and in 1991 in Czechoslovakia. As a stylized fact traded goods sectors have been liberalized before non-traded goods sectors, the soft budget constraint for non-traded goods being retained to ensure the provision of social goods and infrastructure via subsidized losses. This is not to deny that some reforms had occurred in non-traded goods, only that they had gone much further in the traded goods sector. The early opening of the traded goods sector was an easy method of introducing rational commodity prices into a transforming economy. Retention of the non-traded goods sector in public ownership on the other-hand was thought to be desirable because it could be used as a cushion against the harshness of market reforms (e.g., increasing unemployment).

Thus, during the course of the transition market-failures have remained. For example, there was the continuing existence of a large number of monopolized industries, rigid labor markets (Dinopoulos and Lane, 1992), underdeveloped banking systems and capital markets (Hardy and Lahri, 1992), the pre-existence of inefficient and subsidized industries giving rise to moral hazard problems between the government as principal and enterprise managers as agents, and inadequate legal systems. An important element is that non-traded goods production largely remained subsidized through the soft budget constraint within the state sector so as to soak up the labor which was (and is) being released by the liberalized traded goods sector.

The economic implication of the above - captured in our model and exploited in our econometrics - is that, as sequenced reforms allow the market system to spread only slowly, the operation of price equilibrating processes also develop slowly.[1] Good statements of this are: "maintaining price controls in some sectors may diminish the advantages of price liberalization in others. Liberalization must be fairly comprehensive to bring its full efficiency benefits" (Sundakov, Ossowski, and Lane, 1994, p. 431). And, "competition can function in an effective and desirable way only when enterprises have the means and incentives to pursue their individual interests, and when the institutions of financial discipline are in place, such as the absence of systematic subsidies and capricious taxation, the separation of lenders from borrowers, a mechanism to remove unsatisfactory management, and the ultimate threat of bankruptcy" (Hardy, 1992, p. 310-11). The idea that the benefits of improved resource allocation through the spread of the market are achieved gradually is also supported by Flanagan (1995). He notes that employment in the private sector in the Czech economy had increased sharply between 1988 and 1994 (reaching 60%) and draws the conclusion that "new private firms appear to have played a leading role in reversing the wage structure distortions that developed under central planning" (p. 842). He also notes that this evolution of the wage structure raised "productivity through improved allocation of labour" (page 844).

2. MICROECONOMIC-MACROECONOMIC EQUILIBRIUM

In this section we develop a simple economic model in which we can predict the impact of economic liberalization policies on the behavior of a TEs price structure as represented by the equilibrium real exchange rate.

As Williamson (1994) mentions, the literature on real exchange rate determination is split into that part which sees it as being determined by macroeconomic balance, and that which sees it as being determined as the relative price of traded and non-traded goods in microeconomic equilibrium. Here we show that the equilibrium real exchange rate is determined in simultaneous micro-macro-economic equilibrium.

We define the real exchange rate, Q, as the nominal exchange rate, E, weighted by a pair of national relative price levels, P. Thus,

$$Q = EP/P^* \tag{1}$$

[1] According to Sundakov, Ossowski and Lane (1994), even firms in the price-liberalized nonfood traded goods sector (e.g. televisions) may operate perversely. Even though they are free to set market prices shortages still exist. This is because of the distortions caused by the allocation of inputs at below market prices according to perceived need. From the point of view of a firm in the liberalized sector, the lost profit from greater sales at higher prices may be more than balanced by the lower cost of inputs.

where E is the foreign currency price of a unit of domestic currency, and the asterisk denotes the foreign country. An increase in Q - appreciation - reduces a country's international competitiveness. An alternative way of defining the real exchange rate is as the relative price of non-traded good in terms of traded goods. Thus, assuming $P^* = 1$ and defining $P = P^{á}_{T}P^{1-á}_{NT}$ (where ^{á} is the share of traded goods in a country's price index) we have:-

$$Q = P_{NT}/P_T ,\qquad (2)$$

thus, a real appreciation increases the relative price of a country's nontraded goods.

From a Keynesian perspective (Meade, 1993, Corden and Neary, 1982, Salter, 1959, Swan, 1955), when internal and external balance occur simultaneously an economy is in 'macroeconomic equilibrium'. Internal balance occurs when unemployment is at its natural, or, equilibrium, rate. At the corresponding level of equilibrium real GDP, the equilibrium real exchange rate is:-

$$Q = Q(A, U), \qquad Q_A > 0,\ Y_U < 0,\qquad (3)$$

where A is domestic absorption (i.e. real GDP plus net exports) and U the natural rate of unemployment. $Q_A > 0$ is required to keep the level of spending (domestic plus foreign) on domestic product steady at the full employment level. $Q_U > 0$ as a rise in the natural rate of unemployment requires demand to be switched away from domestic goods. In figure 1b II is the internal balance function.

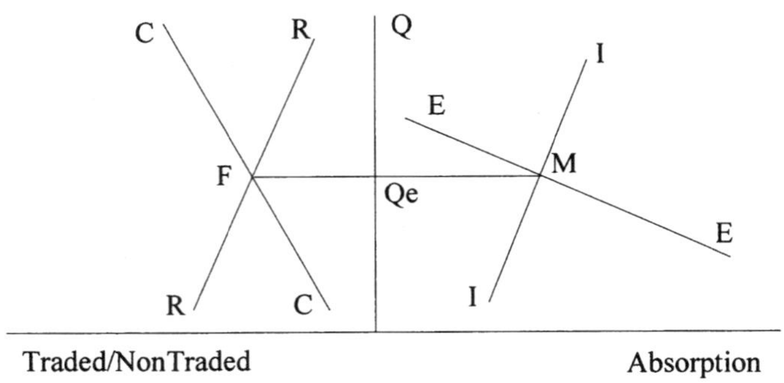

Figure 1a
Resource Allocation

Figure 1b
Internal-External balanc

For external balance the level of Q must yield trade balance, following Williamson (1994), for a given level of 'sustainable' capital inflow. Thus,

$$Q = q(A, K, X, T, S) \quad q_A < 0,\ q_K > 0,\ q_X > 0,\ q_T > 0,\ q_S > 0. \qquad (4)$$

where $q_A < 0$ is necessary as higher absorption increases import demand. The shift factors governing the external balance function, EE, in figure 1b, all of them potentially endogenous to the transition process are: K, the level of 'sustainable' international capital inflow; X, the level of net exports exogenous to Q - depending for example on the modernization of a TEs traded goods sector; T, the level of tariffs and other impediments (such as licenses and quotas) to imports; and S is the level of subsidies on non-traded goods used as inputs into traded goods production. [2]

As the real exchange rate is the relative price of traded and non-traded goods we can write:

$$C_T/C_{NT} = f(Q), \qquad f' > 0, \qquad (5)$$

$$R_T/R_{NT} = g(Q), \qquad g' < 0\ , \qquad (6)$$

where C_T/C_{NT} is the ratio of traded (T) to non-traded (NT) goods in consumption and R_T/R_{NT} their ratio in domestic production (with $C_T + C_{NT} = A$ and $R_T + R_{NT} = Y$). $f' > 0$ as absorption increasingly favors traded goods as Q appreciates and reduces their relative price; [3] and $g' < 0$ as real appreciation reduces the competitiveness of production in the traded goods sector. In figure 1a f is represented by CC and g by RR. Forming

$$B = h[g(Q) - f(Q)] \qquad h' \leq 0 \qquad (7)$$

defines excess supply of traded goods and, therefore, the balance of trade, B. As excess supply is a negative function of Q, the trade deficit above Qe is greater the larger are f' and g' in absolute value, i.e. the flatter are CC and RR.

Crucial to our argument is that in absolute value f' and g' will begin to increase from low values under central planning. We define a situation of 'complete' central planning as $f' = g' = 0$; the central planner being entirely responsible for production and consumption allocation. However, the introduction of market processes into such a system allows

---

[2] The absolute slope of EE is flatter than II as a given change in A needs less adjustment, via a change in Q, of net exports for external balance than is the case for internal balance.

[3] We have assume throughout that substitution effects dominate.

these allocations to become price-sensitive and the signs of the respective derivatives will appear.[4] But the transition in RR is gradual as it is not possible to create a market economy in resource allocation on Western lines all at once. Similarly, *CC* will over time become more responsive to the real exchange rate as domestic consumers and, especially, producers gradually switch from domestic to foreign sources of supply.[5] We liken the gradual increasing slopes of the *RR* and *CC* functions to the slow opening of a fan – see figure 2 - but if a transition is not going well the fan does not open very much.

The slopes of the microeconomic functions in figure 1a govern those of the macroeconomic functions in figures 1b and 2. The more responsive are the shares of traded goods in production and consumption to a change in *Q* the flatter will be the EE function, as any given increase in *Q* will cause a larger trade deficit (in figure 1a) which to maintain external balance will need to be offset by a larger fall in absorption (figure 1b). Similarly with II: the more sensitive are *CC* and *RR* to a change in Q, the flatter is II - as a given increase in *Q* causes a larger trade deficit which needs to be offset by a larger increase in absorption to maintain internal balance.

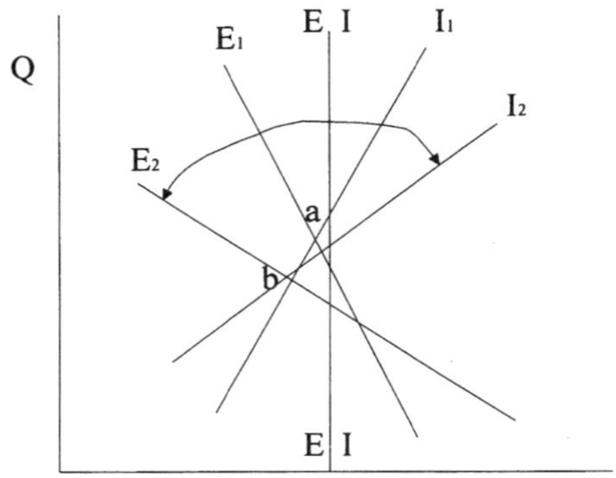

Figure 2: The opening of a "fan": internal-external balance during a transition

[4] Viewed in a different way under 'complete' central planning the production possibility frontier between T and NT goods is rectangular with its interior corner located at the point chosen by the central planners. Changes in relative prices will not alter this allocation. As market processes are introduced, the production possibility frontier gains some curvature - showing that a change in relative prices can affect the allocation of production. Similarly, with 'complete' central planning the community indifference curves are rectangular with the corner point chosen by the central planner. The introduction of market processes again introduces curvature and price responsiveness.

[5] The relative rates at which the slopes of RR and CC increase is not important to our discussion, but it is likely that the rate of change of CC will be faster than RR.

Our hypothesis is that the time series properties of the real exchange rate depend on the relative slopes of the relevant schedules. The intersection of a pair of flattening *II* and *EE* functions in figure 2, driven by the flattening of the underlying *RR* and *CC* schedules, provides a center of gravity to which the real exchange rate may revert. If, for example, *RR* and *CC* are quite flat then a deviation of the actual *Q* from its equilibrium will cause a large balance of trade disequilibrium which will set off strong automatic adjustments - perhaps through changes in the money stock, along the lines of the monetary approach to the balance of payments. Or, a disequilibrium *Q* could be associated with a point off the *II* and *EE* schedules thereby causing strong macro-disequilibrium in labor and commodity markets. Again automatic adjustment, will if allowed, correct the disequilibrium real rate - in the case of unemployment, falling wages and prices. Hence with relatively flat schedules, reflecting the fact that the reforms have begun to bite, we expect the real exchange rate will be mean reverting. In contrast, in a situation where the schedules are still relatively steep, the automatic forces of adjustment are themselves weak. In this case, when the actual real exchange rate is away from the equilibrium rate, *Q* is unlikely to return to equilibrium or if there is a tendency to return it will be a slow drawn-out process. [6] In a time series sense this means the real rate is likely to exhibit considerable persistence in terms of standard statistical tests will appear non-stationary.

Of course, both of the above predictions, but especially the first, are likely to be confounded if as is possible the equilibrium rate for a country in transition moves around a lot. We will let the data be the arbiter for the time series properties of the Visegrad real exchange rates.

3. DATA SOURCES

The real exchange rates have been constructed using the definition for *Q* given earlier. All of the data are taken from the IMF's International Financial Statistics CD-Rom (June, 1996) issue. The nominal exchange rate is line ae and the price series are the consumer price index, line 64, the wholesale price index, line 63, and the real effective index, line 63. All real exchange rates have been transformed into natural logarithms. All data are monthly and for Poland and Hungary start in either January 1980 or 1985 and end in 1995. For the Czech and Slovak Republics the data starts in January 1993 and ends in December 1995. The relatively long runs of data available for Poland and Hungary means that we can examine the time series properties of the real exchange rates both pre and post the

[6] For example, the gap between a pair of near vertical RR and CC functions - even well away from equilibrium - will yield only a small payments deficit, so the adjustment in the money stock is rather minor.

introduction of reforms. The exact sample periods for each series are defined in the relevant Table.

4. ECONOMETRIC METHODS AND RESULTS

In this section we examine the mean reversion properties of the real exchange rates defined above. In testing for the mean-reverting properties of our real exchange rates we use a Dickey Fuller test. Although it is now widely accepted (see, for example, Campbell and Perron (1991) for an overview of the unit root literature) that such a test has relatively low power to discriminate between a series which has exactly a unit root and one which is highly autoregressive, but nonetheless mean-reverting (i.e. has a root close to the unit circle), it is a useful benchmark test in the current application.

Assume that the log of the real exchange rate, q_t, has the following ARMA specification:

$$\phi(B)q_t = \alpha + \theta(B)\varepsilon_t,$$

where B denotes the lag operator and $\alpha = \varphi_0 + \varphi_1 t,$ where t is a deterministic time trend. The easiest way to motivate a test for a unit root in q_t is to assume that it has a purely autoregressive representation which will be the case if the moving average polynomial, $\theta(B)$, in (8) is invertible. Given this assumption we may reparameterise (8) as:

$$\Delta q_t = \gamma_0 + \gamma_1 t + (\beta_0 - 1)q_{t-1} + \sum_{j=1}^{n-1} \beta_{j+1}\Delta q_{t-j} + v_t, \tag{9}$$

where

$$\beta_i = \sum_{j=1}^{n} \phi_j; \quad i = 1,\dots,n, \tag{10}$$

since $\phi(B)$ will contain a unit root if $\sum_1^n \phi_j = 1$, the presence of a unit root is formally equivalent to a test of whether $\beta_0 = 1$ or $(\beta_0 - 1) = 0$. This hypothesis may be tested using a standard t-test although as Dickey and Fuller (1979) and many others note this will have a non-standard distribution and therefore one has to use the percentiles tabulated by Fuller (1976). One may test for two unit roots in the real exchange rate by estimating (9) with all of the q_t terms first differenced again. The inclusion of the correct specification of deterministic variables in (9) is crucial to the power of the test (Campbell and Perron (1991)).

The results from estimating (9) for each of the real exchange rates over the full sample period are presented in Tables 1 through 6. Four different lag length selection criteria have been used: the Akakie Information Criterion (AIC); the Bernanke Information Criterion (BIC); a lagrange multiplier statistic (LM); and a reduction statistic (Red). For Poland (Tables 1 and 2) we note that in levels none of the real exchange rate measures appear stationary (irrespective of the deterministic specification), but there is clear evidence of stationarity when the variables enter the autoregression in differences. For Hungary (Tables 3 and 4) the picture is very similar. The results for the Czech and Slovak Republics (Tables 5 and 6) differ somewhat to the other two countries in the that although the unit root tests on the levels of the real rates all confirm non-stationarity, the tests in first differences also indicate some evidence of non-stationarity (in particular, in half of the cases there is evidence of non-stationarity). However, it is noteworthy that the nonstationarity only occurs in instances where the AIC and BIC criteria are used and in each of these cases the lag length is chosen to be 11; given the relatively short sample period, such a long lag length will in all likelihood lead to an overfitting of the data. The LM and Red criteria, which each indicate a zero lag length, produce what we believe are the more reliable test statistics, and these indicate stationarity of each of the real exchange rates in first differences.

The sub-sample results for the Polish pre-transition period are reported in Tables 7 and 8 and confirm the findings for the full sample period: rates are non-stationary in levels but stationary in differences. However, notice that for the post-reform period (Tables 9 and 10) there is very strong evidence that Polish real exchange rates are stationary in both levels and first differences. A similar picture emerges for Hungary pre and post the inception of reforms. Thus, in Tables 11 and 12 we note that levels are non-stationary and differences are stationary, while in Tables 13 and 14 the t-ratios from the levels equations are close to significance at the 5 per cent level for two measures of the real rate (effective and CPI-based) and are significant at the 10 per cent level (critical value -2.58). Since the unit root test has low power to reject the null, using a 10 per cent critical value does not seem unreasonable.

To summarize the findings of this section, we believe that we have revealed evidence of mean reversion for the real exchange rates of at least two (i.e. Hungary and Poland) of the Visegrad four for the post-reform period. Given that the type of test used has relatively low power to reject the null of a unit root, this would seem to be a strong result. Our failure to find evidence of mean reversion for the Czech and Slovak Republics in all likelihood reflects the relatively small data sample for these countries rather than a failure of the reform process.

5. CONCLUDING COMMENTS

In this paper we have analyzed the real exchange rate behavior of a TE using a simple micro-macro-economic model that reveals the kind of factors generating movements in a TE's equilibrium real exchange rate. We demonstrated, *inter alia*, that the time path of the equilibrium real exchange rate (and the trade deficit, equilibrium unemployment and internal/ external balance) will depend on the sensitivity of resource allocation and the distribution of consumption to changes in relative prices, and on the nature of shocks to the equilibrium level of unemployment. For an economy in transition, the equilibrium real rate will be subjected to successive shocks thereby implying that the permanent component of the real exchange rate will, in all likelihood, dominate the transitory component. This means that it is less likely that TEs real exchange rates will be mean-reverting compared to mature economies real exchange rates (which are known to be non-stationary, at least for the recent floating exchange rate period - see MacDonald, 1995). However, although we did indeed find considerable evidence of non-stationarity across the Visegrad four, there was clear evidence of mean reversion for the real exchange rates of Poland and Hungary in the post-reform period. Given the relatively low power of the tests used, this would seem to be a relatively strong result.

Table 1. Unit Root Tests For Polish Exchange Rates (Whole Sample)

Variable	Sample	No Trend				Trend				
		Test	Lags	ADF	5 %	Test	Lags	ADF	5%	t Statistics on Trend Term
Real ER (Producer Prices)	1982(1) to 1995(10)	AIC	0	-2.6893	-2.88	AIC	0	-2.8581	-3.43	0.9921
		BIC	0	-2.6893	-2.88	BIC	0	-2.8581	-3.43	0.9921
		LB	0	-2.6893	-2.88	LB	0	-2.8581	-3.43	0.9921
		LM	0	-2.6893	-2.88	LM	0	-2.8581	-3.43	0.9921
		Red	0	-2.6893	-2.88	Red	0	-2.8581	-3.43	0.9921
Real ER (Consumer Prices)	1980(1) to 1995(10)	AIC	2	-1.6729	-2.88	AIC	2	-1.3138	-3.43	-0.8889
		BIC	0	-2.0499	-2.88	BIC	0	-1.7976	-3.43	-0.5191
		LB	0	-2.0499	-2.88	LB	0	-1.7976	-3.43	-0.5191
		LM	0	-2.0499	-2.88	LM	0	-1.7976	-3.43	-0.5191
		Red	2	-1.6729	-2.88	Red	2	-1.3138	-3.43	-0.8889
Real ER Index	1980(1) to 1995(10)	AIC	0	-1.5455	-2.88	AIC	0	-1.5648	-3.43	0.3071
		BIC	0	-1.5455	-2.88	BIC	0	-1.5648	-3.43	0.3071
		LB	1	-1.8687	-2.88	LB	1	-1.9135	-3.43	-0.4481
		LM	0	-1.5455	-2.88	LM	0	-1.5648	-3.43	0.3071
		Red	2	-0.9217	-2.88	Red	1	-1.9135	-3.43	-0.4481

Table 2. Unit Root Tests For First Difference In Polish Exchange Rates (Whole Sample)

Variable	Sample	No Trend				Trend				
		Test	Lags	ADF	5 %	Test	Lags	ADF	5%	t Statistics on Trend Term
Real ER (Producer Prices)	1982(2) to 1995(10)	AIC	0	-16.0081	-2.88	AIC	0	-15.9749	-3.43	-0.8019
		BIC	0	-16.0081	-2.88	BIC	0	-15.9749	-3.43	-0.8019
		LB	0	-16.0081	-2.88	LB	0	-15.9749	-3.43	-0.8019
		LM	0	-16.0081	-2.88	LM	0	-15.9749	-3.43	-0.8019
		Red	0	-16.0081	-2.88	Red	0	-15.9749	-3.43	-0.8019
Real ER (Consumer Prices)	1980(2) to 1995(10)	AIC	3	-8.3288	-2.88	AIC	3	-8.4995	-3.43	-1.5335
		BIC	1	-11.6452	-2.88	BIC	1	-11.7435	-3.43	-1.3225
		LB	0	-14.4929	-2.88	LB	0	-14.5480	-3.43	-1.1319
		LM	0	-14.4929	-2.88	LM	0	-14.5480	-3.43	-1.1319
		Red	3	-8.3288	-2.88	Red	3	-8.4995	-3.43	-1.5335
Real ER Index	1980(2) to 1995(10)	AIC	3	-8.6780	-2.88	AIC	3	-8.6567	-3.43	-0.1864
		BIC	0	-11.4257	-2.88	BIC	0	-11.3962	-3.43	-0.1298
		LB	1	-10.1321	-2.88	LB	1	-10.1069	-3.43	-0.1870x
		LM	0	-11.4257	-2.88	LM	0	-11.3962	-3.43	-0.1298
		Red	3	-8.7019	-2.88	Red	3	-8.6815	-3.43	-0.2151

Table 3. Unit Root Tests For Hungarian Exchange Rates (Whole Sample)

Variable	Sample	No Trend				Trend				
		Test	Lags	ADF	5 %	Test	Lags	ADF	5%	t Statistics on Trend Term
Real ER (Producer Prices)	1982(1) to 1995(7)	AIC	0	-1.6420	-2.88	AIC	0	-2.0050	-3.43	1.1891
		BIC	0	-1.6420	-2.88	BIC	0	-2.0050	-3.43	1.1891
		LB	0	-1.6420	-2.88	LB	0	-2.0050	-3.43	1.1891
		LM	0	-1.6420	-2.88	LM	0	-2.0050	-3.43	1.1891
		Red	0	-1.6420	-2.88	Red	0	-2.0050	-3.43	1.1891
Real ER (Consumer Prices)	1980(1) to 1995(7)	AIC	2	-0.4993	-2.88	AIC	2	-0.4993	-3.43	-3.2767
		BIC	0	-0.5364	-2.88	BIC	0	-0.5364	-3.43	-3.2767
		LB	0	-0.5364	-2.88	LB	0	-0.5364	-3.43	-3.2767
		LM	0	-0.5364	-2.88	LM	0	-0.5364	-3.43	-3.2767
		Red	0	-0.5364	-2.88	Red	0	-0.5364	-3.43	-3.2767
Real ER Index	1980(1) to 1995(7)	AIC	0	-1.2411	-2.88	AIC	0	-1.4109	-3.43	0.6894
		BIC	0	-1.2411	-2.88	BIC	0	-1.4109	-3.43	0.6894
		LB	0	-1.2411	-2.88	LB	0	-1.4109	-3.43	0.6894
		LM	0	-1.2411	-2.88	LM	0	-1.4109	-3.43	0.6894
		Red	8	-0.5470	-2.88	Red	8	-0.5448	-3.43	-0.2107

Table 4. Unit Root Tests For First Difference In Hungarian Exchange Rates (Whole Sample)

Variable	Sample	No Trend				Trend				
		Test	Lags	ADF	5 %	Test	Lags	ADF	5%	t Statistics on Trend Term
Real ER (Producer Prices)	1982(2) to 1995(7)	AIC	0	-13.8371	-2.88	AIC	0	-13.8086	-3.43	0.3493
		BIC	0	-13.8371	-2.88	BIC	0	-13.8086	-3.43	0.3493
		LB	0	-13.8371	-2.88	LB	0	-13.8086	-3.43	0.3493
		LM	0	-13.837	-2.88	LM	0	-13.8086	-3.43	0.3493
		Red	0	-13.8371	-2.88	Red	0	-13.8086	-3.43	0.3493
Real ER (Consumer Prices)	1980(2) to 1995(7)	AIC	1	-10.1260	-2.88	AIC	1	-10.4968	-3.43	-2.2968
		BIC	0	-14.1084	-2.88	BIC	0	-14.3542	-3.43	-2.2968
		LB	0	-14.1084	-2.88	LB	0	-14.3542	-3.43	-2.2968
		LM	0	-14.1084	-2.88	LM	0	-14.3542	-3.43	-2.2968
		Red	0	-14.1084	-2.88	Red	0	-14.3542	-3.43	-2.2968
Real ER Index	1980(2) to 1995(7)	AIC	1	-11.1140	-2.88	AIC	1	-11.1143	-3.43	-0.7547
		BIC	0	-13.0104	-2.88	BIC	0	-12.9783	-3.43	0.2246
		LB	0	-13.0104	-2.88	LB	0	-12.9783	-3.43	0.2246
		LM	0	-13.0104	-2.88	LM	0	-12.9783	-3.43	0.2246
		Red	7	-4.0596	-2.88	Red	7	-4.0559	-3.43	-0.2857

Table 5. Unit Root Tests For Czech and Slovak Exchange Rates

Variable	Sample	No Trend				Trend				
		Test	Lags	ADF	5 %	Test	Lags	ADF	5%	t Statistics on Trend Term
Czech Republic	1993(1)	AIC	12	-0.3842	-3.00	AIC	12	-0.8918	-3.60	-1.2810
Real ER	to	BIC	12	-0.3845	-3.00	BIC	12	-0.8918	-3.60	-1.2810
(Producer Prices)	1995(12)	LM	0	-0.9164	-2.93	LM	0	-2.3198	-3.50	-2.1115
		Red	0	-0.9164	-2.93	Red	0	-2.3198	-3.50	-2.1115
Czech Republic	1993(1)	AIC	12	-2.0932	-3.00	AIC	12	-0.9690	-3.60	-0.3293
Real ER	to	BIC	12	-2.0932	-3.00	BIC	12	-0.9690	-3.60	-0.3293
(Consumer	1995(12)	LM	0	-0.2474	-2.93	LM	0	-2.3267	-3.50	-2.3549
Prices)		Red	9	-2.4334	-2.93	Red	9	-2.2272	-3.50	-1.6422
Slovak Republic	1993(1)	AIC	12	-2.0163	-3.00	AIC	12	-1.9457	-3.60	-1.4477
Real ER	to	BIC	12	-2.0163	-3.00	BIC	12	-1.9457	-3.60	-1.4477
(Producer Prices)	1995(11)	LM	0	-0.6781	-2.93	LM	0	-2.2859	-3.50	-2.3398
		Red	11	-2.7749	-3.00	Red	11	-1.6833	3.60	-0.9429
Slovak Republic	1993(1)	AIC	12	-1.9661	-3.00	AIC	12	-1.0561	-3.60	-0.5498
Real ER	to	BIC	12	-1.9661	-3.00	BIC	12	-1.0561	-3.60	-0.5498
(Producer Prices)	1995(11)	LM	0	-0.3027	-2.93	LM	0	-2.2783	-3.50	-2.4134
		Red	0	-0.3016	-2.93	Red	0	-2.3079	-3.50	-2.4313

Table 6. Unit Root Tests For Differences In Czech and Slovak Exchange Rates

Variable	Sample	No Trend				Trend				
		Test	Lags	ADF	5 %	Test	Lags	ADF	5%	t Statistics on Trend Term
Czech Republic Real ER (Producer Prices)	1993(2) to 1995(12)	AIC	11	-1.3665	-3.00	AIC	11	-1.3509	-3.60	-1.0135
		BIC	11	-1.3665	-3.00	BIC	11	-1.3509	-3.60	-1.0135
		LM	0	-5.6678	-2.93	LM	0	-5.5964	-3.50	-0.3355
		Red	0	-5.6678	-2.93	Red	9	-2.1671	-3.50	-1.3178
Czech Republic Real ER (Consumer Prices)	1993(2) to 1995(12)	AIC	11	-1.3796	-3.00	AIC	11	0.9604	-3.60	1.7715
		BIC	11	-1.3796	-3.00	BIC	11	0.9604	-3.60	1.7715
		LM	0	-5.6207	-2.93	LM	0	-5.5443	-3.50	-0.2857
		Red	0	-5.6207	-2.93	Red	8	0.7312	-3.50	1.8503
Slovak Republic Real ER (Producer Prices)	1993(2) to 1995(11)	AIC	11	-0.9107	-3.00	AIC	11	-0.4095	-3.60	1.4748
		BIC	11	-0.9107	-3.00	BIC	11	-0.4095	-3.60	1.4748
		LM	0	-4.6337	-2.93	LM	0	-4.6202	-3.50	-0.6104
		Red	0	-4.7112	-2.93	Red	0	-4.6848	3.50	-0.5260
Slovak Republic Real ER (Producer Prices)	1993(2) to 1995(11)	AIC	11	-0.8159	-3.00	AIC	11	0.4010	-3.60	1.6360
		BIC	11	-0.8159	-3.00	BIC	11	0.4010	-3.60	1.6360
		LM	0	-5.6429	-2.93	LM	0	-5.6449	-3.50	-0.7374
		Red	0	-5.7440	-2.93	Red	0	-5.7385	-3.50	-0.6952

Table 7. Unit Root Tests For Polish Exchange Rates (Pre 1990 Sub-Sample)

Variable	Sample	No Trend				Trend				
		Test	Lags	ADF	5 %	Test	Lags	ADF	5%	t Statistics on Trend Term
Real ER (Producer Prices)	1982(1) to 1995(12)	AIC	2	1.1223	-2.88	AIC	2	-3.3144	-3.43	4.5421
		BIC	1	0.7670	-2.88	BIC	1	-3.7022	-3.43	4.7992
		LB	0	-0.4805	-2.88	LB	0	-5.2738	-3.43	5.9090
		LM	0	-0.4805	-2.88	LM	0	-5.2738	-3.43	5.9090
		Red	12	-0.6948	-2.88	Red	12	-0.9374	-3.43	0.8560
Real ER (Consumer Prices)	1980(1) to 1995(12)	AIC	4	0.2541	-2.88	AIC	4	-2.7058	-3.43	2.9284
		BIC	0	-0.3050	-2.88	BIC	0	-3.6041	-3.43	3.7570
		LB	0	-0.3050	-2.88	LB	0	-3.6041	-3.43	3.7570
		LM	0	-0.3050	-2.88	LM	0	-3.6041	-3.43	3.7570
		Red	4	0.2541	-2.88	Red	4	-2.7058	-3.43	2.9284
Real ER Index	1980(1) to 1995(12)	AIC	7	-0.2423	-2.88	AIC	7	-1.6727	-3.43	-2.5580
		BIC	0	0.0774	-2.88	BIC	0	-1.1725	-3.43	-2.3937
		LB	0	0.0774	-2.88	LB	0	-1.1725	-3.43	-2.3937
		LM	1	-0.1446	-2.88	LM	2	-1.2852	-3.43	-2.2894
		Red	7	-0.2423	-2.88	Red	7	-1.6727	-3.43	-2.5580

Table 8. Unit Root Tests For First Differences In Exchange Rates (Pre 1990 Sub-Sample)

Variable	Sample	No Trend				Trend				
		Test	Lags	ADF	5 %	Test	Lags	ADF	5%	t Statistics on Trend Term
Real ER (Producer Prices)	1982(1) to 1995(12)	AIC	0	-12.7726	-2.88	AIC	0	-13.0600	-3.43	1.8906
		BIC	0	-12.7726	-2.88	BIC	0	-13.0600	-3.43	1.8906
		LB	0	-12.7726	-2.88	LB	0	-13.0600	-3.43	1.8906
		LM	0	-12.7726	-2.88	LM	0	-13.0600	-3.43	1.8906
		Red	1	-13.1533	-2.88	Red	1	-13.0245	-3.43	-0.8425
Real ER (Consumer Prices)	1980(1) to 1995(12)	AIC	3	-5.8546	-2.88	AIC	3	-5.8932	-3.43	1.1184
		BIC	1	-8.1961	-2.88	BIC	1	-8.2381	-3.43	1.1280
		LB	0	-11.0081	-2.88	LB	0	-11.0552	-3.43	1.1035
		LM	0	-11.0081	-2.88	LM	0	-11.0552	-3.43	1.1035
		Red	3	-5.8546	-2.88	Red	3	-5.8932	-3.43	1.1184
Real ER Index	1980(1) to 1995(12)	AIC	6	-2.4299	-2.88	AIC	6	-2.9864	-3.43	1.9344
		BIC	0	-7.7231	-2.88	BIC	0	-7.9877	-3.43	1.8993
		LB	0	-7.7231	-2.88	LB	0	-7.9877	-3.43	1.8993
		LM	0	-7.7231	-2.88	LM	0	-7.9877	-3.43	1.8993
		Red	6	-2.4299	-2.88	Red	6	-2.9864	-3.43	1.9344

Table 9. Unit Root Tests For Polish Exchange Rates (Pre 1990 Sub-Sample)

Variable	Sample	No Trend				Trend				
		Test	Lags	ADF	5 %	Test	Lags	ADF	5%	t Statistics on Trend Term
Real ER (Producer Prices)	1982(1) to 1995(10)	AIC	12	-4.4746	-2.89	AIC	12	-5.0546	-3.45	-2.8062
		BIC	0	-6.0161	-2.89	BIC	0	-6.2836	-3.45	-2.6389
		LB	0	-6.0161	-2.89	LB	0	-6.2836	-3.45	-2.6389
		LM	0	-6.0161	-2.89	LM	18	-5.5293	-3.45	-3.3738
		Red	6	-1.4258	-2.89	Red	6	-1.2026	-3.45	-0.4733
Real ER (Consumer Prices)	1980(1) to 1995(10)	AIC	1	-5.5800	-2.89	AIC	1	-5.3929	-3.45	-2.4883
		BIC	1	-5.5800	-2.89	BIC	1	-5.3929	-3.45	-2.4883
		LB	5	-4.3993	-2.89	LB	1	-5.3929	-3.45	-2.4883
		LM	0	-5.8889	-2.89	LM	3	-4.1201	-3.45	-1.8014
		Red	9	-2.2392	-2.89	Red	9	-2.1649	-3.45	-0.5882
Real ER Index	1980(1) to 1995(10)	AIC	0	-4.2439	-2.89	AIC	0	-3.3823	-3.45	-0.9812
		BIC	0	-4.2439	-2.89	BIC	0	-3.3823	-3.45	-0.9812
		LB	0	-4.2439	-2.89	LB	0	-3.3823	-3.45	-0.9812
		LM	17	-3.8367	-2.89	LM	12	-4.0254	-3.45	-2.4755
		Red	1	-1.8669	-2.89	Red	1	-1.9102	-3.45	0.4427

Table 10. Unit Root Tests For First Differences In Polish Exchange Rates (Pre 1990 Sub-Sample)

Variable	Sample	No Trend				Trend				
		Test	Lags	ADF	5 %	Test	Lags	ADF	5%	t Statistics on Trend Term
Real ER (Producer Prices)	1982(2) to 1995(10)	AIC	6	-7.0586	-2.89	AIC	6	-6.9378	-3.45	0.4977
		BIC	2	-7.8616	-2.89	BIC	2	-7.5074	-3.45	0.6462
		LB	0	-9.4571	-2.89	LB	0	-9.2634	-3.45	0.5793
		LM	0	-9.4571	-2.89	LM	0	-9.2634	-3.45	0.5793
		Red	2	-7.8616	-2.89	Red	2	-7.5074	-3.45	0.6462
Real ER (Consumer Prices)	1980(2) to 1995(10)	AIC	6	-4.3946	-2.89	AIC	6	-4.3079	-3.45	0.8772
		BIC	1	-5.3030	-2.89	BIC	1	-5.5327	-3.45	-1.8240
		LB	0	-6.5015	-2.89	LB	0	-6.6851	-3.45	1.5272
		LM	0	-6.5015	-2.89	LM	0	-6.6851	-3.45	1.5272
		Red	6	-4.3946	-2.89	Red	6	-4.3079	-3.45	0.8772
Real ER Index	1980(2) to 1995(10)	AIC	0	-6.7352	-2.89	AIC	0	-7.4263	-3.45	-2.5099
		BIC	0	-6.7352	-2.89	BIC	0	-7.4263	-3.45	-2.5099
		LB	0	-6.7352	-2.89	LB	0	-7.4263	-3.45	-2.5099
		LM	2	-9.0898	-2.89	LM	0	-7.4263	-3.45	-2.5099
		Red	3	-8.6780	-2.89	Red	3	-8.6567	-3.45	0.1864

Table 11. Unit Root Tests For Hungarian Exchange Rates (Pre 1990 Sub-Sample)

Variable	Sample	No Trend				Trend				
		Test	Lags	ADF	5 %	Test	Lags	ADF	5%	t Statistics on Trend Term
Real ER (Producer Prices)	1982(1) to 1995(12)	AIC	1	-1.6531	-2.88	AIC	1	-2.2178	-3.43	1.4692
		BIC	0	-1.6518	-2.88	BIC	0	-2.1416	-3.43	1.3590
		LB	12	-2.0901	-2.88	LB	12	-2.4254	-3.43	1.2577
		LM	8	-1.4566	-2.88	LM	13	-2.6733	-3.43	1.4957
		Red	12	-2.0901	-2.88	Red	12	-2.4254	-3.43	1.2577
Real ER (Consumer Prices)	1980(1) to 1995(12)	AIC	1	-2.0244	-2.88	AIC	1	-1.7737	-3.43	-0.0156
		BIC	0	-1.9536	-2.88	BIC	0	-1.6548	-3.43	-0.1266
		LB	0	-1.9536	-2.88	LB	0	-1.6548	-3.43	-0.1266
		LM	0	-1.9536	-2.88	LM	0	-1.6548	-3.43	-0.1266
		Red	6	-0.7369	-2.88	Red	6	-2.9193	-3.43	-2.9858
Real ER Index	1980(1) to 1995(12)	AIC	0	-1.2114	-2.88	AIC	0	-3.0051	-3.43	-3.0968
		BIC	0	-1.2114	-2.88	BIC	0	-3.0051	-3.43	-3.0968
		LB	0	-1.2114	-2.88	LB	0	-3.0051	-3.43	-3.0968
		LM	0	-1.2114	-2.88	LM	0	-3.0051	-3.43	-3.0968
		Red	8	-0.9698	-2.88	Red	8	-2.9444	-3.43	-2.9444

Table 12. Unit Root Tests For First Differences In Hungarian Exchange Rates (Pre 1990 Sub-Sample)

Variable	Sample	No Trend				Trend				
		Test	Lags	ADF	5 %	Test	Lags	ADF	5%	t Statistics on Trend Term
Real ER (Producer Prices)	1982(2) to 1995(12)	AIC	1	-7.8769	-2.88	AIC	1	-7.8434	-3.43	-0.2108
		BIC	0	-10.0941	-2.88	BIC	0	-10.0396	-3.43	-0.0166
		LB	11	-2.1648	-2.88	LB	11	-2.1691	-3.43	-0.3008
		LM	2	-6.1805	-2.88	LM	7	-5.4956	-3.43	-0.4924
		Red	12	-0.1131	-2.88	Red	12	-0.1258	-3.43	-0.6009
Real ER (Consumer Prices)	1980(2) to 1995(12)	AIC	1	-7.5797	-2.88	AIC	1	-7.7136	-3.43	-1.3036
		BIC	0	-9.7860	-2.88	BIC	0	-9.8210	-3.43	1.2487
		LB	0	-9.7860	-2.88	LB	0	-9.8210	-3.43	1.2487
		LM	0	-9.7860	-2.88	LM	0	-9.8210	-3.43	1.2487
		Red	0	-9.7860	-2.88	Red	0	-9.8210	-3.43	1.2487
Real ER Index	1980(2) to 1995(12)	AIC	1	-9.3365	-2.88	AIC	1	-9.3769	-3.43	-0.9309
		BIC	0	-10.2072	-2.88	BIC	0	-10.3117	-3.43	-1.3690
		LB	0	-10.2072	-2.88	LB	0	-10.3117	-3.43	-1.3690
		LM	0	-10.2072	-2.88	LM	0	-10.3117	-3.43	-1.3690
		Red	7	-2.9978	-2.88	Red	7	-3.2038	-3.43	-1.1648

Table 13. Unit Root Tests For Hungarian Exchange Rates (Pre 1990 Sub-Sample)

Variable	Sample	No Trend				Trend				
		Test	Lags	ADF	5 %	Test	Lags	ADF	5%	t Statistics on Trend Term
Real ER (Producer Prices)	1982(1) to 1995(7)	AIC	1	-0.8414	-2.89	AIC	1	-2.1113	-3.45	2.4580
		BIC	0	-0.8899	-2.89	BIC	0	-2.1817	-3.45	2.4703
		LB	0	-0.8899	-2.89	LB	0	-2.1817	-3.45	2.4703
		LM	0	-0.8899	-2.89	LM	0	-2.1817	-3.45	2.4703
		Red	1	-0.8414	-2.89	Red	1	-2.1113	-3.45	2.4580
Real ER (Consumer Prices)	1980(1) to 1995(7)	AIC	1	-2.8471	-2.89	AIC	1	-2.9187	-3.45	-1.8973
		BIC	0	-2.8411	-2.89	BIC	0	-3.4924	-3.45	-2.4716
		LB	0	-2.8411	-2.89	LB	0	-3.4924	-3.45	-2.4716
		LM	0	-2.8411	-2.89	LM	0	-3.4924	-3.45	-2.4716
		Red	2	-0.1507	-2.89	Red	2	-2.2679	-3.45	-2.5956
Real ER Index	1980(1) to 1995(7)	AIC	0	-2.7687	-2.89	AIC	0	-1.1760	-3.45	-0.2483
		BIC	0	-2.7687	-2.89	BIC	0	-1.1760	-3.45	-0.2483
		LB	0	-2.7687	-2.89	LB	0	-1.1760	-3.45	-0.2483
		LM	0	-2.7687	-2.89	LM	0	-1.1760	-3.45	-0.2483
		Red	8	-1.2378	-2.89	Red	8	-1.4415	-3.45	-0.7787

Table 14. Unit Root Tests For First Differences in Hungarian Exchange Rates (Pre 1990 Sub-Sample)

Variable	Sample	No Trend				Trend				
		Test	Lags	ADF	5 %	Test	Lags	ADF	5%	t Statistics on Trend Term
Real ER (Producer Prices)	1982(2) to 1995(7)	AIC	0	-8.5136	-2.89	AIC	0	-8.7192	-3.45	1.4946
		BIC	0	-8.5136	-2.89	BIC	0	-8.7192	-3.45	1.4946
		LB	0	-8.5136	-2.89	LB	0	-8.7192	-3.45	1.4946
		LM	0	-8.5136	-2.89	LM	0	-8.7192	-3.45	1.4946
		Red	6	-2.3911	-2.89	Red	6	-2.3879	-3.45	0.1438
Real ER (Consumer Prices)	1980(2) to 1995(7)	AIC	1	-7.9314	-2.89	AIC	1	-8.3563	-3.45	2.0474
		BIC	0	-10.9600	-2.89	BIC	0	-11.2718	-3.45	1.7914
		LB	0	-10.9600	-2.89	LB	0	-11.2718	-3.45	1.7914
		LM	1	-7.9314	-2.89	LM	2	-5.7189	-3.45	1.9596
		Red	0	-10.9600	-2.89	Red	0	-11.2718	-3.45	1.7914
Real ER Index	1980(2) to 1995(7)	AIC	0	-6.4907	-2.89	AIC	0	-9.2566	-3.45	-2.3854
		BIC	0	-6.4907	-2.89	BIC	0	-9.2566	-3.45	-2.3854
		LB	0	-6.4907	-2.89	LB	3	-5.7385	-3.45	-2.6451
		LM	0	-6.4907	-2.89	LM	0	-9.2566	-3.45	-2.3854
		Red	8	-2.0056	-2.89	Red	8	-1.9835	-3.45	-0.0675

REFERENCES

Begg, D,, L. Halpern and C. Wyplosz (1999), "Equilibrium Exchange Rates", Chapter 2 of *Monetary and Exchange Rate Policies, EMU and Central and Eastern Europe*, Forum Report of the Economic Policy Initiative, No. 5, EastWest Institute, New York.

Berg, A. and O. Blanchard (1994), in *The Transition in Eastern Europe: Country Studies*, University of Chicago Press, Chicago.

Blanchard, O., S. Commander and F. Coricelli (1994), *Unemployment, Restructuring, and the Labour Market in Eastern Europe and Russia*, World Bank, Washington DC.

Borensztein, E., D. G. Demekas and J. D. Ostry (1993), "An Empirical Analysis of the Output Declines in three Eastern European Countries", *IMF Staff Papers*, 40 (1), March, 1-31.

Branson, W. and J. B. De Macedo (1995), "Macroeconomic Policy in Central Europe", *CEPR Discussion Paper*, No 1195.

Brown, A. N. (1999), *When is the Transition Over?*, Upjohn Institute, Kalamazoo.

Calvo, G. A. and F. Coricelli (1993), "Output Collapse in Eastern Europe", *IMF Staff Papers*, 40 (1), March, 32-52.

Campbell, J. Y. and P. Perron (1991), "Pitfalls and Opportunities: What Macroeconomists Should Know About Unit Roots", in O. J. Blanchard and S. Fisher, (eds), *NBER Economic Manual*, Cambridge, MA.

Corden, W.M. and J.P. Neary (1982), "Booming Sector and Deindustrialization in a Small Open Economy", *Economic Journal*, 92 (4), December, 825-48.

Dickey D., and W. A. Fuller (1979), "Distribution of the Estimators for Autoressive Time Series with a Unit Root", *Journal of American Statistical Society*, 74, 427-31.

Dinopoulos, E. and T. D. Lane (1992), "Market Liberalization Policies in a Reforming Socialist Economy", *IMF Staff Papers*, 39 (3), September, 456-494.

Flanagan, R. J. (1995), "Wage Structures in the Transition of the Czech Economy", *IMF Staff Papers*, 42 (4), December, 837-53.

Fuller, W. A. (1976), *Introduction to Statistical Time Series*, New York, Wiley.

Genberg, H. (1991), "On the Sequencing of Reforms in Eastern Europe", *IMF Working Paper*, WP/91/13.

Halpern, L. and C. Wyplosz (1997), "Equilibrium Exchange Rates in Transition Economies", *IMF Staff Papers*, 44 (4).

Hardy, D. C. (1992), "Soft Budget Constraints, Firm Commitments, and the Social Safety Net", *IMF Staff Papers*, 39 (2), June, 310-29.

Hardy, D. C. and Lahari (1992), "Bank Insolvency and Stabilization in Europe", *IMF Staff Papers*, 39 (4) December, 778-800.

Krajnyak, K. and J. Zettelmayer (1998), "Competitiveness in Transition Economies: What Scope for Real Appreciation?", *IMF Staff Papers*, 45 (2), June, 309-362

MacDonald, R. (1995), "Long-run Exchange Rate Modeling: A Survey of The Recent Evidence", *Staff Papers of the International Monetary Fund*,

Meade, J. (1993), ""The Meaning of Internal Balance", *American Economic Review*, December. (Reprinted Nobel lecture, 1977).

Salter, W. E. G. (1959), "Internal and External Balance: The Role of Price and Expenditure Effects", *Economic Record*, August, 226-38.

Svejnar, J. (1999), "The Transition Is Not Over, but Note the Merits of the Central European Model". In Brown, op cit., pp 77-98.

Sundakov, A., R. Ossowski and T. D. Lane (1994), "Shortages Under Free Prices: The Case of Ukraine in 1992", *IMF Staff Papers*, 41 (3), September, 411-24.

Swan, T. (1956), "Economic Control in a Dependent Economy", *Economic Record*, November, 230-56.

Williamson, J. (1994), *Estimating Equilibrium Exchange Rates*, Institute for International Economics, Washington DC.

Chapter 4

MONETARY CONTROL ON THE PATH TO EU AND EMU MEMBERSHIP

Rod Cross
Department of Economics and ICMM, University of Strathclyde

ABSTRACT

This chapter summaries some of the main issues surrounding monetary control in the Visegrad economies, focusing on the ability of the countries to satisfy EMU admission criteria.

1. INTRODUCTION

For the "Visegrad" countries - the Czech and Slovak Republics, Hungary and Poland - accession to the European Union (EU) is seen as an important intermediate step in the process of economic transition. Eleven of the fifteen members of the EU joined an economic and monetary union at the start of 1999, with the common euro interest rate and exchange rate to be cemented by the abolition of separate national currencies at the start of 2002. Whilst the possibility exists that some existing EU members will remain outside the EMU by the time the six countries (Poland, Hungary, the Czech Republic, Slovenia, Estonia and Cyprus) fast-tracked for membership join the EU, the ability of these countries to satisfy EMU membership criteria needs to be taken seriously.

The Maastricht requirements that fiscal deficits and debt ratios be less than 3% and 60% of GDP are considered elsewhere in this volume. The other requirements for entry into EMU are that the rate of inflation is no more than 1.5% above the EU average in the three lowest inflation countries; that nominal long-term interest rates are no more than 2% above the average of the three lowest EU member rates; and that the nominal exchange rate has been maintained within some European Monetary System (EMS) bands for at least two years without realignment. The European Central Bank (ECB) has interpreted its target of price stability as being an inflation rate of 0-2%. In 1999 inflation rates were at the lower end of this range in the lowest inflation EMU countries, so the

R. MacDonald and R. Cross (eds.), Central Europe Towards Monetary Union: Macroeconomic Underpinnings and Financial Reputation, 59–70.

Maastricht inflation criterion for EMU entry is likely to involve an inflation rate of no more than 2%. European Bank for Reconstruction and Development (EBRD) projections for inflation rates in the Visegrad countries in 1999 were Slovakia (14.5), Hungary (8.0), Poland (6.5) and the Czech Republic (3.5). Slovakia has not been fast-tracked for EU membership because of its failure to satisfy "political" criteria. Hungary and Poland clearly have still to undergo a sizeable process of disinflation in order to satisfy EMU entry criteria. An EMS Mark II began in 1999 with Denmark and Greece as its initial members, and this will presumably be the vehicle for satisfying the exchange rate requirements for EMU entry. Exchange rate crises, such as those experienced by several EMU members in the run up to 1999, and by the Czech Republic in 1997, could well present problems on the trajectory to EMU membership. If accession to EU membership occurs in 2002-2004, one scenario would involve EMU membership being considered two years later.

This chapter offers an overview of some of the main issues surrounding the ability of the Visegrad countries to have sufficient monetary control to achieve the inflation criteria for EMU membership. As Keynes remarked, "...the ideas of economists and political philosophers, both when they are right and when they are wrong, are more powerful than is commonly understood ..." (Keynes 1936, pp. 383-4). At the time the Visegrad economies embarked on transition Keynesian ideas had ceased to exert much influence on policy making in the market economies, being supplanted by reformulations of "classical" doctrine. This has almost inevitably conditioned the monetary control frameworks established in the transition economies. In the following discussion some of the main elements in this conventional wisdom regarding macroeconomic policy are reviewed.

2. MONETARISM

According to monetarist doctrine, "inflation is always and everywhere a monetary phenomenon". For this doctrine to apply, several conditions need to hold: the axiom of monetary neutrality, so that shocks in the monetary sector have potentially lasting effects on inflation, but not on "real" variables such as output and employment; stable demand for real money balance relationships, so that changes in velocity do not offset, in an unpredictable manner, shocks emanating from the supply side of the monetary sector; and exogeneity in the processes determining the nominal money supply, so that the predominant arrow of causality runs from money to prices, and not vice-versa. Taking logs and time derivatives in Irving Fisher's quantity theory equation gives:

$$\dot{p} = \dot{m} + \dot{v} - \dot{t} \tag{1}$$

where $\dot{p}$ is the rate of inflation, $\dot{m}$ is the rate of change of the nominal money stock, $\dot{v}$ is that rate of change of velocity and $\dot{t}$ is that rate of change of "real" economic transactions or activity. Referring to expression (1), the monetary neutrality axiom serves to fix the value of $\dot{t}$ independently of $\dot{m}$ and $\dot{p}$ once expectations are realised; the stable demand for real balances postulate serves to pin $\dot{v}$ as a stable function of, usually, opportunity cost and scale variables; and exogeneity in the money supply process serves to introduce exogenous shifts in $\dot{m}$ which, given the other assumptions, can only lead to corresponding shifts in $\dot{p}$. Hence the monetarist causality $\dot{m} \rightarrow \dot{p}$.

The above is the monetarist story for a closed economy, or for an economy with a freely floating exchange rate, and so no central bank intervention in the foreign exchange market. In such a world the exchange rate depreciates/appreciates to reflect any excess/shortfall of domestic monetary expansion and inflation relative to that in the rest of the world. With a fixed exchange rate, and central bank intervention in the foreign exchange market, the money supply can no longer be controlled independently of the exchange rate peg, but instead becomes demand-determined. The change in the money supply is now:

$$\dot{m}^S = \dot{d} + \dot{f} \tag{2}$$

where $\dot{d}$ is the rate of domestic credit expansion, and $\dot{f}$ is the rate of change of central bank foreign exchange reserves. In this fixed exchange rate set-up the "law of one price" is used to fix the domestic rate of inflation equal to that in the countries to whose currencies the exchange rate is pegged, and the endogenous variable is now the change in foreign exchange reserves:

$$\dot{f} = \left[\dot{p} + \dot{t} - \dot{v}\right] - \dot{d} \tag{3}$$

where the term in brackets represents the change in the demand for nominal money balances. Thus changes in domestic credit creation now drive the extent of foreign market intervention required, i.e. $\dot{d} \rightarrow \dot{f}$.

Whilst all four countries have maintained fixed exchange pegs for at least some of the period since 1990. Poland and Hungary have crawling pegs which are devalued at pre-announced rates, the Czech Republic moved to a managed float designed to stabilise the Koruna against the DM in 1997, and Slovakia widened its intervention bands to ±7% in 1997. Thus the relevant logic is some mixture of the fixed exchange rate monetarism, summarised in equation (2), and of the closed economy/floating exchange rate monetarism, summarised in equation (1).

3. RATIONAL EXPECTATIONS

The complaint from within the classical camp was that simple monetarism lacked foundations in terms of individual optimising behavior, particularly with regard to expectation formation (Lucas 1972, for example). The obvious problem of aggregating over heterogeneous agents is ignored by assuming a representative agent. The following is the Sargent (1995) two-period analysis. The representative agent maximises a utility function:

$$In\left[2w_1 - m_t / p_t\right] + In\left[2w_2 + m_t / p^*_{t+1}\right] \tag{4}$$

Here the agent is choosing the nominal money balances m_t to carry over to period $(t+1)$, $2w_1$ is a measure of the resources available to consume or save in period t, $2w_2$ is the resources available in $(t+1)$, with the "2" coefficients being designed to cancel out the "2" m's which would otherwise appear in (5) below, p and p^* are the actual and expected price levels, and the overlapping generations structure gives $w_1 > w_2$. This optimisation exercise yields:

$$m^D_t / p_t = w_1 - w_2 p^*_{t+1} / p_t \tag{5}$$

Thus the demand for money depends on the resource or net worth scale variables w_1 and w_2, and on the "own" rate of interest p^*_{t+1} / p_t. The money supply is determined by the monetary authority as:

$$m^S_{t+1} = \alpha m^S_t \tag{6}$$

The representative agent believes that the price level is related to the money supply as:

$$p_t = \beta m^S_t + \gamma^t k \tag{7}$$

where β, γ and k are constants summarising the agent's beliefs, $\beta, \gamma > 0$, $k \geq 0$. If the agent knows the value of α in (6), the rational expectation of the price level is:

$$p^*_{t+1} = \beta \alpha m^S_t + \gamma^{t+1} k \tag{8}$$

Substituting (8) into (5) and (7) yields:

$$m^D_t = \beta\left[w_1 - w_2 \alpha\right] m^S_t + \gamma^t \left(w_1 - w_2 \gamma\right) k \tag{9}$$

The equilibrium $m^D_t = m^S_t$ will occur only when:

$$\beta = \left[w_1 - \alpha w_2 \right]^{-1} \tag{10}$$

and $$\gamma = w_1 / w_2 \tag{11}$$

Substituting (10) and (11) into (7) gives:

$$p_t = \left[w_1 - \alpha w_2 \right]^{-1} m_t^S + \left(w_1 / w_2 \right)^t k \tag{12}$$

The parameter α describes the money supply process in (6), and is given, but k, which comes from (7), can take any value $k \geq 0$. Thus there is one equilibrium in which prices are proportional to the money supply, i.e. when $k=0$, but a continuum of other possible equilibria in which the price level rises in speculative bubbles (see Sargent 1995, p. 13, from which this model is taken). The point is that expectational beliefs condition equilibria under rational expectations, with the money supply no longer necessarily pinning down a unique value for the price level.

4. HETEROGENEOUS EXPECTATIONS

The standard rational expectations model assumes homogeneous expectations. Once heterogeneous expectations are introduced the axiom of monetary neutrality does not necessarily hold. Consider the consequences of monetary policies designed to reduce inflation rates in the Visegrad four to EMU levels. One pessimistic group of agents does not expect the anti-inflation policy to be successful, the other group are optimistic about the chances of the policy succeeding (see Calvo 1989). In the face of such diverse expectations, the nominal yields on savings deposits and bonds will have to be raised to cover some weighted average of the inflation expectations of the pessimists and optimists. If the anti-inflation strategy turns out to be successful, the ex post real interest rate will be high because the nominal interest rate contained a premium to cover the pessimistic inflation expectation that did not materialise. The high real interest rates would thus impact on the real economy by way of bankruptcies and unemployment, and a banking crisis could further depress the "real" economy once the commercial banks have a heavier burden of non-performing or bad debts (see Sachs 1995). Or, alternatively, the transmission mechanism might operate via the nominal exchange rate, a tougher nominal exchange rate being required to reassure the pessimists, with the resulting ex post exchange rate premium causing problems in the traded goods sector.

5. RELIABILITY OF MONETARY INDICATORS

The preceding analytical models assume that there is some unique measure of money. This obviously begs the questions of which measure of the money supply is relevant in the sense of having a causal influence on prices and economic fluctuations, and of whether such a measure of the money supply would continue to have the same causal influences were it to be controlled.

A necessary condition for some measure of money to have predictable, in the sense of reliable, effects on prices and economic fluctuations is the existence of a stable demand for money or velocity function. In the wake of liberalisation and innovation in systems of financial intermediation, demand for money relationships in many market economies have proved to be unstable. Thus the introduction of new types of bank deposit, interest-bearing chequing accounts for example, lead to reallocations of asset portfolios which change the relationships between the different measures of money and the income/wealth and interest rate differential explanatory variables. Such shifts in velocity functions are likely to characterise the Visegrad economies as the banking systems are restructured and as new financial assets and hence new forms of holding wealth become available. The short runs of data available since liberalisation also make it difficult to draw reliable inferences regarding the demand for money or velocity relationships. To circumvent this problem data sets which span both the planning and liberalisation eras can be employed, with proxies for shortages controlling for "monetary overhangs" under central planning (Chawluk and Cross 1997, Nijsse and Sterken 1996).

Even if stable demand for money functions could be found, it would not necessarily follow that the relationships would remain stable if the monetary magnitudes in question were used as instruments of monetary control. "Goodhart's Law" states that a monetary magnitude will behave differently if it is subjected to control (Goodhart 1984). The underlying problem is that of disintermediation. Thus if the central bank operates a target for, say, the rate of growth of domestic currency M2, the domestic banks could avoid any undesired restrictions on their ability to lend by offering loans via foreign branch offices, or loans denominated in foreign currencies. The restrictions on bank lending could also be circumvented by the establishment of new financial intermediaries outwith the M2 net.

For these reasons it would be imprudent for the Visegrad countries to rely solely on money supply targets as their sole means of controlling their rates of inflation. Instead a more eclectic approach to monetary control has been adopted, with targets for monetary growth being complemented by other instruments of monetary control.

6. THE NATURAL RATE HYPOTHESIS

An important role in monetary policy in market economies is played by the natural rate of unemployment or output concept (see Stiglitz 1997). The natural rate of hypothesis can be expressed as:

$$\Delta p = f(u - u^*) + \Delta p^e \tag{13}$$

$$u^* = g(r) \tag{14}$$

$$u^* A u \tag{15}$$

where $\Delta p = p - p_{-1}$, where p is the log of the price level, $\Delta p^e = p^e - p_{-1}$ where p^e is the log of the expected price level, u and u^* are the actual and natural rates of unemployment, r is a vector of "real", i.e. non-monetary, variables which determine u^* and A means "is an attractor for". If the rate of inflation follows a unit root process, $\Delta p = \Delta p_{-1} + \phi$ where ϕ is a random term, and if the expected price level is geared purely to this process, then $E[p] = p^e = p_{-1} + \Delta p_{-1}$. Thus $p - p^e = p - (p_{-1} + \Delta p_{-1}) = \Delta^2 p$, where $\Delta^2 p = \Delta p - \Delta p_{-1}$, and (13) can be written as:

$$\Delta^2 p = f(u - u^*) \tag{16}$$

with $f(u-u^*) \lesseqgtr 0$ as $(u - u^*) \gtreqless 0$ and $f(0)=0$.

The implication of the natural rate hypothesis (NRH) for policies to reduce rates of the inflation in the Visegrad countries is clear: as expression (16) indicates, $\Delta^2 p < 0$ will require $u > u^*$. Thus if the NRH holds, the Visegrad countries could well have to operate restrictive monetary policies, in the form of higher interest rates for example, in order to engender the lower inflation expectations required to reduce their rates of inflation to EU or Maastricht levels. If restrictive demand policies have to be used to hold unemployment above natural rate levels, several important issues arise.

A central problem is knowing what the natural rate of unemployment is. The US literature on what determines the natural rate has been dominated by the "triangle" model (Gordon 1997), and the European literature by the "battle of the mark ups" model (Layard, Nickell and Jackman 1991).

The "triangle" model sees inflation as determined by a triad of factors: "demand", in the form of $(u-u^*)$ deviations; "supply", in the form of a vector of supply side variables, x; and "intertia", in the form of lagged values of inflation. A simplified version of this model, in which the natural rate is constant, $u^* = \bar{u}$, can be written as:

$$\Delta^2 p_t = \sum_{i=1} \alpha_i (u_{t-i} - \bar{u}) + \sum_{i=0} \beta_i x_{t-i} + \sum_{i=1} \gamma_i \Delta^2 p_{t-i} + v_t \tag{17}$$

where v is an error term. In (17) the natural rate enters non-linearly as $\sum_{i=1} \alpha_i \bar{u}$, so it is difficult to estimate this relationship. The regression equation usually estimated is:

$$\Delta^2 p_t = \mu + \sum_{i=1} \alpha_i u_{t-i} + \sum_{i=0} \beta_i x_{t-i} + \sum_{i=1} \gamma_i \Delta^2 p_{t-i} + v_t \tag{18}$$

where $\mu = -\sum_{i-1} \alpha_i \bar{u}$. Thus the estimate of the natural rate derived from this model is:

$$\hat{u}^* = -\hat{\mu} / \sum_{i=1} \hat{\alpha}_i \tag{19}$$

Thus the estimate of the natural rate is a non-linear function of the parameters. Such functions usually have non-normal distributions, so the confidence intervals around the estimated natural rate cannot be ascertained from the test statistics usually reported. Staiger, Stock and Watson (1997) have used the "Fieller method", which involves generating confidence intervals by a "suck it and see" method of trying all the possible values of u^*, to calculate confidence intervals for various specifications of u^* in the US. The finding is that the intervals are large, the typical 95% confidence interval being around 40% of the point estimate of u_t^*. Cross, Darby and Ireland (1997) extended this work to the G7 countries using various time-varying specifications of u_t^*, and found that, with the possible exception of Germany, the confidence intervals were even larger outside the US, though tighter confidence intervals can be identified for the US, at around 25% of the point estimate. A basic problem is that the α_i coefficients on the unemployment terms in (17) and (18) above are not particularly well-determined, so uncertainty surrounding these parameter values is transmitted into uncertainty about the natural rate.

The "battle of the mark-ups" model can be written as:

$$p\text{-}w = a_0 - a_1 u - a_2(p-p^e) + a_3 z_p + v_p \tag{20}$$

$$w\text{-}p = b_0 - b_1 u - b_2(p-p^e) + b_3 z_w + v_w \tag{21}$$

where p and p^e are the logs of the actual and expected price levels, w is the money wage level, z_p and z_w are price and wage push variables and v_p and v_w are error terms. Setting $p\text{-}p^e = \Delta^2 p$ and solving (20) and (21) for u^* gives:

$$u^* = (a_0 + a_3 z_p + b_0 + b_3 z_w)/(a_1 + b_1) \tag{22}$$

Thus, as in the "triangle" model, the natural rate is a non-linear function of the parameters estimated in regression equations, with again the coefficients on unemployment appearing in the denominator. If the z_p and z_w variables do not track the putative movements in u^* particularly well, and if the coefficients on unemployment are not particularly well-defined, the confidence intervals surrounding natural rate estimates are likely to be large.

Identifying the likely time paths for natural rates of unemployment in the Visegrad countries presents obvious difficulties in the face of the massive shifts in resources from state to private sectors, and the learning processes involved in relation to the newly established social safety nets for the employed and unemployed and new methods of wage bargaining. On an optimistic scenario, natural rates would fall in the coming years as "mismatch" problems become less severe. This would allow inflation rates to fall without requiring higher actual unemployment. Even with this optimistic scenario problems could arise as inflation rates fall to EU or Maastricht levels. The question is whether the natural rate is independent of the rate of inflation as very low rates of inflation are approached. If firms are reluctant to cut money wages, firms needing to reduce real wages in order to survive in the face of adverse shocks will experience greater difficulties as the rate of inflation approaches zero. In the Akerlof, Dickens and Perry (1996) model of monopolistically competitive firms with heterogeneous wage setting, the equilibrium rate of unemployment is higher by 1-2% in their simulation model, and higher by 2.6% in their US empirical estimates, if inflation falls from a steady rate of 3% to zero. Rates of unemployment in many of the EU countries rose substantially as they moved towards EMU and disinflation towards the German rate of inflation. The non-neutrality suggested by Akerlof, Dickens and Perry (1996) may help explain the high unemployment in the EMU zone as a whole, and may present problems for the Visegrad countries should they zero in on such low rates of inflation.

On a pessimistic scenario the natural rates of unemployment do not fall. In this case reducing the rates of inflation in the Visegrad countries would require contractionary monetary policies to raise actual above natural rates of unemployment. There are substantial risks to the real economies under this scenario, and the higher unemployment may not be just temporary if hysteresis effects are present. If workers are scarred by the experience of unemployment, if investment projects abandoned or delayed are not restored once the lower rates of inflation are achieved, or if firms that go into liquidation are not balanced by new firms coming into business when the level of real demand recovers, the legacy would be a higher equilibrium rate of unemployment in the new lower inflation equilibrium (see Cross, Darby and Ireland 1996).

7. CENTRAL BANK INDEPENDENCE AND MONETARY CONTROL

At the time central banks were established as entities separate from the rest of their banking systems in the transition economies the fashion in many advanced market economies and developing countries was to bestow greater degrees of independence on their own central banks. Several developments contributed to this movement, such as breakdown of the Bretton Woods system of fixed exchange rates in 1971-73, and the rise in influence of the doctrine of monetary neutrality (see Cukierman 1996). Various studies indicated a negative correlation between indices of the extent of central bank independence and the rate of inflation (Grilli, Masciandro and Tabellini 1991, for example), so central bank independence was seen as a way to obtain the natural rate "free lunch" of lower inflation. Causality, of course, might run in the opposite direction, with governments wanting lower rates of inflation granting more independence to their central banks. Independent central banks tend to have achieving low inflation as their overriding goal, so whether greater independence compromises the objective of stabilising real output is a moot point (see Debelle and Fischer 1994).

In the context of the accession of the Visegrad countries to the EU, central bank independence is virtually a *sine qua non*. If causality runs from independence to inflation, independence is seen as necessary to reduce inflation rates to EMU or Maastricht levels; independence from national political control is obviously involved in the transfer of power over monetary policy to the ECB.

The interaction between political and central bank influences on monetary policy can be seen in a flow of funds identity for the change in the broad domestic money supply:

$$\Delta m=[(g+rb-t)-\Delta b-\Delta fd]+\Delta bles+\Delta blps+\Delta fxr \qquad (23)$$

where Δm is the change in broad money, g is government spending, rb is interest payments on government debt, t is taxation revenue, Δb is sales of government debt outside the banking system, Δfd is funding of the fiscal deficit by foreign loans or assistance to the government, $\Delta bles$ and $\Delta blps$ are the changes in bank lending to the enterprise and personal sectors respectively and Δfxr is the increase in central bank foreign exchange reserves. The term in square brackets in (23) represents the unfunded component of the government's fiscal deficit. If the fiscal deficit $(g+rb-t)$ is too high, funding the deficit will present too great a problem for the central bank and monetary control will be lost. The Maastricht fiscal criteria that $(g+rb-t)/y \leq 3\%$ and $b/y \leq 60\%$, where y is GDP, impose limits on the extent to which the money supply can increase as a result of monetisation of fiscal deficit.

The second source monetary expansion is the change in the banking sector's lending to the enterprise and personal sectors (*Δbles* and *Δblps*). The standard instruments of controlling such lending are reserve ratios and the central bank's discount policy on loans to the banking sector. Problems in the Visegrad economies have arisen from inter-enterprise debts, non-performing loans to state enterprises and the under-capitalisation of the banking sector.

The third main source of domestic monetary expansion is the foreign exchange market intervention of the central bank (*Δfxr*). In the mid-1990s this has been a major problem for the Visegrad countries because of the substantial inflows of foreign capital. Such capital inflows play a key role in restructing the real economies, yet boost the domestic money supply when the central bank intervenes to keep a fixed exchange rate (as was the case in the Czech and Slovak Republics) or a pre-announced rate of devaluation (Hungary and Poland). Widening the permitted margins of exchange rate fluctuations (the Czech and Slovak Republics), or changing the pre-announced rates of devaluation (Hungary and Poland) can ease the problem temporarily, but the underlying dilemma remains.

REFERENCES

Akerlof, G. A., W. J. Dickens and G. L. Perry (1996), "The Macroeconomics of Low Inflation", *Brookings Papers on Economic Activity*, 27.1, 1-26.

Calvo, G. (1989), "Incredible Reforms", in G. Calvo, R. Findlay, K. Pentti and J. Bragade de Macredo eds., *Debt, Stabilisation and Development*, Basil Blackwell.

Chawluk, A. and R. Cross (1997), "Measures of Shortage and Monetary Overhang in Poland", *Review of Economics and Statistics*, February, 79.1, 105-115.

Cross, R., J. Darby and J. Ireland (1996), "Hysteresis and Ranges or Intervals for Equilibrium Unemployment", Robert Schuman Centre Discussion Paper, European University Institute, Florence.

Cross, R., J. Darby and J. Ireland (1997), "Uncertainties Surrounding Natural Rate Estimates in the G7", CEPR Conference on Unemployment Dynamics, May.

Cukierman, A. (1996), "The Economics of Central Banking", Centre for Economic Research, Discussion Paper No. 9631, Tilburg University.

Debelle, G. and S. Fischer (1994), "How Independent Should a Central Bank Be?", in J. C. Fuhrer ed., *Goals Guidelines and Constraints Facing Monetary Policy Makers*, Federal Reserve Bank of Boston, MA.

EBRD, *Transition Report 1999*, EBRD, London.

Goodhart, C. A. E (1984), *Monetary Policy in Theory and Practice*, Macmillan, London.

Gordon, R. J. (1997), "The Time-Varying NAIRU and its Implications for Economic Policy", *Journal of Economic Perspectives*, Winter, 11.1, 11-32.

Grilli, V., Masciandro D. and Tabellini G. (1991), "Political and Monetary Institutions and Public Financial Policies in the Industrial Countries", *Economic Policy*, 13, 641-392.

IMF (1999), *World Economic Outlook*, April, IMF, Washington DC.

Keynes, J. M. (1936), *The General Theory of Employment Interest and Money*, Macmillan, London.

Krugman, P. (1991), "History versus Expectations", *Quarterly Journal of Economics*, May, 651-667.

Layard, R., S. Nickell and R. Jackman (1991), *Unemployment: Macroeconomic Performance and the Labour Market*, Oxford UP.

Lucas, R. E. Jr. (1972), "Expectations and the Neutrality of Money", *Journal of Economic Theory*, April, 103-124.

Nijsse, E. and E. Sterken (1996), "Shortages, Interest Rates and Money Demand in Poland 1969-1995", CCSO Series No. 25, Universiteit Twente, Rijksuniversiteit Groningen.

Sachs, J. D. (1995), "Russia's Struggle with Stabilisation: Conceptual Issues and Evidence", *World Bank Annual Conference on Development Economics*, 57-91.

Sargent, T. J. (1995), *Bounded Rationality in Macroeconomics*, Oxford UP.

Staiger, D., J. H. Stock and M. W. Watson (1997), "The NAIRU, Unemployment and Monetary Policy", *Journal of Economic Perspectives*, Winter, 11.1, 33-50.

Stiglitz, J. (1997), "Relections on the Natural Rate Hypothesis", *Journal of Economic Perspectives*, Winter, 11.1, 3-10.

Chapter 5

IMPACT OF CAPITAL INFLOWS INTO THE CZECH REPUBLIC AND POLICY RESPONSES

Miroslav Hrncir
Czech National Bank

1. STAGES OF CAPITAL FLOWS

Prior to 1990, i.e. prior to the start of transition in the former Czechoslovakia, capital flows were strictly controlled and their macroeconomic importance was rather limited. Transition brought a reversal, both the volume and forms of capital flows have expanded and diversified within a few years. Since early 1990s, capital flows became a major factor of economic developments and a major issue of policy-making.

However, the causal factors, forms of capital flows and their impact went through several development stages. Those stages reflected

- the advancing institutional frameworks and the gradual up-grading of financial openness of the Czech economy related, in particular, to the sequence of liberalisation steps,
- the shifts in the macroeconomic situation from the structural depression of 1991-2 to the recovery of 1993-4 and robust growth of 1995-6,
- related shifts in macroeconomic policies, from a tough restrictive stance at the start of transition to gradual easing in the follow-up stages.

The stages of capital flows in the period 1990-1996 developed as follows:

- "infancy" stage of 1990-92
- capital inflow "episode" of 1993-95
- 1996: a medium term standard?

1.1 "Infancy" stage of 1990-92

In that stage in the conditions of underdeveloped financial infrastructure and only partial foreign exchange liberalisation capital flows were mostly confined to long-term official inflows combined with occasional short-term capital flight.

R. MacDonald and R. Cross (eds.), Central Europe Towards Monetary Union: Macroeconomic Underpinnings and Financial Reputation, 71–87.

The long-term official inflows resulted from the endeavour of monetary authorities to replenish the unsatisfactory low level of foreign exchange reserves. At the same time, they reflected the support extended by international institutions to the initiated transition process.

Table 1. Consolidated Capital Account in 1990-1992 (in US$ mil.)

	1990	1991	1992
Capital Account	504.8	-1331.0	1.9
Direct Investment	132.6	513.1	982.9
Portfolio	..	..	-26.0
Other long term	370.3	1142.4	319.7
Short term	1.9	-2986.3	-1274.7

Note: Data represent the share of the Czech Republic in capital flows of the former Czechoslovakia
Data Source: Czech National Bank

Opposite to official capital inflows, the private community reacted through short-term capital outflows to the conditions of uncertainty, shocks and devaluation expectations of the initial transition stage. The country's international reserves under pressure especially when the waves of capital flight emerged. The first occurred in the second half of 1990, prior to the implementation of the sweeping liberalisation "package" linked to the "pre-announced" (!) devaluation of the Czechoslovak koruna. The second one developed two years later, once the forthcoming split of the federal republic and of the common currency became evident. [1] In both cases capital flight materialised, notwithstanding as yet relatively rigid capital controls.

Those short-term capital outflows were not equally matched by long-term inflows and, as a result, the cumulated capital account in convertible currencies showed a deficit for the period 1990-92.

1.2 Capital inflow "episode" of 1993-95

Since the second half of 1993 the importance, volume and structure of capital flows substantially changed. Unlike the former period, private capital flows started to dominate and, at the same time, massive inflows resulted in an unprecedented capital account's surplus. It increased from US$ 3 bn in 1993 to US$ 8.2 bn in 1995 on consolidated basis (in both convertible and non-convertible currencies). As a result, the official foreign exchange reserves surged from US$ 0.8 bn in January 1993 to

[1] In 1990, under the pressure of rapidly diminishing reserves an additional "unplanned" devaluation of CZK was effected in October 1990.

In January 1993 the official reserves of the Czech Republic dropped to US$ 0.8 bn only. The newly established Czech central bank, CNB, had to turn to international markets to replenish the reserves drained by capital flight sparked by the expectations of the forthcoming dissolution of former Czechoslovakia and of its currency.

USD 14 bn at the end of 1995. In 1995 alone, when the inflows culminated, the official reserves increased by US$ 7.8 bn.

Table 2. Foreign Debt and Foreign Exchange Reserves

	As of 1.1.1993	1993	Change in 1994	1995	As of 31.12.1995	Change in 1996	As of 31.12.1996
Gross Foreign Debt	7.1	1.4	2.2	5.6	16.3	3.5	20.4
Short term	1.8	0.2	0.9	2.1	5.0	0.9	5.9
Long-term	5.3	1.2	1.3	3.5	11.3	3.0	14.5
Foreign Exchange Reserves	3.5	2.8	2.6	8.5	17.4	-0.5	16.9
Official reserves (CNB)	0.8	3.1	2.3	7.8	14.0	-1.6	12.4
Commercial banks	2.7	-0.3	0.2	0.7	3.3	1.2	4.5

Data Source: Czech National Bank

The causes of inflows may be external or internal. The capital inflow episode which developed in the Czech Republic since the latter half of 1993 was specific to the country. Compared to previous years, the early 1990s witnessed a remarkable return of capital to emerging market economies (EMEs), i.e. to mostly middle income countries. This shift reflected to some extent factors external to those countries, notably the low level of U.S. interest rates.

The external motives of inflows coincided with domestic causes in transition economies. The progressing transformation and external opening of the former centrally planned economies offered new investment opportunities. In the Czech case the incentives to invest were on the one hand related to the successful stabilisation and to restoration of currency stability, to the advancing privatisation and liberalisation of both external flows and domestic economy. At the same time, capital inflows were also called for by a rather constrained domestic supply of financing, in particular of long-term credits, and by a much wider interest rate differential compared to standard conditions. That differential, linked with the nominal stability of the fixed exchange rate which had already earned some credibility, provided a "one way bet" for speculators. Thus the causes of capital inflows derived both from the success of stabilisation as well as from the implied imbalances and constraints inherent transition, which offered profit until corrected.

The role of the mentioned causal factors diverged in individual stages and, moreover, their impact overlapped. As a result, the quantitative assessment of their relative weights is difficult. Nevertheless, the changing shares of the various forms of capital inflow may be taken as yielding some information on the underlying causes and their relative importance.

The net values of four basic forms of capital flow, i.e. of foreign direct investment, portfolio capital, other long term capital and short term capital developed in the capital inflow episode of 1993-1995 as follows (in cumulative terms):

Table 3. Net Capital Inflows in 1993-1995 (US$ bn)

Foreign direct investment	3.8
Portfolio investment	3.8
Other long term capital	5.3
Short term capital	1.7

Data Source: Czech National Bank

(i) Other long term capital

As indicated, "other long term" capital was the dominant form of net capital inflows in the period examined. It reflected rapidly an increasing volume of credits contracted by the Czech entities (companies, municipalities, banks) abroad. The reasons behind the surging volume of this form were threefold:

- limited supply of medium and long-term financing by domestic banks, especially in the early stage. Given the lack of products for long-term savings, domestic banks borrowed short but lended mostly short as well, failing to provide a maturity transformation of savings,
- foreign credits were increasingly available for credit-worthy (big) clients. Thanks to the gradual up-grading of the state's, banks' and (selected) companies' ratings, those credits were significantly cheaper compared to domestic interest rates,
- while borrowing abroad the Czech entities mostly disregarded the implied exchange rate risk. This can be at least partly explained by the environment of nominal exchange rate stability of the Czech koruna (CZK) maintained since the very start of transition. Given the lack of experience with exchange rate fluctuations there were hardly any incentives for domestic entities to calculate exchange rate risk and to hedge.

Thus, the surging volume of foreign credits contracted by Czech companies and banks was to some extent controversial. On the one hand these credits provided a substitute for the lack of domestic savings and enabled an increase in domestic absorption (investment and private consumption) beyond the domestic limits and, as a result, an acceleration in economic recovery. At the same time, however, the relief gained from the foreign exchange constraint implied increasing indebtedness of domestic borrowers and, consequently, increasing potential vulnerability of the national economy.

(ii) Foreign direct investment

The entire inflow of FDI to the Czech Republic in the period 1990-1996 amounted to US$ 7.1 bn, of which US$ 4.2 bn materialised in 1993-1995. In comparative terms, this inflow was higher than in some other countries of Central and Eastern Europe but much lower than in Hungary and, especially in 1996, also well behind Poland and Russia. By all measures (volume, share of GDP, annual flows on a per capita basis) Hungary surpassed all other countries in the region in attracting foreign direct investment, between 1990 and 1995 it accumulated US$ 11.2 bn, i.e. almost double the US$ 5.7 for the Czech Republic and well over the US$ 7.1 bn for Poland. However, unlike some other EMEs, including Hungary and Poland, the Czech authorities did not provide any special incentives to foreign investors (e.g. tax holidays).

(iii) Short term capital

Volatile short term inflows were attracted by a large interest rate differential[2] combined with a fixed exchange rate of CZK whose nominal stability has been maintained since the start of transition and earned some credibility. Moreover the developing expectations tended to assume a nominal appreciation. The shift towards an increasing share of short term capital inflows materialised towards the end of 1994 and in the first half of 1995. As a result, the short term debt increased from US$ 1.8 bn at the beginning of 1993 to US$ 5.0 bn at the end of 1995, implying an increased ratio of short term debt to total indebtedness from 25% to 31%.

2. POLICY RESPONSES TO CAPITAL FLOWS

As elsewhere, a range of various policies and instruments has been applied in the Czech Republic to cope with capital flows and with their impact. The lessons from other parts of the world economy suggested that it was well advised to combine a number of instruments into a policy-mix and to apply several, not only one, "line of defence" (Williamson J., 1994).

The policies and instruments used were of both a macroeconomic and structural nature. The former included monetary policies (sterilisation), exchange rate and fiscal policies, while the latter were targeted to increase the absorption capacity of the economy, to ease restrictions on capital outflows and to place some impediments to short-term volatile capital inflows.

[2] 3 month PRIBOR minus weighted average of US$ (LIBOR) and DM (FIBOR) developed in the range of 6-8.5% in 1995-96.

2.1 Sterilisation of capital inflows

Since 1993 the first line of defence to cope with increasing capital inflows has been sterilised intervention. Given the existing rigid fixed exchange rate regime (allowing for exchange rate fluctuations only in the narrow band of ± 0.5%) and its fixing arrangement, the central bank had to be permanently present on the foreign exchange market and to intervene accordingly, buying and selling foreign exchange. In 1993-96 a substantial share of those interventions was sterilised.

The extent of sterilisation reflected the monetary policy targets. In the Czech case monetary policy has been geared to quantitative targets for monetary aggregates, M2. Accordingly, the extent of sterilisation resulted in an emerging diversion between the actual trends in money supply developments and intermediary targets of monetary policy in terms of M2.

Sterilisation can be defined narrowly as offsetting the effect of forex interventions on the monetary base via corresponding domestic transactions in securities (open market operations). The other, broader option, refers to offsetting transactions for the money supply aggregate, including also changing minimum reserve requirements and a shift of public deposits from commercial banks to the central bank.

The scope of sterilisation in the narrow concept is identified in Table 4, based on the central bank balance sheet data. The values of the sterilisation ratio, defined as the ratio of the change in central bank NFA to that in reserve money (monetary base) reflected two different periods and situations:

- In 1993-95 increases in central bank foreign exchange reserves accounted for more than the entire increase in the monetary base (though with downward trend) as the central bank was slashing domestic money creation.
- In 1996 the situation was reversed, the impact of the fall in NFA on monetary base was almost compensated by increased domestic money creation.

Table 4. Central Bank Balance Sheet: Scale of Sterilisation of Foreign Exchange Flows (End of period, in CZK bn)

	A	B	A/B	C
	ΔNFA	ΔMonetary Base	Sterilisation Ratio*	ΔNDA
1993/92	64.3	43.2	1.49	-21.1
1994/93	96.3	67.0	1.44	-29.4
1995/94	181.8	162.3	1.12	-18.9
1996/95	-22.6	-9.2	(2.46)	13.4
1995/92	342.4	272.5	1.26	-69.4
1996/92	319.8	263.3	1.21	-56.0

* Ratio of the change in NFA to that in the monetary base

Note: NFA is net foreign assets of the central bank (its net international reserves), NDA is its net domestic assets.
Data Source: Czech National Bank

The broader concept of sterilisation is applied in Table 5. Apart from the impact of open market operations, i.e. of selling and buying of bills and bonds denominated in domestic currency, it covers the impact of:

- changes in minimum reserve requirements on primary deposits of commercial banks;
- the shift of government (FNP) owned deposits to the central bank and of the parallel arrangement for the Telecom deposit; [3]
- diminished refinancing of commercial banks.

Table 5. Drainage and Injection of Liquidity in 1990-1996 (Annual averages, CZK bn)

Year	Liquidity injection (+) refinancing Injection (+)	Liquidity drainage (-) Open market operations	Minimum reserves requirements	Deposits with CNB	Balance
1990	17.4	0.0	0.0	0.0	17.4
1991	21.1	0.0	21.8	0.0	-0.8
1992	15.1	11.8	25.3	0.0	-22.0
1993	6.5	26.4	40.0	0.0	-58.8
1994	7.1	70.4	47.2	0.8	-111.3
1995	7.3	89.4	64.3	20.6	-166.9
1996	13.4	138.4	94.6	..	..
Change in period					
1990	17.4	0.0	0.0	0.0	17.4
91/90	3.7	0.0	21.8	0.0	-18.2
92/91	-6.0	11.8	3.5	0.0	21.2
93/92	-8.6	13.6	14.7	0.0	-36.8
94/93	0.6	45.0	7.2	0.8	-52.5
95/94	0.2	19.0	17.1	19.8	-55.6
96/95	6.1	49.0	30.3	..	..

Data Source: Czech National Bank, Selected Indicators of Monetary Development, Czech National Bank

[3]The Telsource investment into the Czech Telecom represented the largest foreign direct investment on the Czech territory amounting to US$ 1.1 bn.

Table 6. Reserve Requirements on Primary Deposits of Commercial Banks

As of 1.1.1994	demand deposits	9%
	term deposits	3%
Changes		
from 4.8.1994	demand deposits	12%
	term deposits	3%
from 3.8.1995	building societies and Czech-Moravian Guaranty and Development Bank	4%
	all other banks and savings banks	8.5%
from 1.8.1996	building societies and Czech-Moravian Guaranty and Development Bank	4%
	all other banks and savings banks	11.5%

Data Source: Czech National Bank

As indicated in Table 6, since 1994 minimum reserve requirements were adjusted each year upwards. The tightening impact of these changes is identified in Table 5. As a result, the relative share of reserve requirements on the total drainage of liquidity has been increasing and at the end of 1996 it surpassed the role of short-term securities in the portfolio of commercial banks (CNB, Treasury and FNP bills), as apparent in Table 7.

Open market operations represented the main form of sterilisation. As the data suggest, their volume was steadily increasing up to mid 1996, since then the trend has been reversed. Due to the balanced budget policy the volume of Treasury bills was restricted and, consequently, CNB had to start to issue its own bills to sterilise the massive capital inflows of 1993-95. In the course of time, their share in open market operations became dominant, as can be inferred from the data in Table 7.

Table 7. Sterilisation in 1995-96: Open Market Operations and Reserve Requirements (Monthly averages CZK bn)

	3/95	6/95	9/95	12/95	3/96	6/96	9/96	12/96
Treasury, CNB and FNP bills	79.9	86.6	86.4	137.6	145.6	152.9	126.3	112.9
of which: CNB bills	49.7	55.8	50.8	101.7	101.9	98.0	81.6	64.4
Minimum reserve requirements	56.6	58.0	73.5	75.7	79.8	82.7	112.9	115.5

Data Source: Czech National Bank

The constraints of sterilisation policies are related especially to their (i) effectiveness and (ii) implied costs.

(i) Effectiveness of Sterilisation

The lessons from elsewhere suggest that the potential of massive sterilisation tends to be eroded in the course of time. The causal factors of its diminishing effectiveness are related to the increased incentives to further inflows, which have their origin in sterilisation operations themselves. The argument is, in particular, that sterilisation measures put upward pressure on the interest rates prevailing in the domestic market. This can be expected to happen especially when markets are thin, as was the case in the Czech Republic. Moreover, as it is short-term interest rates which are pushed up, the structure of inflows is likely to become increasingly biased towards the short end, which is just the opposite to the desirable outcome.

The indicator of the central bank's ability to contain capital inflows via sterilisation operations, i.e. offset coefficient, was calculated for the Czech Republic in 1994 and 1995 in the range of 0.3 - 0.6 (compare Šmídková K.,1995).[4] This result would imply that sterilisation operations were relatively effective and could be used further. [5] In advanced market economies, where capital mobility is expected to be high, sterilisation has been as a rule regarded as ineffective, apart from a very short-term effect. The Czech data would suggest, on the other hand, the continued - though limited - ability to achieve the goals of sterilisation.

(ii) Costs of Sterilisation

Apart from the limits in effectiveness of sterilisation, the other constraining factor is its costs, which inhibit its wider use and which may lead central banks to abandon this "first line of defence" against capital inflows. The concepts which can be applied for the identification of the costs range from the narrow flow measure of the quasi-fiscal cost of open market operations to various forms of opportunity costs of wider sterilisation policies.

The quasi fiscal costs of open market operations (borne by the central bank, but ultimately affecting budgetary flows) resulted from the difference between the interest liabilities on the securities issued and interest earned on the forex reserves which were traded for domestic securities, i.e. from uncovered interest rate parity plus the risk premium on domestic securities. Providing that the given nominal value of the pegged koruna (CZK) exchange rate was credible (the expectations inclined rather to its nominal appreciation) and the domestic nominal deposit rate around 7-8% in 1994-95, the uncovered interest rate parity condition was violated by several percentage points. With capital inflows in the range of 9.5% of GDP in 1994 and 18.4% of GDP in 1995, the flow costs alone could be calculated at around 1% of GDP if all the inflows had been sterilised by open market operations. However, this was not the case and the IMF study estimated the quasi-fiscal flow cost at 0.3 % of GDP in 1994 and about 0.5% of GDP in 1995.

---

[4]The IMF report on the Czech Republic placed the value of offset coefficient close to the ceiling of that corridor.

[5]Values close to 0 indicate high degree of central bank autonomy in developing money supply as its operations do not evoke additional capital inflow, while values close to 1 imply an opposite situation.

Apart from open market operations, the CNB applied in a parallel way other instruments to control the impact of capital flows on domestic liquidity (consult Table 5 for the identification of their role). These operated on the money multiplier instead of offsetting the effects on the monetary base and represented sterilisation measures in a wider sense. Though those instruments moderated the costs of sterilisation via open market operations borne by the central bank, they had costs of their own. The increased non-renumerated reserve requirements, for example, replaced part of the quasi fiscal costs of the central bank (tax on the government) with an implied tax on commercial banks.

2.2 Macroeconomic and Structural Policies Accompanying Sterilisation

(i) Exchange rate regime and policies

The experience from elsewhere in EMEs suggests that the adjustment of exchange rate regimes and of exchange rate policies has been a standard element of a policy-mix addressing increased capital mobility and the impact of massive capital inflows on both the monetary and real dimensions of the national economy. In that respect the distinguishing feature of the Czech developments was the commitment to a rigidly fixed exchange rate regime. Since the very start of transition, the adopted band allowed for fluctuations in the range of ±0.5% only. The other EMEs of Central and Eastern Europe with pegged exchange rates, for example Poland and Hungary, reacted already in the early 1990s to the persistent real exchange rate appreciation by shifting to more flexible exchange rate regime options.

Unlike those countries, the Czech authorities maintained the initial rigid fixed exchange rate regime unchanged up to the end of February 1996, despite the increasing pressures arising from massive capital inflows in the years 1993-1995. Only on February 28, 1996 was the applied band of the CZK widened to ±7.5% but the previous level of the central parity was maintained and the horizontal type of the band untouched. This was the period when the expectations of nominal exchange rate developments reflecting the diverging trends in current and capital accounts were more or less balanced. As a result, the shift to the new regime was smooth and a success. With the benefit of hindsight it can be claimed that both the type of regime change and its timing were chosen properly.

The main causal factor behind that regime shift was the increasing inconsistency between massive capital inflows and the goals of monetary stability. In this period the Czech economy and its foreign exchange sphere underwent substantial liberalisation. The new foreign exchange law (No. 219/1995) which came into force on October 1, 1995 provided for current account convertibility status in accordance with Article VIII of the IMF and, at the same time, it went beyond that status by extending liberalisation to a number of capital account items.

However, the advanced stage of financial openness of the Czech economy proved to be increasingly inconsistent with the rigid fixed exchange rate regime. On the one hand, the inherent properties of an economy in transition persisted, in particular large inflation and interest rate differentials vis a vis a basket of currencies. In those conditions the prospects of fixed exchange rate regime sustainability together with an open capital account and increasing capital mobility were rather slim. At the same time, the rigid fixed exchange rate regime severely constrained the autonomy of domestic monetary policy. It could not effectively correct the biased incentives of capital inflows nor cope with the pressures arising from their massive flows and volatility. The substantial widening of the band (from ±0.5 to ±7.5%) lessened these pressures, provided room for manoeuvre and enhanced the autonomy of monetary policy. The width of the band, together with the declaration of the central bank that it was prepared to make use of it, increased the implied uncertainty for currency speculators and helped to deter the short-time volatile capital inflows. As a result, a significant outflow of short-term capital was registered in the first half of 1996. Of course, however useful such a regime change was, it was not a panacea: it could neither solve the implied imbalances nor be a substitute for a policy mix which addressed them.

(ii) Fiscal policy stance

In the Czech Republic a balanced budget policy was adhered to from the start of transition. It implied a relatively tight fiscal stance compared to some other economies in transition. When capital inflows started to develop, this policy provided a positive contribution to the stabilising efforts and helped to cope with the side-effects of capital inflows. However, in the course of time, under the increasing pressures of political cycle considerations (1996 was the year of two general elections, into the lower and upper chambers of the Parliament) a tendency to a deficit in the consolidated budget started to develop [6]. However moderate the final state budget deficit was (after the correcting cuts in expenditures imposed in the course of the year it was in the range of 0.1% of GDP), in terms of the change with respect to the previous stage the deterioration was significant. The surge of capital inflows (especially in 1995) required just the opposite trend, i.e. an increasing budget surplus. This would make lower interest rates feasible, lower volatile inflows and, consequently, lower inflationary pressures. In reality, the main burden of coping with capital inflows was borne by monetary policy which could not be considered an optimal policy mix.

[6] At the same time, the extra-budgetary funds, in particular the use of proceeds from privatisation by the Fund of National Property financed some of the outlays which otherwise would have been financed by budgetary expenditures.

(iii) Liberalisation and deregulation together with temporary controls

As elsewhere in parallel circumstances, the range of applied policies also included steps towards liberalisation of outflows on the one hand and some "throwing of the sand into the wheels" of capital inflows. The relaxation of outward controls developed step by step for a longer period. However, the adoption of the new foreign exchange law in 1995 considerably extended and legally codified the scope of capital flow liberalisation. Concerning outflows, according to the law full liberalisation has been applied in particular to foreign direct investment by residents, to financial credits from non-residents as well as to purchase of real estate by residents abroad. A substantial relaxation was also made in the rules for purchasing foreign securities.

Liberalisation and deregulation steadily progressed also on the inward side. Nevertheless, reflecting the temporary need to weather massive inflows of capital, in particular volatile and speculative short-term forms, administrative barriers were also imposed to make the short-term flows less attractive. In April 1995 the central bank introduced a fee (margin) of 0.25 percent on its transactions in foreign exchange with commercial banks. However, given the degree of financial integration already reached, on the one hand, and the existing interest rate differentials on the other, such a "sand" was of rather small importance. Later on, in August 1995, the central bank imposed a quantitative limit on the net short term open positions (liabilities) of banks to non-residents. Those positions must not exceed either of two ceilings: 30% of the value of the bank's balance sheets' short-term assets and liabilities; or CZK 500 mil.

The rationale was to discourage massive short-term inflows. Though the measure could be relatively easy circumvented, it helped to some extent to correct the implied bias towards an increasing share of short-term inflows. This control represented a possibly "third best" policy, ineffective in longer run, but it proved workable in the short run. Moreover, it was adopted in the conditions when the legal framework did not allow for the more standard forms of control applied elsewhere in EMEs, such as an obligatory deposits on capital inflows (possibly limited to some forms and/or maturities of capital inflows). Though the situation has changed with the new foreign exchange law and when the imposition of obligatory deposits became feasible since 1995, the Czech monetary authorities have not used them. Moreover, the commitment resulting from the OECD code of behaviour requires the formal suspension of provision.

(iv) Structural policies

Apart from the above identified policies, an important role in capital flows management and control in EMEs can be attributed to structural policies. Unlike sterilisation and various impediments to inflows, they address the causes rather than the symptoms of capital flows. As elsewhere, also in the Czech Republic a considerable part of capital inflows was biased due to the remaining domestic distortions and inefficiencies. The latter arise in particular in financial intermediation and banking services and products (e.g. as yet wide margins between borrowing and lending rates). It follows that policies promoting increasing the absorption capacity of the domestic economy, including financial market reforms and enhanced efficiency of banking intermediation, as well as improvements in physical infrastructure, should be an integral, priority part of the policy mix.

While sterilisation and control measures are quick and relatively easy to impose and implement (legal and other institutional conditions allowing), their potential is as a rule increasingly eroded in the course of time. They are therefore usually resorted to as the first line of defence. Instruments and policies aiming at an enhanced absorption capacity of the domestic economy are just the opposite: it takes time to make them effective, but their impact is also of a longer-term nature.

3. The impact of capital inflows on macroeconomic variables

The issue of capital inflows into EMEs, including the EMEs of Central and Eastern Europe, and of the policies to cope with their impact may appear controversial. The countries have been undercapitalised, the heritage of the past implied obsolete technology, underdeveloped infrastructure and the need for extensive restructuring. The level of domestic capital and of domestic savings could hardly match the requirements of speeding up economic recovery and sustainable growth. From this "real" economy point of view capital inflows into the Czech Republic since 1990 may appear lower than desirable, though their per capita volume was larger than in some other Central and European countries.

At the same time, capital inflows became one of the major challenges for economic and monetary policies. First, the absorption capacity of the domestic economy has been limited, constrained by the existing rigidities. Second, the capital inflows' side-effects on "non-real" (monetary) dimensions of economic development had to be dealt with to avoid or, at least to ease, their destabilizing impact. The "standard" problems relating to capital inflows also proved relevant in the Czech case.

(i) Impact on money supply

Data on the money supply show that the targeted corridor for M2 was repeatedly exceeded and ex post (in the course of the given year) amended in the period 1992-95 (Table 8). In strict terms the target was adhered to only in 1996. As the years of money supply overshooting coincided with the episode of capital inflow (despite the large extent of implemented sterilisation as identified above), a causal link may be inferred. As follows from Table 9, the increases of M2 in the years 1993-95 were increasingly due to the net foreign assets. The situation reversed in 1996 when capital inflows decreased from 18.4% of GDP in 1995 to just 5.8% of GDP. Given the surging current account deficit, the money supply grew entirely because of domestic credit formation.

Table 8. Monetary Targets and Actual Developments of M2

	Monetary target		Actual M2
	Initial	Corrected	
1992	12	17.5	22.8
1993	17	19	20.3
1994	12-15	17	20.8
1995	14-17	14-17	19.4
1996	13-17	13-17	10-11*

* Preliminary
Data Source: Czech National Bank

Table 9. Net Foreign Assets (NFA), Domestic Credits (DC) and Money Supply (M2) Developments

	ΔNFA	ΔDC	ΔM2	ΔNFA/ΔM2	ΔDC/ΔM2
1993/92	54.1	110.3	121.8	44.4	90.6
1994/93	105.1	103.6	150.0	70.1	69.1
1995/94	116.7	112.0	169.2	69.0	66.2
*1996/95	-44.5	101.0	77.8	-57.2	129.8

* Preliminary
Data Source: Report on the Monetary Development in the Czech Republic Czech National Bank

Massive inflows posed two interrelated problems for monetary policy with respect to the money supply: what level of money supply target to choose; and the controllability of the money supply by domestic authorities. The surging money supply and weakened monetary control were transmitted into the level of aggregate demand, with the risk of overheating in the domestic economy and increased inflationary pressures. Though the inflation record of the Czech Republic could be considered a success compared to some other economies in transition, an inflation inertia at the level of around 9-10% apparently developed, with only relatively modest decreases in inflation rates since 1992.

However, apart from time lags involved, the impact of money supply developments on the course of inflation is subject to a number of qualifications. The assessment of money demand function itself is not straightforward in the conditions of economies in transition. Accordingly, the changing institutional environment of the Czech economy (rapidly increasing number of market agents in the initial transition stage) and the implied changes in velocity of money (its downward trend) could hardly be adequately reflected ex ante in the targeted M2 values. A possible interpretation may therefore view the overshooting of M2 targets, at least to some extent, as a spontaneous correction for the ex ante unaccounted factors.

(ii) Capital inflows and real exchange rate appreciation

Massive capital inflows, are as a rule, associated with real exchange rate appreciation, but - as the experience elsewhere in the world economy showed - the countries with the largest inflows were not necessarily those with largest real exchange rate appreciation. What mattered in particular were the fiscal policies, countries with a decreasing share of government consumption experiencing lower real appreciation, and vice-versa.

Given the nominal exchange rate stability and the much higher domestic inflation compared to the countries to which the currency was tied, the process of real appreciation materialised in the Czech economy at the start of transition. The analytical issue is to what extent that process was accentuated by capital inflows. Though some additional impetus to real appreciation was hardly avoidable, the standard indicators in terms of CPI, PPI and unit labour costs (compare Hrnèíø M., 1996) signalled a rather persistent rate of real appreciation than a speeding up. The relatively tight monetary and fiscal policies might have counteracted and eased the pressures arising.

Under the conditions of a rigidly fixed exchange rate, the impact of capital inflows could assert itself only via real appreciation up to February 1996. After widening the band, a nominal appreciation also became possible. As for the latter period, since mid 1996 the CZK was in the stronger part of the band and its rate of appreciation increased in the first months of 1997, exceeding 5%, despite increasing deficits on trade and current accounts. In those conditions the impact of capital inflows (increasingly through emissions of eurobonds denominated in CZK) on nominal exchange rate appreciation was evident.

(iii) Capital inflows and the current account deficit

One of the alternative approaches to the explanation of the increasing trade deficit developing since 1994, and the current account deficit since 1995, i.e. with one year time lag, was the causal link to capital inflows. The argument is that thanks to capital inflows a rising domestic absorption could be financed.

Data on macroeconomic developments in the Czech economy showed (compare Hájek M., 1997) that quickly growing aggregate demand was increasingly matched by foreign supply since late 1993. The transmission of the emerging excess of domestic demand over domestic supply proved to be channelled more into trade and current accounts deficits than into surging inflation.

Whether, and to what extent, capital inflows should be allowed to be translated into a larger current account deficit to finance increased domestic absorption is considered a matter of strategic decision. Two principles can be inferred from the discussion in other countries, as a guidance:

- sustainability, i.e. in principle long term flows may be allowed, under certain qualifying conditions, to be translated into a higher real exchange rate or current account deficit,
- provided public finances are in principle balanced, current account deficits reflect the difference between private domestic investment and savings, an issue which should be of less concern (Lawson doctrine).

Apart from the fact that the maturity and sustainability of capital inflows are always hard to assess, the non-standard conditions and rigidities of economies in transition constrained the usefulness of the above guidance. The extent, trends and time horizon of current account imbalances should be a matter of concern, even if public finances are balanced. By the same reasoning, it matters what kind of excess domestic absorption is financed by external inflows: whether investment or consumption; and also what type of investment is implemented, i.e. orn ot the potential for a future repayment of foreign debt is created.

REFERENCES

Hajek, M. et al (1997), "Macroeconomic Analysis of the Czech Economy", *Institute of Economics*, Prague.

Hrncir, M. (1996), "Exchange Rate Regime and the Stages of Transition", Conference Paper, Prague.

IMF (1996), *Czech Republic - Recent Economic Developments*.

Smidkova, K. (1995), "Offset Coefficient for the Czech Republic", *Czech National Bank*, Prague.

Chapter 6

REFORMS AND DEVELOPMENT OF THE BANKING SYSTEMS IN TRANSITION ECONOMIES

Éva Várhegyi
Center for International Private Enterprise

ABSTRACT

The Central and Eastern European (CEE) countries in transition faced two-fold task: getting rid of the inheritance of the centralised model and creating sound, market-oriented financial sector at the same time. Transition from the old monobank system of a centrally planned economy to the two tier banking system of a market economy was accompanied by market imperfections and cost a lot. Though the roots of the problems were similar in the region, the answers given by the individual governments were quite different. The differences lie in the sequence of the reform steps rather than in the characteristics of the steps themselves.

The general tasks which each country had to solve by reforming the banking system are described below:

- establishing the institutions and rules which ensure soundness and competitiveness of the banking system
- dealing with the inherited financial weaknesses of the banks and their clientele
- privatising the former state-owned banks in order to hamper the reproduction of the weaknesses deriving from the irresponsible ownership and dependence on political powers.

The governments of CEE countries analysed here have to face special pressure coming from the intention to become members of the EU and speeding up the transition process. The association agreements of these countries with EU requires further steps of harmonisation and liberalisation in the regulation of the banking system. Creating free market entrance is particularly urgent in those countries (Czech Republic and Hungary) which have become members of OECD. The quick liberalisation of the financial markets means however further challenge for these countries because of strengthening the international competition on the domestic market.

R. MacDonald and R. Cross (eds.), Central Europe Towards Monetary Union: Macroeconomic Underpinnings and Financial Reputation, 89–120.

This overview part of this chapter intends to describe the general characteristics of the transition process in the banking systems of CEE countries. The following parts will give more detailed description of individual country experiences, with special consideration of efficiency and regulation of the banking market.

1. INSTITUTIONAL AND REGULATORY CHANGES AND THEIR EFFECTS ON COMPETITION

The reforms of the banking system in CEE started with splitting the former monobank, issuing new licensing for the establishment of new banks and deregulating the financial markets. Creating two-tier banking system and free market entrance aimed at business-like behaviour and competition of banks.

Since under the monobank system of the centrally planned economy the state was involved directly in the allocation of funds, they were allocated without the consideration of repayment possibilities. Since central bank had the exclusive right of debiting the firms accounts or revolving the credit, no loans were classified as non-performing.

The two-tier banking systems were established between 1987 and 1990. The former monobanks were split into 3 to 9 commercial banks and the central bank. Though the methods of splitting were different, their effects on competition were equally weak. While the break-up of Polish and Czechoslovakian monobanks resulted in the organisation of commercial banks on a regional basis, the Hungarian method split the central bank into commercial banks by the economic branches. In each model of transition competition was hindered by the strongly segmented market. As the monopoly status of national savings banks with almost unique access to household deposits survived, commercial banks remained in strong dependence on refinancing facilities of central bank and - later on - the interbank market.

Competition was also mitigated by the high concentration of the market, the dominance of big state owned banks. At the beginning of transition these banks grew rapidly and realised high profits as a consequence of the increasing activity of financial intermediation and the weak regulation.

As a second step of the reform of the banking sector new banking law, accounting system and supervisory regulations have been issued, covering the basic principals of prudential banking. Banking Supervision has been established to strengthen the quality of the system and of the individual banks. Deposit protection schemes have been set up in order to ensure depositors in the situation of bank failures.

The new banking laws enacted between 1989-1991 and gradually amended later usually set up requirements for the establishment and the operation of financial institutions in conformity with EC's banking provisions and standards. Concerning the treatment of foreign investors, the laws followed rather the EC's First Banking Directive than more liberal Second Banking Directive. [1] The rules of prudential regulation were more and more following the standards recommended by Basle Committee and getting close to the implementation of later European directives. In the first phase of the banking reforms, the norms of accounting and portfolio classification were, however, looser than in the EC and the existing banks were granted a transitional adjustment period to meet the required capital adequacy ratio of eight per cent. (See table 1.)

Simultaneously with the establishment of prudential rules of banking regulation, a process of deregulation went on in the monetary policies of transition economies. Ceilings for interest rates and credit volumes were gradually abolished, offering a larger scope for market signals in the monetary policy and the banking activities as well.

In spite of some discriminatory provisions against foreigners built in the laws, the licensing and ownership rules in totality were quite liberal. The authorised activities of banks were set up according to the universal banking model which lets banks trade in securities, expect Hungary, where banks had to establish separate institution for this activity. Subsidiary of foreign banks was allowed to open according to the same licensing procedures as in the case of a bank. Though in the Czech Republic and the Slovak Republic foreign banks were given permission to set up branch offices, the authorities could require the transfer of certain financial means up to CZK 500 million (about ECU 14 million), which meant the same capital requirement than during establishing banks.

The easy entrance to the market at the beginning of the reform has strengthened the competition to different extent in various fields of banking activities. Subsidiaries and branches of foreign banks usually occupied the most favourable segments of the markets: the best clients (joint ventures with stable export markets) and the less risky products (such as interbank lending and short term credits). [2] On the other hand, domestic banks caught up less profitable and riskier clientele of indebted and insolvent state-owned enterprises and of newly emerging private entrepreneurs with small capital and uncertain prospects.

According to some opinions the sequencing of market access in banking was counterproductive and contributed to the frequent bank failures in some transition countries. 'Entry regulation was very liberal at the beginning of the financial reforms, whereas in the last two to three

[1] See Várhegyi, É. (1996).

[2] See Ábel, I., P. I. -Székely, (1994), Hrnčíř, M. (1994).

years regulation has become increasingly rigid, sometimes to the point of practically preventing any access to banking market.' [3]

Due to the weak regulation and control in the first years of the reform, banks could be established without proper initial capital and owners, and even fraudulently. The high number of bank failures in some countries were due not only to the collapse of the former East-European markets of the indebted enterprises and the deep recession in the region but to the imprudent behaviour of the banks as well.

At the beginning of the transformation, the inheritances of the old regime and the unsettled market accompanied by weak regulation led to market imperfections and ineffectiveness which could have only been treated by well co-ordinated policy. As the experiences show, the policies pursued by the governments were occasional, sometimes confused, and lacked of proper foresight. The learning process took too much time.

2. TREATMENT OF THE INHERITED WEAKNESSES

Besides creating an entirely new set of institutions, procedures and rules for operation of banks, the other key task for the governments of the transition countries was to assure soundness of the banking system. They had and, in some respects still have, to solve the problems of banks, deriving from their insufficient capital, insolvency and bad quality of portfolios, as well as the distortions of the market characterised by the high level of concentration, segmentation and imperfect competition.

In first years of transition the banking sector expanded rapidly in each country. The expansion was partly due to transition itself, namely the growing role of the banking sector in the economy. As the widening and deepening of the financial intermediation preceded the establishment of strict regulation and close control, banks increased their lending without prudential consideration. The level of the risk reserves and loan loss provisions kept step neither with the increase nor the deterioration of the bank assets. At the beginning of transition, the lack of competition and proper rules resulted in high profitability of the banks in these countries, often exceeding the international average of ROAs and, in particular ROEs.

On the other hand, the expansion of the banking sector in the first years of transition derived from the liberal licensing policy and the gradual opening of domestic financial markets, which quickly increased the number of actors. Due to easy entry and low capital requirements, and high profitability, private newcomers and foreign banks entered the market inducing some kind of rivalry. Though the competition was

---

[3] CEPR - IEWS (1996). This rigidity is reflected in the fact that the Czech authority stopped granting new banking licences at the end of 1993 (see in the survey chapter).

mitigated by concentration and segmentation of the banking market, the entry of foreign banks more or less contributed to the deterioration of position of big state-owned banks.

The bright period of banking at the beginning of transition was followed by a deterioration in the portfolios and a decline in capital adequacy, which led to a fall in profitability in some cases. Without the help of the state bank consolidation programmes, the erosion of banks' own capital sooner or later would have resulted in technical insolvency. The strong neccessity of portfolio cleaning and/or capital injection revealed that the high profits reported earlier were mostly due to the inadequate accounting system, which had allowed banks to fail provisioning and to show the unrealised interest as income. The deterioration of capital adequacy of some banks were equally due to the inherited weaknesses of balance sheets (namely insufficient capital, bad portfolios), the lack of well-suited regulation and control, the lack of prudent bank management and the collapse of the Eastern market with its consequences (namely the fall of export demand and industrial output, the growth of internal and external imbalances).

Though the open crisis reached the segment of the newly established small banks, mostly owned by domestic private entities, a sort of *hidden crises* was observable in the case of big banks owned by the state itself and state-owned enterprise and/or other partly state-owned banks. (This cross-ownership relation of banks was typical in the Czech Republic, due to the voucher privatisation and the operation of national investment funds.[4]) As the largest part of the doubtful and bad loans concentrated in the balance sheets of big state owned banks derived from the former central bank, the responsibility of their treatment belonged to the state.

The erosion of capital of the banking sector was due mostly to overindebted enterprises, among them the giant SOEs being the main clients of the giant banks. The bank portfolios deteriorated both because of the losses on the loans inherited and of the continuing losses of the clientele inherited.[5] As 'too big to fail' was the basic principle of banks in bailing out large companies, to cut back the credit lines of them seemed to be impossible in the first year of transition. In addition to this mentality, in some transition countries the implementation of bankruptcy legislation was postponed in the spirit of gradualism.

During the process of transition in EEC economies, indebtedness of enterprises accelerated and led to insolvency in large numbers. As parallel with worsening macroeconomic conditions the rules of portfolio classification gradually closed to international standards, the proportion of classified assets in the banks' balance sheets, in particular the bad and doubtful claims, increased quickly. The velocity of this increase depended

---

[4] See Bonin, J. P. (1995).

[5] See Király, J. (1995).

partly on the aggravation of the asset classification, provisioning regulation and accounting system, partly on the revealing of the crisis in the sphere of the real economy, which was also in close connection with the regulation (namely the accounting law and the implementation of bankruptcy legislation). The differences between the appearance of the bad loan problem and its acceleration in the individual countries are well reflected in the trends of deterioration of banks' assets. While for example, in Hungary the deterioration in the banks' portfolio culminated in 1993 and was decreasing later on, the process started later and lasted longer in the Czech Republic and the Slovak Republic. [6]

The governments had different options to treat the deepening problems. There was an option to prevent the crisis of the banking sector by *cleaning up portfolios*. An other option to avoid massive state intervention was to put the burden on depositors by *inflating simultaneously bad debt and deposits*. Elements of both solutions were applied in all countries to some extent.

The possibility of concealing and inflating the bank crisis highly depended on the strictness of regulation and control. As soon as severe rules of portfolio classification had been introduced in the practice, weaknesses of teh banking sector were revealed. The first appearance of the alarming weaknesses of a number of large banks was observable in Hungary, where the rigorous provisions of the bankruptcy, accounting and banking laws came into force at the beginning of 1992 revealed the technical insolvency's in the first place, and cried for quick state intervention.[7]

The methods of state interventions in treating insolvency and capital problems of banks were different, and most of them were applied in most countries. One usually applied form of state intervention was the so-called loan consolidation program, which aimed at cleaning up the banks' portfolio. There were two types of approaches in the issuing of bad debts: the centralised and the decentralised one. Both models were applied to certain extent in each country, but the sequence and the combination of them was different.

The aim of the *centralised approach* was to clean up the bank's balance sheets of non-performing loans and transfer them to a 'restructuring agency'. This type of institution was the Consolidation Bank in the ex-Czechoslovakia where an amount of about eight per cent of all bank credits to enterprise was allocated for banks' recapitalisation and write-offs through debt-for-bonds swaps at the end of 1991. [8] A part of

---

[6] In the Czech Republic the bad loans stood at 19 % of the total granted credits in 1992, 24 % in 1993, 25 % in 1994 and 26 % in 1995. See Šmídková, K. (1996).

[7] Though in the ex-Czechoslovakia the Consolidation bank was established in 1991, its immediate role was, however, to take over perpetual credits for inventories from commercial banks, and only later extended its activities to non-performing loans. (Hrnčíř, M. (1994), p. 229).

[8] See Hrnčíř, M. (1994), p. 230.

these claims might be restructured in co-operation with the debtor enterprises, another part might be written off. The assumed advantage of the centralised model was to accelerate the restructuring and privatisation of enterprises, but in the practice these expectations has not been justified because of the insufficient means and interest of state agencies. In Hungary bad claims of HUF 100 billion face value were converted to state bonds at a price of 60 to 100 per cent. Though a state agency (the Hungarian Development and Investment Bank) was commissioned to manage the claims, it was allowed to co-operate with the banks originally owned them. Consequently this method can be seen as a kind of the semi-centralised model.

In the *decentralised model* of consolidation the responsibility for the solution of bad loan problem was assumed by the banks. Banks got capital injections from the State in order to recapitalize themselves and fill up their loan-loss provisions. The decentralised method was adopted in Poland as the single tool of the Restructuring Program coming into force in 1993. The program intended to offer a chance to those debtors that showed potential for future growth and were capable of preparing a realistic business plan and financing strategy, on the one hand, and to improve the health of the financial sector by substantially eliminating the problem of bad debts, on the other. In Hungary the decentralised method was applied in the Bank and Debtor Consolidation Program of 1993-1994, which followed the semi-centralised model of the Loan Consolidation Scheme of 1992. Decentralised restructuring model was intended to follow the earlier centralised one at the end of 1995 in the Slovak Republic.

The countries examined here applied different models and methods of restructuring the banking sector. As the order of time of the restructuring was also different, the comparison of the costs and benefits can hardly be given. While global balance sheets of the individual banking sectors show the degree of the improvement until the end of 1995, they reflect not only the effects of restructuring but that of the privatisation and the strengthening competition as well. (See table 2.) In Hungary, for example, where data reflect a considerable improvements in the quality of banks' portfolio, besides the consolidation program the market structure of the banking sector was significantly changed, due to the quick expansion of banks with foreign participation simultaneously with the contraction of problem banks' market share.

3. PRIVATISATION

Restructuring programs usually aimed at bringing banks in position that is suitable for their privatisation. It has to be mentioned, however, that privatisation of the banking sector does not mean only the privatisation of state-owned banks but also the promotion of entry of private banks into the market. Most countries applied both methods of privatisation in order to improve the efficiency of credit allocation. In the first years of banking reforms, the share of privately owned capital in the banking sector increased rather as a result of newly established domestic and foreign banks than that of privatisation. In the Hungarian case, moreover, the improvement of the banking sector was mostly due to the competitive environment stemming from the entrance of foreign banks.

Concerning methods of bank privatisation in the narrower sense, there are three approaches that have been applied so far in CEE countries: (1) the sale of shares through public offers on domestic stock market to small investors, (2) the sale of a large stake to strategic foreign investors, and (3) the use of the so called voucher privatisation. [9]

The *first method* was basically applied in Poland. The privatisation program for the nine commercial banks intended to sell 40-50 per cent ownership to domestic investors by initial public offers on the Warsaw Stock Exchange, 10-20 per cent to bank employees and 10-20 per cent to foreign investors, reserving 30 per cent for the state. [10] A similar structure of ownership was created in the case of the largest Hungarian bank, the National Savings Bank (OTP), by public offering of 28 per cent ownership to a dispersed group of foreign investors.

The *second model* of privatisation was generally applied in Hungary. Making portfolios attractive by the loan and bank consolidation programs, the government intended to search for strategic financial investors for each bank. With the exception of OTP, the Hungarian government gave up reserving any stake in the commercial banks. Until the end of 1996, three of the four large commercial banks were sold in this way. In all cases the foreign strategic owners got the majority of the shares.

Though the overall result of the privatisation can be seen yet neither in Poland, nor in Hungary, some advantageous effects of the foreign strategic owners have appeared. The changes among the member of board and the management strengthened the prudent behaviour of banks which resulted in an improvement both in the quality of portfolios and profitability. [11] The more severe lending attitude also increased the efficiency of credit allocation which undoubtedly contributed to the improvement of the banks performance, but made the access to credit sources more difficult for newly established small and medium sized enterprises, lacked of enough capital.

The Czech and the Slovakian experiences were principally based on mass privatisation (*third model*). The majority of large state-owned banks went through voucher privatisation: the state kept from 26 to 67 per

---

[9] See Bonin, J. P. (1995).

[10] See IEWS (1995).

[11] See survey chapter.

cent of the shares in the large banks and the others were sold by vouchers.[12] Since the large banks collected the major stake of vouchers through the investment privatisation funds founded by themselves, significant cross-ownership evolved between the banks and their clients, on the one hand, and among the banks, on the other. As the state remained the largest owner while private ownership became dispersed and disturbed by the cross-ownership relation between banks and clients, this method of privatisation failed to create proper ownership control of banks, and therefore could not prevent the reproduction of the bad loan problem.

Table 1. Comparison of the legal system in the Czech Republic (CZ), Hungary (H), Poland (P) and the Slovak Republic (S) with the EC banking directives
(As in 1996)

Area of regulation	EC directives	Comparison
Access to market	Directive 77/780/EEC (First Banking Directive)	Partly harmonised. Different criterion of economic need when applying for the authorisation.
Providing of banking services	Directive 89/646/EEC (Second Banking Directive)	Principle rules for providing with banking services are harmonised
Pursuit of business	Directive 89/299/EEC on the own funds	Remaining discrepancies are of technical nature
	Directive 89/647/EEC on solvency ratio	Roughly harmonised in CZ, H and S. Partly harmonised in P, where asset quality is evaluated only in terms of loan portfolio quality
	Directive 92/121/EEC on large exposures	Principal rules are harmonised, some technical differences have remained
Supervision	Directive 92/30/EEC on consolidated supervision	Under harmonisation
Money laundering	Directive 91/308/EEC on money laundering	Harmonised
Deposit guarantee	Directive 94/19/EEC	Partly harmonised, different subjects and limits of guarantee

Sources: BIS (1995), CNB (1996), Mervart, J. (1996), NBS (1996), Várhegyi, É. (1996)

[12] See Šmídková, K. (1996).

Table 2. Methods, cost and results of banks' restructuring

	Czech and Slovak Republic	**Hungary**	**Poland**
Model of restructuring	centralised	combined	decentralised
State agencies involved into the process	Consolidation Bank recapitalized by the National Property Funds	Ministry of Finance, Hungarian Investment and Development Bank	Ministry of Finance
Methods and cost	1991: swapping bad loans for state bonds, amounting to CZK 38 bn (USD 1.4 bn) plus capital injection of CZK 12 bn (USD 0.4 bn) 1992-1995: na	1992: swapping bad loans of 14 banks and 68 savings co-operatives for state bonds, amounting to HUF 98 bn (USD 1.2 bn) 1993: swapping debts of 13 big state-owned companies for HUF 57 bn (USD 0.6 bn) of state bonds 1993-94: capital injection of HUF 153 bn (USD 1.5 bn) into 8 banks 1995-96: state guarantee for bad loans of some privatised banks, amounting to HUF 30 bn (USD 0.2 bn)	1993: swapping bad loans of 7 regional banks for 11 trillion zloty (USD 5 bn) of state bonds 1994: injecting 25 trillion zloty (USD 10 bn) of state bonds into 2 specialised banks
Total cost (USD bn)	na	1992-95: USD 3.5 bn	1993-94: USD 15 bn
Cost to GDP of 1995 (%)	na	9.2	12.6
Source of recapitalisation	revenue of small-scale privatisation	state budget	state budget
Bad loans to total loans, end of 1996 (%)	Czech Republic: 28.1 Slovak Republic: 31.8	7.2	14.7

Source: CEPR - IEWS (1996), CNB (1996), Hrnčíř, M. (1994), NBH (1996), NBS (1996), EBRD (1999).

4. ESTABLISHMENT OF THE TWO-TIER BANKING SYSTEM

The first important step in the modernisation of the Hungarian financial sector was the *creation of the two-tier banking system*, more adapted to the market environment. Following two years of preparation, the new system of the NBH, performing primarily central bank functions, and the institutionally separated commercial banks was set up on January 1 1987. At the same time State Banking Supervision was created from a department of the Ministry of Finance. The tasks and the scope of activities were stipulated partly by the Act on Public Finances, and partly by a Government Decree.

At the beginning the activity scope of the financial institutions was strictly regulated. Certain types of banks were allowed to operate with determined range of clientele and banking operations. The limitations of the business activity led to segmentation of the market and hindered competition. The loosening of the market segmentation started around 1989 through the integration of the retail market. Commercial banks originally having corporate clientele were admitted to the retail market, while retail financial institutions were given commercial banking licenses. At the same time the banks were given more and more freedom to perform trade related foreign exchange transactions. Competition was also increased by the entrance of new foreign owned and joint venture banks, as well as subsidiary banks founded by large banks specialising in particular business lines.

The number of financial institutions, 21 in 1987, has doubled since; as a result, 43 banks and specialised financial institutions, 205 savings and 8 credit co-operatives were in business by the end of 1999. During that time the number of financial institutions was increased by several new entrances and decreased by some M&As, bankruptcies and market exits. (See Table 3.)

The Hungarian banking system includes seven types of financial institutions:

1. Commercial banks authorised to perform all activities set forth in the Banking Act
2. Specialised financial institutions with limited authorisations according to lower minimum equity requirements and operating facilities
3. Investment banks
4. Mortgage banks (this type exists since 1998)
5. Building societies (this type exists since 1997)
6. Savings co-operatives
7. Credit co-operatives (this type exists since 1994).

Table 3. Number of banks

Type of banks	1990	1992	1994	1996	1998	1999
Commercial banks	28	30	36	33	32	30
Specialised financial institutions	4	5	7	9	6	6
Investment banks	-	1	1	1	1	1
Mortgage banks	-	-	-	-	1	2
Building societies	-	-	-	-	4	4
Banks total	*32*	*36*	*44*	*43*	*44*	*43*
Savings co-operatives	260	257	254	247	236	205
Credit co-operatives			4	8	8	8
Co-operatives total	*260*	*257*	*258*	*255*	*244*	*213*

Source: National Bank of Hungary

However, the institutional and regulatory changes, which undoubtedly created a better basis for the operation of the banking system, were not adequate in themselves to substantially improve the effectiveness of monetary regulations and the efficiency of capital allocation (Várhegyi, 1993, 1994). The reasons included the limited autonomy of the NBH, the subordination of monetary policy to fiscal considerations, on the one hand, and the survival of previous behaviour of banks whose share were owned in large percentages by their commercial customers, the enterprises, on the other. It was not until the nineties that notable changes commenced in this respect.

5. ESTABLISHMENT OF LEGAL FRAMEWORK FOR THE HUNGARIAN BANKING SYSTEM

The most important milestone in creating the legal framework for the banking system *in conformity with European standards*, was the enactment of the Act on the National Bank and the Act on Financial Institutions at the end of 1991. These Acts played a dual role. On the one hand, the regulation of participants of the banking sector on the legislative level gave more *effective protection* against the political pressures, affording more opportunities to operate in accordance with their economic functions. On the other hand, they might facilitate *the integration* of the Hungarian banking system into the capital markets of developed economies. Two other acts, the new Accounting Act promoting the transformation into market economy and the Bankruptcy Act are also worth highlighting from the institutional modernisation process of the nineties as laws influencing the operating conditions of the banking sector.

The *Act No. LX of 1991 on the National Bank of Hungary* brought about considerable changes after the previous ex-lex situation. Previously the NBH operated under the supervision of the Government, meaning not only that its President was appointed by the Prime Minister, but also that the government had the right to approve the monetary and credit policy guidelines. Thus monetary policy was subordinated to the economic policy of the government even in the formal sense. The NBH had to provide unlimited financing not only to the budgetary deficit, but also for economic programs considered a priority by the Government.

In theory the Act on the NBH, effective from December 1991, put an end to the subordination of the Central Bank. Following the liberal German model, the Act ensures a legal status to the NBH which is extremely important for the responsible operation of the central bank in the still heavily centralised Hungarian economy. According to the Act, the President of the NBH reports solely to Parliament. The central bank has the independent tool of interest rate policy to influence the economy. In addition, the NBH can decide independently about its policy towards banks, on refinancing, the compulsory reserve requirements and the daily liquidity reserve requirements. Even though the Act provides that the exchange rate policy is the joint competence of the Government and the NBH, in reality the government cannot take decisions to adjust the exchange rates without the consent of the NBH.

The *Act No. LXIX of 1991 on Financial Institutions and Financial Institutional Activities (hereinafter: Banking Act)* was also an important milestone in bringing Hungarian banking system closer to Western style banking. The Act imposes obligations on banks which can be met only by putting prudential considerations on top of their list of priorities. The requirement of eight percent solvency ratio, as well as the control of owners and large borrowers constitute the legal conditions for prudential banking operations.

Though the Banking Act was modelled after EC's banking provisions and standards, the course defined by the Act does not fully reflect the trends prevailing in Europe. In some respects the Act followed rather the EC's First Banking Directive [13] than the more liberal Second Banking Directive. [14] Notable restrictions were set up partly concerning the treatment of foreign investors, and partly concerning the authorised banking activities.

The main question of the banking model was decided one year earlier, at the time when the Act on Securities was established. The Securities Act, enacted in June of 1990, allowed only those organisations to trade with securities who were active *exclusively* in that field. This regulation limited the application of universal banking model.

In some aspect the Hungarian regulations were different from EU directives concerning credit institutions. While the conditions of establishment of a bank were quite liberal, each bank is formed in a separate process. Furthermore, since the notion of branch was not recognised by Banking Act, it followed that there was no way to authorise the opening of a branch of foreign credit institution. The Act originally

[13] 77/780/EEC (1977) (hereinafter First Banking Directive).

[14] 89/646/ EEC (1989) (hereinafter Second Banking Directive).

made the acquisition of holdings in excess of 10% by foreigners subject to the prior conceptual consent of the Government. This restriction was abolished in 1996 as a consequence of Hungary's joining OECD.

The principle of *national treatment* was not however fully maintained by this step of liberalisation because the Hungarian Banking Act sets more than usual requirements to foreign investors. These regulations were revised in the new law to be enacted in 1997. The *new act on credit institutions* has meant an improvement in the harmonisation of legislation to EU and brought the Hungarian financial system closer to the universal banking model. As the OECD-membership required to abolish any kind of restrictions against foreigners, the establishment of branches of foreign credit institutions was allowed from the end 1997.

6. CHANGES IN THE OWNERSHIP STRUCTURE

Privatisation began very early, already in the late 1980s, when minority holdings in some banks (Inter-Európa Bank, General Banking and Trust Ltd., General Enterprise Bank, Postabank) were sold to foreign investors. These early privatisation deals all raised the capital of the banks in question. In addition, the foreign equity holding in some mixed banks (Unicbank, CIB, Citibank, BKD, and European Commercial Bank) was increased. Certain portions of bank shares went into private hands through the privatisation of corporate owners. This "spontaneous privatisation" was stopped in 1992 by the centralisation of bank shares owned by state-run companies. The budding privatisation process was also halted by the bank consolidation program. As an inheritance of the imprudent banking in the 80s, and a consequence of the transition including the strict Bankruptcy Law and the Banking Law with prudential requirements most state owned banks lost their capital due to the huge amount of bad and doubtful loans by the end of 1992. The consolidation program consisted of two phases, a so-called loan consolidation in which banks portfolios were cleaned-up from bad loans followed by the so-called bank consolidation in which banks gave capital injection from the state.

Before the bank consolidation had been completed, only two relatively healthy banks could be considered for sale. Privatisation raised two crucial policy issues, notably whether (1) Hungarian banks must be sold to strategic or portfolio investors, and (2) concentrated or diversified structures must be developed. At the end of 1993, after lengthy debates, the government resolved that it preferred to involve strategic investors into the bank privatisation. In practice, the most suitable investors were selected in tender bids. This policy was applied in the partial privatisation of the Hungarian Foreign Trade Bank (HFTB) in the summer of 1994, in which the state owner intended to ensure profit-oriented operations, balanced ownership structure and capital resources required for development through the simultaneous involvement of strategic and institutional investors. The Bayerishe Landesbank as the strategic and the EBRD as the financial investor jointly submitted the best bid.

The privatisation of the consolidated banks generally followed the same pattern: participants were selected on the basis of the price offered and the capital injection promised. This is how the Budapest Bank (GEC, EBRD) was sold in 1995, then the Hungarian Credit Bank (ABN Amro) in 1996, and the Savings Bank (DG Bank), the K&H Bank (Kredietbank, Irish Life) and Mezőbank (Erste Bank) in 1997. The strategic investors mostly acquired majority stakes or were granted an option for future purchase (GEC), and effected large capital injections.

Attempts at selling some crisis-hit small banks failed: only the viable businesses of Dunabank were sold to a private owner (ING), while three were led out of the market with government assistance. Two small banks were taken over by the state-owned Hungarian Investment and Development Bank.

Generally based on strategic investors and producing concentrated holdings, the Hungarian bank privatisation includes two exceptions: OTP and Postabank, the two largest retail banks. A government decision excluded the involvement of strategic investors into the privatisation of the OTP Bank, which began in 1995, and aimed at creating a diversified ownership structure with the domination of institutional-financial investors. Consequently, in addition to the 10 percent holding of the two social insurance funds each, OTP was given away in private placement to foreign institutional, Hungarian institutional and private investors, employees and the management. (In Postabank, a less conscious government policy produced a similar ownership structure because the exit of former strategic investors also had a role to play.)

The privatisation of the Hungarian banking system had practically finished by the end of 1997. The state holdings in banks with strategic majority shareholders will soon be sold either through the stock exchange or by the exercising of the options. Only banks with special functions will remain in state ownership (Eximbank, Hungarian Development Bank, Land Credit and Mortgage Bank). The future of the Postabank, in which the state has acquired a majority interest in a bailout action required by capital loss, is still open.

By the end of 1997, the share of state property within Hungarian banking, including the holdings of social insurance funds, had dropped to 21 percent. At the same time the share of foreign capital had risen to over 60 percent. The influence of foreign investors increased in 1998 and 1999 as a result of some capital increases and the sale of the state's minority interests.

It is not only the dominance of foreign capital that is a striking feature of Hungarian banking but also the low share of Hungarian non-state owners. Private individuals hold a mere 2.5 percent of the banking capital, and within "other domestic organisations", which account for 12 percent of the total, the state-owned Hungarian Development Bank and some companies with a majority state holding have the most. These two features of the ownership structure are interdependent. Foreign owners had to gain control, as in the absence of domestic private capital there was no other option (Várhegyi, 1998).

Within foreign ownership, banks, which qualify as strategic investors, are in the majority, and the share of portfolio investors is low. This is a direct result of the method chosen to sell consolidated banks: only strategic investors were invited to submit tender bids. Financial investors were important in the privatisation of OTP.

Although most of the strategic investors are West European banks, the structure is very diverse. No country dominates the Hungarian banking system (German banks, which carry the largest weight, control less than 20 percent of the market) and no foreign institution has a market share over 8 percent through its Hungarian bank. The majority of the larger banks are owned by German (BLB, DG, Commerzbank, Hypobank, Dresdner, WestLB), Austrian (BA-CA, RZB, Erste), Dutch (ABN Amro), Belgian (Kredietbank), Italian (Banca Commerciale, Sao Paolo di Torino) and U.S. (Citibank, GEC) financial institutions. The ownership structure fits the pattern of Hungarian trade, two-thirds of that is done with the EU countries. However, the dominance of the European Union does not mean exclusiveness: the U.S., Russia (Gazprom Bank) and Asia (Daewoo, IC Bank, Nomura) are also present on the market, though the latter in investment banking mostly.

Table 4. Ownership structure of the Hungarian banking sector by registered capital (distribution in %)

Type of owner	1993	1994	1995	1996	1997	1998
I. Hungarian owners	86.7	83.5	63.9	50.5	37.3	37.0
State and social securities	67.7	65.8	41.8	35.6	20.4	21.7
Other Hungarian institutions	17.9	15.1	17.8	11.6	15.2	12.3
Private persons	1.1	2.5	4.2	3.2	1.7	3.0
II. Foreign owners	12.4	16.0	35.7	45.8	60.6	60.4
Foreign banks	9.9	13.9	26.8	38.9	48.5	50.0
Other foreign institutions	2.6	2.2	8.8	10.1	12.1	10.4
III. Other (preferential shares, own shares of banks)	0.9	0.5	0.4	3.7	2.1	2.6
Total	100.0	100.0	100.0	100.0	100.0	100.0

Source: National Bank of Hungary

The government adopted two types of privatisation. The minority share of the National Savings Bank (OTP) was sold to foreign and local institutional investors (30 per cent), and to employees and management (5 per cent), the 40 per cent was allocated to the social insurance administrations and the public in compensation note swap transaction, while 25 per cent was reserved in long-lasting state ownership. The majority share of the other banks were sold to foreign strategic and institutional investors. The Hungarian Foreign Trade Bank (MKB) was sold to Bayerische Landesbank (51 per cent) and EBRD (17 per cent) during 1994 and 1995. The Budapest Bank was bought by EBRD (32.5 %) and General Electric Capital Services (27.5 %) at the end of 1995, while Hungarian Credit Bank was fully sold to ABN-Amro Bank at the end of 1996.

7. OVERCOMING THE INHERITED PROBLEMS

The development of the two-tier bank system and the establishment of a legal environment adjusted to the requirements of market economy led to functional improvements in the financial system of Hungary. However, the historical problems of the banking sector were not managed and the banks were not disburdened from *inherited non-performing loans*.

Problem loans inherited from the preceding period were dramatically increased by the financial problems of enterprises during the rapid transformation process started in the early 1990s. The position of the banks without sufficient capital or risk provisions was aggravated by the severe Bankruptcy Act introduced in 1992 without considering the interests of lending banks.

As by 1992 the fast growth of bad loans became one of the most critical obstacles to the operation of the Hungarian banking system, it was necessary to start the consolidation process. However, the fire fighting loan consolidation programme did not bring about the desired long term improvement in the positions of either the banks or their debtors. Therefore further one (namely: the bank consolidation programme) was implemented in 1993 and 1994.

7.1 Loan consolidation programme of 1992-1993

In December 1992 the government decided to help banks by loan consolidation programme. Bad loans of 14 commercial banks and 68 savings co-operatives showing capital adequacy ratios below 7.25 % were bought by the government in the total face value of HUF 102.5 billion for HUF 80 billion *consolidation bonds* with 20 years maturity. In addition, the government purchased the bank debts of 12 large enterprises selected by the administration. HUF 57 billion consolidation bonds were paid by the government to lending banks for these debts representing HUF 62 billion total face value.

The results of the loan consolidation program can be characterised by the following highlights (Balassa, 1996):

- The process was followed by considerable *short term improvement* in the position of the banking system. The required amounts of risk provisions were lowered and the capital adequacy ratios increased.

- However, the benefits of loan consolidation *did not last long*. The portfolios retained by the banks continued to deteriorate because of more rigorous criteria and poor debtor positions. The process did not address the bad undercapitalisation of the banks, neither the ownership and management problems.
- The government failed to clearly define the future of debts removed from bank portfolios or the debtor organisations. The actual commencement of debt management and business reorganisation was delayed by *two years of hesitation* and this generated substantial loss.
- The debt cancellation of some important enterprises translated into carrying on the historical *bargaining mechanism* between companies and the government.

7.2 Recapitalisation of banks in 1993-1994

In spite of portfolio cleaning by loan consolidation, the total problem debt portfolio in the banking system increased to HUF 436 bn by the end of 1993, amounting to 29 per cent of the outstandings of banks, 16 per cent of banking assets total and 12 per cent of the GDP. As a consequence of the risk provision requirements, the equity balances of many banks (including leading state owned banks) *became technically insolvent*. The government decided to take another consolidation step by *recapitalisation to compensate the loss of equity*.

The key characteristics of the so called *bank consolidation programme* approved in December 1993 are reviewed below (Balassa, 1996):

- Involved banks were required to produce risk provisions by December 31 1993 according to international standards.
- In Phase 1 the banks were recapitalised through the acquisition of share by the government (new share issue) to 0% capital adequacy ratio as of December 31 1993.
- In Phase 2 it was specified as a general principle to increase the capital adequacy ratios of big banks to 8% and of small banks to 4% through share sale followed by subordinated loans.
- Share sale and subordinated lending was performed by the transfer of consolidation bonds.

In the first step the total equity amount of 8 banks was increased by HUF 115 bn. Following these transactions the equity share of the government increased to not less than 75% in 7 out of the 8 concerned banks.

Under the bank *consolidation agreements* executed at the end of 1993 bank managements are obliged to improve the performance of the banks. Each bank had to develop a consolidation programme to formulate the strategy of the bank, improve the cost management process, rationalise the organisation and develop the qualification and credit rating systems. Subject to the performance of these objectives the additional equity raises promised to the banks were actually implemented in May and December 1994.

While the new government entering into office in 1994 promised that the bank consolidation process was completed by the final capital injection at the end of 1994, it continued to support the banks during 1995 and 1996. HUF 9 billion equity was committed to support the merger of two undercapitalised banks, namely, Mezôbank and Agrobank. The government also indicated that it may underwrite the bad debts of certain banks to facilitate their privatisation sale.

7.3 Impacts consolidation programmes on banks

The consolidation bonds issued by the government and used in the consolidation processes added HUF 350 billion, amounting to *7 per cent of the GDP*. In 1994 and 1995 the interests of consolidation bonds was estimated at 2 per cent of the GDP each year.

According to actual data the substandard, doubtful or bad debt portfolios of the banks were gradually reduced both in absolute terms and in terms of shares in total accounts receivable. The impacts of consolidation processes are reflected by the faster than average reduction rate of the doubtful and bad debts of involved banks. (See Table 5.)

As a result of the consolidation process banks were theoretically enabled to enhance their lending activity. However, this effect was offset by the high share of consolidation bonds in bank portfolios. As the market is unwilling to absorb this volume of bonds of unusually long maturity, the banks are unable to replace new loans for the bad ones removed from their portfolios. Consequently the level of business lending of banks involved in consolidation is decreasing.

In conclusion the consolidation process improved the balance sheets of banks in terms of equity and portfolio quality. On the other hand the consolidated banks typically adjusted to the new situation by *lower lending activity*.

Table 5. Quality of the portfolio of the banking system (per cent)

Item	1993	1995	1997	1998
No problem	70.7	83.4	92.8	91.9
Special attention	6.8	7.3	4.6	5.3
Substandard	2.9	1.7	0.8	1.0
Doubtful	6.1	2.4	0.6	0.9
Bad	13.5	5.2	1.2	0.9
Total outstandings	100.0	100.0	100.0	100.0
Problem loans as % of total outstandings	29.3	16.6	7.2	8.1
Problem loans as % of balance sheet total	20.7	15.1	6.8	7.9
Problem loans as % of GDP	15.4	7.3	4.4	5.1

Source: National Bank of Hungary

8. MARKET STRUCTURE AND COMPETITIVENESS

The Hungarian banking system has not developed in the course of a spontaneous process. The reform, aimed at the establishment of a two-tier banking system, has not eliminated the distortions deriving from the inherited structures and artificial division of the market till our very days. This has several consequences which prevent the development of a healthy competition and slow down the emergence of a viable market structure.

This chapter investigates the manifestations of power relations developing on the Hungarian banking market, the causes and tendencies of their coming about through presenting concentration, segmentation and income polarisation.

8.1 The development of the banking sector

The Hungarian banking sector showed a moderate quantitative development after 1990. The growth of the balance sheet total fell behind that of GDP. The relatively slow development of the banking sector was however illusive and reflected the cleaning up of banks portfolios from nonperfoming loans. Owing to the more and more rigorous banking regulation and the recession of the economy, the activity of the banking sector grew narrow during the last years. On the other hand, however, the cleaning of the market resulted in a *healthier structure* of banks capable of development. (See Table 6.)

Table 6. Progress of the Hungarian banking sector, 1992-1998*

	1992	1993	1994	1995	1996	1997	1998
Number of banks	36	42	44	43	43	43	44
Balance sheet total, HUFbn	2,276	2,631	3,072	3,693	4,499	5,688	6,559
Balance sheet total as percentage of GDP	77.3	74.1	70.4	66.4	67.2	67.2	68.2
Share capital, HUFbn	109	257	296	220	222	306	326
Equity, HUFbn	167	148	209	296	377	550	571
Profit after taxation**, HUFbn	-2.9	-154.0	12.3	44.1	61.4	58.7	40.1
Bad and doubtful loans as percentage of total assets	8.5	20.0	11.5	7.4	4.0	3.2	1.8
Capital adequacy ratio	8.8	11.5	15.6	18.3	18.9	17.3	9.9
ROA**	-0.1	-5.8	0.5	1.6	1.9	1.6	0,9
ROE**	-2.7	-100,3	6.2	21.3	23.0	19.1	11.1
Operating cost as percentage of total asset	N.a.	2.9	3.2	3.7	3.6	3.8	4.0
Net interest margin	N.a.	4.3	4.3	4.7	4.0	4.6	4.5
Number of employees (thousand)	33.1	35.0	36.3	35.8	33.3	32.4	30.3
Asset/ employee (HUFmn)	69	75	85	103	135	175	216

*Banks without savings cooperatives
**In 1997 and 1998: without Postabank, MFB and Realbank which produced losses amounted to HUF 128 billion as a consequence of bad loan policies of several years and resulted in bankruptcy of Realbank and state consolidation steps of the two other banks.
Source: State Banking Supervision and National Bank of Hungary

The economic weight of Hungarian banking is still smaller than in the industrialised countries: the total bank assets account for less than 70 percent of GDP. The portfolio cleaning, which accompanied the bank consolidation, actually made the ratio fall before it began to pick up in 1997. The low weight of Hungarian banking can be seen in terms of deposits and loans alike: bank loans represent 26 percent, deposits 38 percent of GDP. The low volume of loans is due to the poor credit rating of most Hungarian companies, although 1997 brought dynamic growth. Apart from low incomes and slim propensity to save, the scarcity of individual deposits is due to the rising popularity of insurance products (insurance companies, pension funds) and mutual funds, augmented by tax allowances. The Hungarian market was also quite late to accept in broad cash-less means of payment, though Hungary is now the first by the number of banking cards in the East European region.

The development of the banking services was hindered by the distortions of competition and the deteriorating earnings position of the banking sector. The 15 banks which cover one third of the banking market made a loss in 1993. In 9 of them the loss exceeded the size of their equity; all of these banks are majority state owned, with three large, four medium sized and two small banks among their ranks. As the aggregate losses made by the banking sector in 1993 exceeded the total equity of the sector. The erosion of capital of the banking sector was attributable to banks with significantly different earnings positions.

The losses were caused primarily by the rocketing provisioning requirement owing to the surfacing of previous latent losses, which came to light because of the Acts on financial institutions, accounting and bankruptcy, as well as the real deterioration of the market conditions and the absence of adaptation strategies in banks. The 'losers' included primarily the banks financing the traditional Hungarian corporate customers, while the profitable banks consisted mainly of the joint venture banks with select clienteles.

Though in 1994 and 1995 some of the recapitalised banks produced a moderate profit again, banks confined to the Hungarian funding and asset markets had no opportunity to improve their profitability even after the bank consolidation schemes. One reason for this is because given the increasing financing needs of the budget, the cost of funds for banks could not be expected to decline to any significant extent. Even though with the higher equity/debt ratios after the equity increases, the interest expenses did not hit banks' profitability quite as severely, but the banks working with high cost ratios could have eliminated the still substantial expensive funding only if they could accelerate the repayment of the already on-lent credits.

The *benefit of the privatisation and the liberalisation* of the banking sector can be seen in the improving ratios of capital adequacy and profitability reflecting the increasing stability of the banking sector, as well as the in decreasing net interest margin reflecting the effect of the wider competition. As competition has intensified for business with high profile corporate clients, spreads and fees have decreased. Availability of bank loans for domestic firms has become easier which is reflected in the rapid increase of credit stock: its real value doubled between 1995 and 1998. At the same time household savings to banking sector increased by 50 percent in real term while the product range has become wider and more sophisticated.

8.2 Market structure

Even though the number of financial institutions has doubled since 1987, the Hungarian banking market is still dominated by the financial institutions which emerged from the previous mono-bank structure. Even in 1998 more than half of the banking market as measured by the balance sheet total was covered by the National Savings Bank (OTP), the Foreign Trade Bank (MKB) and the three banks separated from the NBH, ABN AMRO (Hungarian) Bank (the successor of Hungarian Credit Bank), the National Commercial and Credit Bank (K&H) and Budapest Bank (BB), inherited their clientele from the mono-bank system together with all the benefits and problems.

The banking market is still heavily *concentrated*, despite the growing number of financial institutions. Over half of the financial institutions had less than 1% market share in 1998. The relatively high concentration of the Hungarian banking market is not the result of competition, as it happened in more developed banking systems in recent years. Instead, it was formed by artificially created monopolies. This is why the degree of concentration decreased rather than increased between 1987 and 1998,[15] partly because of the slowly emerging competition, partly due to the involuntary contraction of the corporate banking market and the devaluation of receivable. In other words, high concentration in Hungary is a heritage which market forces weakened rather than created. (See Tables 7 and 8.)

Table 7. Market concentration

	1990	**1993**	**1994**	**1995**	**1996**	**1997**	**1998**
First 5 banks	83%	69%	64%	61%	59%	56%	54%
First 10 banks	93%	84%	81%	80%	77%	74%	69%

[15] In 1987, after the creation of the two tier banking system, the five largest banks dominated 90 percent of the total market, while by 1998 their markets share had fallen to 54%.

Table 8. Size distribution of commercial banks above 1% market share (according to the total assets)

Banks	*1998*	*1993*	*Change in position*
National Savings Bank (OTP)	25.1	31.6	-6.5
Hungarian Foreign Trade Bank (MKB)	9.2	9.1	+0.1
Commercial and Creditbank (K&H)	7.9	8.8	-0.9
CIB Bank	5.9	4.2	+1.7
Postabank and Savingsbank	5.8	6.4	-0.6
ABN Amro Bank (in 1993: Hungarian Credit Bank)	5.7	13.6	-7.9
Budapest Bank	4.1	6.0	-1.9
BA-CA (in 1993: Creditanstalt)	3.5	1.0	+2.5
Hungarian Development Bank (MFB)	3.2	0.8	+2.4
Raiffeisen Bank (in 1993: Unicbank)	3.0	1.4	+1.6
General Banking and Trust Co. (ÁÉB)	2.6	1.0	+1.6
Citibank	2.4	1.4	+1.0
ERSTE Bank Hungary (in 1993: Mezőbank)	2.1	1.3	+0.8
ING Bank Hungary	2.0	0.8	+1.2
Inter- Európa Bank	2.0	1.5	+0.5
Commerzbank Budapest	2.0	0.4	+1.6
Hypo-Bank Hungaria	1.9	-	+1.9
Bank of Hungarian Savings Cooperatives	1.7	1.4	+0.3
BNP-Dresdner Bank	1.1	0.6	+0.5
WestLB Hungaria	1.1	0.4	+0.7
Banking sector total	*100.0*	*100.0*	-

Source: Reports of banks

A key feature of the changes in the 1990s is the modification of the excessively *segmented market structure* of the earlier period. The rapid liberalisation of regulation and licensing enabled banks with appropriate capital and professional-technical facilities to perform more diverse activities and serve a wider clientele. After 1989 banks were licensed to offer retail-banking services, while retail banks were granted a full commercial bank license. Foreign operations were also gradually liberalised: in 1990 18 of the 26 financial institutions could carry out almost the full range of such operations, whereas in 1991 27 of the 36 organisations had a foreign exchange license.

Despite the softening in the segmented market, Hungarian banking had been strongly polarised in terms of profitability for a long time (Várhegyi, 1993, 1995). The profitability of financial institutions with foreign owners was much higher than that of state-owned banks. The relatively strong capital position of the former also contributed to their increasing market shares.

8.3 Profitability and cost effectiveness

Initially, the Hungarian banking sector experienced extensive development, with quality improvements made in recent years only. Since the largest banks were still state-owned in the mid-1990s, they operated with imprudent cost management; poor branch utilisation and, consequently, lower efficiency than banks, which were smaller but foreign-owned. The profitability of retail banks was also reduced by mass banking products, which are very costly if performed with underdeveloped technologies, while the income of large banks serving the corporate sector was drained by their huge reserves for bad debts. It was only mostly foreign-owned banks with a handpicked clientele that could benefit from the rapid growth.

Significant changes were only seen following the consolidation as a result of privatisation. As from 1996-97, Hungarian banking, deprived of the ill heritage but exposed to increasing competition, began to improve in quality. In addition to the general practice of privatisation, relying on capital-rich strategic investors, the openness of the market and the rising liberalisation of capital movements helped to bring about positive changes. The positive picture was overshadowed by serious problem of two banks (Postabank and Realbank) which loose all of there capital in 1997 and 1998. Losses of both banks may explained by non transparent and unclear ownership structure and the close ties between banks and clients. Postabank being the second largest retail bank was bailed out at first by the state bank, the Hungarian Development Bank, and later on by the state while Realbank went bankruptcy.

Following the low point of the banking crisis through 1996 profitability in the sector gradually increased and, in terms of return on assets, exceeded the average in banking sectors in developed countries. Improvements in profitability and the relatively high average profitability were observed in banks with foreign shareholders. The average profitability ratios between 1994 and 1997 were much higher in banks operating with majority foreign shareholders and banks founded by foreigners than in institutions privatised later or those where no shareholder control was established following privatisation (Postabank, Realbank). (See Table 9.)

Table 9. Interrelationship between profitability and ownership

Bank	ROA* (average between 1994 and 1997)	ROE** (average between 1994 and 1997)	Number of years of majority foreign ownership during the period 1994-97
Raiffeisen Unicbank	4,98	38,8	4
Citibank	4,83	35,9	4
CIB Hungária	3,69	35,2	4
CIB Bank	3,14	24,3	4
Daewoo	2,16	14,4	4
Creditanstalt	2,08	19,7	4
ING	2,04	29,1	4
WestLB	1,92	13,2	4
Inter-Európa Bank	1,78	16,6	4
BNP-Dresdner	1,71	20,6	4
Crédit Lyonnais	1,57	20,1	4
Hungarian Foreign Trade Bank	1,44	16,5	2,5
Budapest Bank	1,42	12,3	2
Hypo-Bank	1,23	7,5	4
Commerzbank	0,87	14,1	4
National Savings Bank	0,80	19,1	0
General Banking and Trust Co.	0,67	7,7	1,4
Commercial and Creditbank	0,57	13,6	0,3
Bank of Hungarian Savings Cooperatives	0,29	8,9	0,5
ABN Amro (Hungarian) Bank (until 1996: Hungarian Credit Bank	0,21	6,4	1
Volksbank	0,12	0,9	4
ERSTE Bank Hungary (until 1996: Mezőbank)	-0,18	-81,3	1
Postabank and Savings Bank	-0,38	-11,5	0
Realbank	-1,16	-8,2	0
Polgári Bank	-1,78	-19,1	0
Konzumbank	-3,39	2,2	0

Source: Reports of banks

We can therefore surmise that there is a close correspondence between profitability and shareholders' background. The best performers comprise only those banks which were controlled primarily by foreign strategic investors in the entire period under review (and perhaps even before that). The 'medium' group contains Inter-Európa Bank, which operated with a minority foreign control for a longer period, and the Hungarian Foreign Trade Bank, Budapest Bank and OTP, which were privatised in the first wave in 1995.

It may seem paradoxical that a decline in the profitability of the banking system can be observed in 1997 when, due primarily to the effects of consolidation and privatisation, capital positions and portfolios indicated stabilisation of the sector. Individual bank data indicate that the decline was general: it equally affected those banks which previously had good results as well as the less profitable banks; differences in capital structures did not appear to play a major role. (See Table 10.)

Table 10. Profitability of major commercial banks

Banks	ROA			ROE		
	1996	1997	1998	1996	1997	1998
National Savings Bank (OTP)	0.79	1.34	1.56	19.7	31.1	32.6
Hungarian Foreign Trade Bank (MKB)	2.17	2.31	1.51	24.9	21.8	16.2
Commercial and Creditbank (K&H)	0.74	0.57	-0.63	15.7	7.9	-10.9
CIB Bank	N.a.	3.95	2.21	N.a.	36.9	19.4
ABN Amro (Hungarian) Bank	1.21	-0.53	-0.88	25.5	-4.9	-9.9
Budapest Bank	2.32	1.48	1.20	18.8	13.2	10.4
BA-CA	2.04	1.56	1.81	19.6	17.8	23.8
Raiffeisen Bank	5.05	4,25	3.23	35.0	34,6	26.9
General Banking and Trust Co. (ÁÉB)	0.21	2.16	3.35	2.9	21.8	33.5
Citibank	4.25	4.85	1.98	39.2	37.4	16.3
Erste Bank	0.66	0.12	-2.81	15.8	3.2	-53.6
ING Bank (Hungary)	2.56	0.39	0.03	33.0	4.6	0.4
Inter-Európa Bank	1.76	1.98	0.42	18.75	22.4	4.4
Commerzbank (Budapest)	1.40	0.35	0.27	24.2	4.3	4.0
Hypo-Bank Hungaria	0.87	0.55	0.07	12.1	3.4	0.7
Bank of Hungarian Savings Cooperatives	0.27	0.90	0.40	8.3	20.4	9.7

Source: Reports of banks

The deterioration in profitability in 1997 was due primarily to intensified competition. This is reflected above all in the decline in average interest margins, as this decline indicates that competition from the non-banking sectors poses an increasing challenge to banks. Interest income relative to total assets in the banking sector has been declining since 1995 and was not offset by non-interest type incomes (fees and commissions).

The general decline in profitability was also due to increases in specific expenditures. In some banks this arose from heightened competition, as a result of which investments in modernisation and network development became necessary (e.g. at ABN AMRO the new Dutch shareholder spent considerable amounts on developing retail business – and in assuming resultant losses).

By international standards expenses in the Hungarian banking sector, measured as a share of total assets, are high (Szelényi 1998. p.12). However, as a net effect of declines in income and increases in expenses, expenses as a share of gross income do not reach the 60–70 percent typical in the banking sectors of developed European countries. On the other hand, high incomes previously enjoyed in the context of weak competition made it possible to retain low cost efficiencies; these conditions are disappearing due to heightened competitive conditions existing today.

Efficiency indices in the Hungarian banking sector are in line with Claessens' (1998) observation – supported by empirical experience based on examination of the situation at 7,900 banks in 80 countries – that entry of foreign banks will increase efficiency in the Hungarian banking system. His conclusions also show that competition generated by foreign banks will decrease profitability of Hungarian banks, non-interest incomes and operating expenses.

According to Claessens' observations, foreign banks attain different levels of efficiency in developed countries compared to those in developing countries. In the former case foreign banks operate at lower levels of efficiency, while in the latter they operate with higher efficiency than Hungarian banks. This is related to the fact that banks entering the developed markets operate primarily in the more competitive wholesale markets, where technical advantages are not sufficient to offset the knowledge of the market in Hungarian banks. In contrast the information disadvantage of foreign banks entering the developing and transition economies is offset by the fact that they are not bound by loan allocation constraints. This may explain the changes in the efficiency indices in the Hungarian banking system which has, since 1997, been dominated by foreign-owned banks.

During the 1980s and the first half of the 1990s foreign banks entering the Hungarian market were able to avail themselves of the income generation advantages of a less developed market. However, as a result of the consolidation of the previously significant Hungarian market participants and their sale to well-positioned strategic shareholders, this option disappeared with effect from 1997. Foreign entrants now face the same competitors in the Hungarian banking market as in developed countries. Presence in a prime location (e.g. Budapest or a county seat) and offering products that are more developed than those offered by Hungarian competitors, targeting limited market segments (e.g. multinationals or high net worth private individuals), no longer suffices.

Activities must be extended to all market segments such that the advantages of economies of scale can be reached.

8.4 Standard of Services

Of critical importance is whether improvements in the quality of the Hungarian banking system, in the context of greater competition, have been reflected in services. The decline in interest margins is an improvement ispo facto as both depositors and borrowers gain from the lower expense of intermediation. However there are also signs indicating that banks able to bear expenses and enjoying good shareholding and management backgrounds can and do improve the standard of their services in response to heightened competition. This has been shown not only in the appearance and rapid dissemination of more sophisticated products and services (e.g. ATM cards, electronic links, telephone services, bank insurance products, investment services) but also in the fact that the majority of banks in Hungary now extend their services to a wide range of customers.

Banks with foreign shareholders generated greater competition primarily in the market for corporate banking services. With the entry of new participants this greater competition could be felt in the first half of the 1990s in services available for creditworthy customers with high account turnover. During the last two years, in order to acquire good quality corporate clients, banks were in some cases willing to accept even loss making instruments.

Because of the saturation of the corporate market and in order to achieve economies of scale, foreign-owned banks have in recent years become very active in the area of retail services. This entry of foreign players with more developed banking technology has forced those retail banks which had previously enjoyed monopoly status to improve their services (improvements in services at OTP have been due to these developments, in addition to increased efficiency constraints following privatisation).

Rapid development of the Hungarian market over the last two years has also multiplied the number of products available in retail bank accounts and related services, though not enough to approach anywhere near the number of products offered in Western Europe (Mérő, 1998). Current account services offered by banks, aiming for the widest possible range of customers (and their technical support), showed clear improvements during the last two years in terms of both branch independence and an increase in account-related services (cards, transfers, loans, telephone and computer banking). In addition to deposit collection and account services, consumer lending has increased in the retail market, reflected also in the increasing number of financial institutions specialising in such lending (Opel, Porsche, Ford, Cetelem).

The spectacular banking investments made in the last two years and often aggressive customer 'acquisitions' (manifested in occasionally less-than ethical advertising and telephone enquiries) indicate that foreign banks which have established operations in Hungary view their presence here as a long-term strategic objective. This is also reflected in efforts to extend branch networks and in the formulation of plans which call for diverse services to be offered to the widest possible range of customers. Such plans are being prepared as the majority of banks are working to make their services universal, to be achieved via acquisition of non-banking institutions (broker firms, investment fund managers, leasing companies, pension funds, insurance companies) and the integration of their activities.

9. LIKELY FUTURE MARKET TENDENCIES

The Hungarian banking market shows the symptoms of both saturation and insufficiency at the same time. From the perspective of the developed countries, both the quality and the quantity of the banking services are far from being satisfactory. However, the boundaries for the Hungarian banking market are set on the demand side by the volume of the *savings* streaming into the banking sector on the one hand and by the creditworthiness of the enterprises and households on the other. The solvent demand for banking services generating non-interest-type of revenues is also restricted by the probably lasting stagnation of the economy and of the standard of living. Therefore it cannot be expected short-term, that the market for the banking industry will significantly grow. Moreover, it could also happen that the development of the *non-banking intermediary* system will lead to the banking sector being absolutely pushed to the background, while the capital market slowly starts growing.

In spite of the low use of bank credits of the corporate sector the net banking debt portfolio of the corporate sector is not expected to grow significantly in the near future. The impacts of the factors working against the increase of the banking debts of the enterprises can already be observed. With the high costs of financial intermediation the banking borrowings of the enterprises will not grow, moreover, with the access to other alternative resources the demand for bank credits can be expected to decrease.

As the business volume of the Hungarian banking market will not grow significantly in the near future and thus the non-efficient structures (like the small banks with relatively expanded branches, or specialised financial institutions without competitive products) will not be able to survive in their current form, a *concentration process* will inevitably start which will result in the decrease of the number of independent banking organisations.

REFERENCES

Ábel, I, P. I. -Székely, (1994), "Market Structure and Competition in the Hungarian Banking System", in J. P. Bonin, I. P. Székely, (eds.), (1994).

Balassa, Ákos (1996), "Consolidation of the Hungarian Banking system and its present situation" (in Hungarian), Külgazdaság No. 4 and 5.

BIS (1995), Report on Banking Supervision in Central and Eastern European Countries, Basle, April.

Bonin, J. P., I. P.-Székely, (eds.) (1994), "The Development and Reform of Financial Systems in Central and Eastern Europe", Edward Elgar Publishing Ltd.

Bonin, J. P. (1995), "Banking in Transition: Privatizing Banks in Hungary, Poland and Czech Republic", Mimeo.

CEPR - IEWS (1996), "Banking Sector Development in Central and Eastern Europe", Lorand Ambrus-Lakatos and Mark E. Schaffer. CEPR - Institute of East West Studies.

Claessens, Stijn (1998), "How does Foreign Entry Affect the Domestic Banking Market? The World Bank", *Policy Research Working paper 1918*, June.

CNB (1996), Banking Supervision in the Czech Republic, Czech National Bank.

EBRD (1999), Transition report 1999, Ten years of transition.

Hrnčíř, M. (1994), "Reform of the Banking Sector in the Czech Republic", in J. P. Bonin, I. P. -Székely, (eds.), (1994).

IEWS (1995), "Accelerating Bank Privatization in Central and Eastern Europe", IEWS Banking and Finance Centre.

Király, J. (1995), "Permanent Banking Crises? Central and East European Banking in the 90s", Mimeo.

Mérő, Katalin (1998), "Retail banking in Hungary" (in Hungarian), *Bankszemle* No. 4.

Mervart, J. (1996), "The Czech Banking Sector in the Period of Convergence to European Union Conditions", Ceská Národní Banka. Institut Ekonomie.

NBH (1996), Annual Report, 1995, National Bank of Hungary.

NBS (1996), Annual Report, 1995, Narodna Banka Slovenska.

Šmídková, K. (1996), "The Emergence of Financial Markets in Transition - The Czech Experience", Ceská Národní Banka. Institut Ekonomie.

Szelényi, Endre (1998), "The EU-ripeness of the Hungarian banking system in the mirror of data of banks" (in Hungarian), *Bankvilág No.2*.

Várhegyi, É. (1996), "Harmonisation of Legislation in the Hungarian Banking Sector", in Monetary Policy in Central and Eastern Europe: Challanges of EU Integration, Oesterreichishe Nationalbank and The Vienna Institute for Comparative Economic Studies, Vienna.

Várhegyi, Éva (1993), "The Modernisation of the Hungarian Banking Sector", in I. P. Székely and D. M. G. Newbery (eds.), Hungary: an Economy in Transition, Cambridge University Press, 1993.

Várhegyi, Éva (1994), "The 'Second' Reform of the Hungarian Banking System", in J. P. Bonin and I. P. Székely (eds.), The Development and Reform of Financial Systems in Central and Eastern Europe, Edward Elgar Publishing Ltd., 1994.

Várhegyi, Éva (1995), "Banks in competition" (in Hungarian), *Financial research Ltd.* Budapest.

Várhegyi, Éva (1998), Bankprivatizáció, *Kulturtrade*, Budapest.

Chapter 7

FINANCIAL FRAGILITY OR WHAT WENT RIGHT AND WHAT COULD GO WRONG IN CENTRAL EUROPEAN BANKING?*

Christian E. Weller
University of Bonn

Jürgen von Hagen
University of Bonn

ABSTRACT

Despite the fact that banks in Central Europe are still struggling with bad loan burdens, and that capital controls have slowly been eliminated, the South East Asian and Russian crises have not led to a massive failure of banks in the region. In this paper, we study economic trends and policies that may have helped to insulate CEECs from international financial contagion. Using data available from the IMF, and the BIS for nine Central European economies (Croatia, Czech Republic, Estonia, Hungary, Latvia, Lithuania, Poland, Slovak Republic, and Slovenia), our results indicate that an economic constellation unique to the early transition period rather than deliberate policy decisions have stabilized the CEECs. Specifically, the lack of recent banking crisis can be attributed to a lack of speculative financing, to underdeveloped asset markets, and to more long-term international capital flows. Future problems may arise as banks are beginning to extend credit more to an expanding real sector than in the past, as asset markets become more developed, or as export growth to the EU may decline with European growth slowing down.

*An earlier version of this paper was presented at the II. International Conference AEconomic System of the European Union and Adjustment of the Republic of Croatia, in Rijeka, Croatia, in April 1999.

R. MacDonald and R. Cross (eds.), Central Europe Towards Monetary Union: Macroeconomic Underpinnings and Financial Reputation, 121–148.

1. INTRODUCTION

The banking systems of the transition economies have compiled bad loan ratios in the double digits during the early transition years. Almost all transition economies recently experienced serious banking sector problems. Regulation and supervision in most transition economies do not appear to be up to the task of ensuring a stable banking sector, and finally, capital controls have gradually been removed. The combination of these factors signal weak financial systems, which should have been destabilized by the financial contagion from the South East Asian and Russian crises. Yet, the transition banking systems have not experienced bank runs or massive bank failures. Only the failure of the fifth largest Latvian bank can in fact be directly linked to the Russian crisis. What is it that has saved these economies from the fate of other emerging economies in the wake of financial crises elsewhere?

The risk that an economy's banking system will fail is directly linked to a number of risks banks are exposed to in open economy. With internal and external liberalization, which the transition economies have implemented over the past few years, the exposure to default, maturity, interest rate, and exchange rate risk should grow. The experience in other emerging economies has shown that the chance of a banking crisis consequently grows after financial liberalization. Thus, the lack of recent financial crises in the transition economies seems even more perplexing as they changed their financial systems from integral parts of a planned economy to market based institutions, while simultaneously eliminating internal and external restrictions rather rapidly?

Understanding the lack of banking crises in the transition economies is not only of interest to the economies themselves, but also to their EU neighbours. Banking crises in Central Europe seem to hit closer to home than financial turmoil in South East Asia as many investors learned after the Russian crisis. Hence, it is important to identify the factors, which insulated the banks from financial contagion to ensure that slower transition economies will also become or remain stable, and to correct possible shortcomings, which could lead to instabilities in the future.

2. BANKING CRISIS AFTER FINANCIAL LIBERALIZATION

Banking crises are hard to identify on a comparative basis, largely because of data limitations. For our purposes, banking crises are defined as "bank runs that lead to closure, merging or takeover by the public sector of one or more financial institutions, [or].. if there are no runs, the closure, merging, takeover, or large-scale government assistance of an important financial institution (or group of institutions), that marks the start of a string of similar outcomes for other financial institutions"

(Kaminsky and Reinhart, 1996:6; Sundararajan and Balino, 1992; Lindgren, Garcia and Saal, 1996; Sheng, 1996). Large bad loan ratios, as they are common in CEECs, are not considered crises, but significant banking sector problems (see table 1). So far, only three cases, namely Estonia, Latvia, and Lithuania in 1995 are classified as banking crises (Lindgren, Garcia and Saal, 1996). Similarly, even though banks in Estonia and Latvia encountered problems in the wake of the Russian crisis, none of them are classified as crises.

In recent studies the chance of crisis has been linked to financial liberalization (FL). The radical financial market changes, which have occurred in CEECs, including bank privatization, easing of entry restrictions, creation of market based lending rules, or elimination of interest rate ceilings, fall under the definition of FL. In addition to reducing domestic restrictions, FL often comprises external liberalization, as it does in the CEECs, creating more capital mobility, and entry opportunities for multinational corporations (MNCs) and multinational banks (MNBs).

How does FL affect the stability of the banking sector? Generally speaking, FL exposes banks to greater default, maturity, exchange rate and interest rate risks. Broadly speaking, internal liberalization allows for more financing to go to productive as well as speculative investments, thereby raising the chance of borrower default. With external liberalization, international loans, which are used to finance these investments, are more easily withdrawn in case of eroding economic fundamentals, thereby increasing the maturity and exchange rate risk. With higher the chance of a crisis rises, too. Obviously, FL does not inevitably lead to crises, but in order to prevent a crisis, a number of stabilizing institutions have to be in place, among them market transparency, adequate regulation and supervision, or a lender-of-last-resort.

Banking crises after FL could arise from an initial "deregulation euphoria", leading to more speculative investments. As financial markets are liberalized, credit is expanded to sectors that were previously credit constrained since the reductions of interest rate ceilings or lending requirements promise higher profits to lenders. More credit may increase investment, thus possibly leading to an output increase (Calvo and Corricelli, 1993; Weller, 1999a). Some of the additional financing, though, is used to fund speculative projects, which is often aided by the lack of adequate regulation and by the prospect of high returns in the short run (Kaminsky and Reinhart, 1996; Lindgren, Garcia and Saal, 1996; Sheng, 1996; Benink and Llewellyn, 1994b; Balino and Sundararajan, 1991). With higher real rates and with expanding real and financial sectors, more funds should be attracted from overseas. More capital inflows from abroad, in turn, may lead to a currency appreciation in real terms, hence attracting even more international capital.

However, rather than a stable equilibrium, changes in economic fundamentals may merely produce periods of tranquillity (Minsky, 1986). Because the continued overvaluation of a currency helps to attract capital, governments may find themselves maintaining an overvalued exchange rate to bring in new capital despite the fact that it leads to deteriorating current account balances (Kaminsky and Reinhart, 1996). Thus, the real sector may slow down, even though lenders still expand their credit. Similarly, the more financing finds its way into speculative projects, the harder it may become for borrowers to repay their loans if their profit expectations are not met. Thus, the banking sectors in liberalized economies become more exposed to a number of risks.

First, the risk that borrowers will default on their loans becomes larger because more credit is extended, possibly to a real sector, which is already slowing down in the wake of an overvaluation, or for speculative purposes. The further the real sector and the financial sector drift apart, the faster default risk grows. Similarly, the more funds are channelled into speculation, the higher the chance of borrower default if short-term profit expectations are not met. With a greater default risk, the chance that international funds are withdrawn increases, and thus maturity and exchange rate risks are directly linked to increases in default risk.

Second, maturity risk may grow after FL, which is the risk that enough short-term bank liabilities, which have been used to fund long-term assets, are withdrawn, such that banks are forced to recall part of their outstanding loans. Importantly, international loans may be withdrawn if investors anticipate economic difficulties, which may result from a continued overvaluation that capital inflows helped to create in the first place.

Third, banks may be exposed to greater exchange rate risk, which is the risk that a currency will be devalued, thus making the repayment of foreign currency denominated loans harder. Since a currency may initially appreciate due to improving fundamentals and due to capital inflows, domestic banks may be enticed to finance domestic assets with foreign liabilities (BIS, 1997; Grabel, 1998). If emerging market currencies become overvalued, more speculative investments may attract more international capital inflows with the promise of short-term gains (Dornbusch, Goldfaijn and Valdés, 1996; Kaminsky and Reinhart, 1996). To avoid capital outflows in case of weakening fundamentals monetary authorities may try to maintain an overvaluation by selling reserves or by tightening money. A devaluation may ultimately become unavoidable as reserves are depleted or the economic performance begins to slow down.

Fourth, interest rate risk grows, which is the possibility that outside rates rise resulting in capital outflows. The more banks borrow abroad, the greater the exposure to interest rate risk.

As for possible stabilizing factors, we find that the risks banks incur may decline due to more international competition (Weller, 2000; Weller and Scher, 1999). It is possible that banks in CEECs reduce their loan and risk exposure once they compete with well-capitalised MNBs. If a bank's net worth is above its safety threshold for prudent lending, more international competition may lead a bank to reduce its loans, such that it can lower its risk exposure. The loan reduction will be greater if MNBs "cherry pick", leaving only borrowers of lesser quality for domestic banks. Obviously, the more a bank reduces its loans the less likely it is to experience default risks, and thus any of the other forms of risks.

Another possible source to reduce the risk exposure of banks are government funds. However, as banks become more vulnerable to crises, government revenues are declining, too, because of slow down of the real sector (Kaminsky and Reinhart, 1996).

Finally, a number of policies, such as monetary policy, exchange rate regimes, capital controls or financial market regulations and supervisions can ensure the stability of a banking system. As the term FL already indicates, a number of these policies, in particular, capital controls and regulations are reduced rather than increased. Whether this leads to more instabilities, though, depends on other factors, such as improving supervision or adequate exchange rate regimes.

3. TRENDS AND POLICIES IN CENTRAL AND EASTERN EUROPE

Even though all signs indicate a greater likelihood of banking crises in CEECs, we are still left looking for an explanation, why the South East Asian and Russian crises have not spilled over into the CEECs. This lack of contagion may either result from effective policies, or from a constellation of economic fundamentals unique to the CEECs.

Our sample consists of nine CEECs, which have moved towards market based economies. In particular, the three Baltics, Estonia, Latvia, and Lithuania, the four Central European economies, Poland, the Czech Republic, Slovakia, and Hungary, and two former Yugoslavian republics, Croatia and Slovenia, are included. In reporting figures for the region, the totals are given for the entire area, while ratios are reported as GDP weighted averages (Tables 2, 5 and 6). By using GDP as weight, we control for contagion effects within the region. Thus, we can trace out some common trends of the nine CEECs, while accounting for regional interdependence.

Policies, which reduce the risks banks are exposed to include monetary policy, exchange rate regimes, capital controls, and adequate supervision and regulation. Through a tightening of monetary policy it may be possible to stabilize a currency, thereby reducing exchange rate risk, while possibly raising the default risk as financing becomes more expensive. Further, some exchange rate regimes may reduce the exchange rate risk, such as currency boards where autonomous monetary policy becomes curtailed, or flexible exchange rates, where currency devaluations are impossible. Next, capital controls limit capital mobility, and lower maturity, interest rate and exchange rate risks. Finally, regulation and supervision can reduce speculation and ensure stability by limiting default risk, and in turn lowering maturity, and exchange rate risks.

Monetary policy in CEECs remains largely focused on price and exchange rate stability for most of the transition period (Abel, Siklos, and Szekely, 1998; Hoen, 1998; Mygind, 1997; Rybczynksi, 1997; Skreb, 1997; Norgard, 1996; Bruno, 1993; Calvo and Corricelli, 1992). Tight monetary policy has been implemented early to curtail high inflation in the wake of price liberalizations (OECD, 1997; Banerjee et al., 1995), and to help the credibility of newly established currencies. Between 1990 and 1993, inflation rates have been high and accelerating due to price liberalizations, and due to a uncertainty about each economy's future (Table 2). A firm stance on money, particularly in 1992 with an average interest rate of 331%, has lowered inflation in the following years. After an initial increase in both M1 and M2 relative to GDP, both decline after 1992 until 1995, and M1 even until 1996. Once inflation rates have become more stable, monetary policies have become less restrictive in 1997, as M1 and M2 grow quite rapidly.

A decline in the exchange rate risk in CEECs may not only result from tight monetary policies, but also from different exchange rate regimes, such as limited convertibility, currency boards, or flexible exchange rates. Table 3 provides an overview of changes in the exchange rate regimes in nine CEECs. First, throughout the period most economies are loosening their restrictions on currency convertibility. Second, while currency boards, flexible exchange rates or managed floats are implemented in five economies, Hungary, Poland, Slovakia and Croatia maintain pegs. While Hungary, Poland, and Croatia have stabilized their exchange rates, the Slovak Republic seems to be struggling. While exchange rate risk may be reduced in most CEECs due to the monetary policies and exchange rate policies, future instabilities may lurk if pegged exchange rates in the larger economies become harder to maintain in a more open environment.

CEECs seem to have indeed become more open economies during the transition years. While some of the CEECs have initially introduced inward and outward capital controls (Abel, Siklos, Szekely, 1998; Druzic, 1997; Leinela and Sutela, 1997; Mygind, 1997; Radosevic and Dyker, 1997; CNB, 1995), these are largely lifted over time (Table 4). Remaining capital controls may come in the form of limitations on the ability of residents to move capital abroad (Radosevic, 1997; BOS, 1998), or as requirements to obtain foreign exchange licenses (NBS, 1995). Thus, capital mobility has increased, consequently raising exchange rate, maturity and interest rate risks.

Whereas all risks grow, bank instabilities could be curtailed through improvements in bank regulation and supervision. A number of remaining problems in the supervision and regulation of banks in CEECs have been identified (Bonin, Miszei, Szekely, and Wachtel, 1998). Among them are the lagging application of international accounting standards, and the prohibition of orderly exit of domestic banks. Overall, it seems that "the infrastructure for bank supervision and regulation has not developed as quickly as it should" (Bonin et al, 1998:1). The lack of adequate supervision and regulation comes at a time, when the need for it is still high, especially from the persistently high bad loan ratios (Table 1). Only after the South East Asian crisis, have a number of CEECs announced improvements in their banking regulation. For instance, the capital adequacy ratio for Estonian banks was increased from 8% to 10%, and subsequently a requirement to create a general 2% reserve fund was introduced (European Commission, 1998b).

Overall, policies, which could help to ensure a stable banking sector, have been gradually reduced. For instance, monetary authorities have eased on their tight monetary stance in 1997 and thereafter. Also, most capital controls have been virtually eliminated by 1996 or 1997. In contrast, bank regulation and supervision appear to be inadequate, and small improvements have only been introduced after the South East Asian or Russian crisis. Finally, the largest economies, Poland and Hungary, have established viable pegged exchange rates, which could, however, come under attack should economic fundamentals deteriorate.

If potentially stabilizing policies are unlikely to have played a major role in ensuring the stability of the banking sectors in CEECs, other factors must have been stabilizing factors. Among them, international financial competition, which has significantly increased in CEECs (Table 6). In all CEECs, MNB entry has been introduced as a mainstay of economic reform. Hungary, for instance, promoted foreign ownership of domestic banks forcefully (Anderson and Kegels, 1998). By 1994, about 15.1% of all Hungarian banks were already foreign-owned, with a further increase to 35.6% in 1995 (Abel, Siklos and Szekely, 1998). Similarly, by early 1998, MNBs owned one third of the share capital of Lithuanian banks, and had controlling stakes in the two largest banks. Further, as a result of MNB entry, credit relative to GDP has declined, for instance, in Poland (Weller, 2000). MNB presence may have a stabilizing impact either through reducing overall loans, or by making loan allocations more prudent through joint ventures. However, the stability that MNBs bring appears to be a trade-off against a declining credit supply, which may have real consequences (Calvo and Corricelli, 1993; Cornelli, Portes and Schaffer, 1996; Weller, 1999).

Other factors, besides growing international financial competition, may have contributed to the CEECs' recent insulation. Banks in CEECs may have so far remained stable thanks to a constellation of economic fundamentals unique to the transition period. For instance, default risk appears to be low for a number of reasons. First, the real sector has been expanding in CEECs, especially after 1994 (Table 5), while the ratio of credit to GDP has been declining until 1996, and only been growing in 1997 (Table 2). Second, asset market speculation, even where it exists, appears to have little real implications as stock and real estate markets are underdeveloped (Table 6). When, for example, corporate malpractice, speculative operations and faulty controls in financial firms were revealed in Estonia in the second half of 1997, the stock market took a hit (European Commission, 1998) without a noticeable impact on the real economy. On the contrary, Estonia's economy grew 11.4% for 1997 (BCE, 1999). Similarly, the attractiveness of Slovakian shares for foreign investors has been declining due to legal protections for minority shareholders. The Slovakian stock index dropped from a high of 405 in February 1994 to less than 100 in October 1998 (European Commission, 1998g), while the Slovakian economy continued to grow above 6% a year (BCE, 1999). Also, opportunities for real estate investments are hampered by legal uncertainties or restitution claims. For example, by 1998 only 55% of the land for which claims have been made in Lithuania were returned to private owners (European Commission, 1998e).

As default risk is low, maturity risk should also be low. This would explain, among other factors, why the rapid increase in short-term debt to CEECs after 1994 following a steady decline, has not had a destabilizing impact (Table 7). Additionally, other forms of more long-term capital flows have gained in importance. FDI flows steadily grew until they reached almost $10 billion in 1995, and remained above $7 billion per year, and long-term debt has continued to grow from 1990 to 1995 (Table 7). Thus, international investors appear to have taken a more long-term outlook as far as CEECs are concerned, thereby reducing the maturity risk.

Does the lack of default and maturity risk suggest that transition economies are generally more stable than other emerging economies? Interestingly, all stabilizing trends in CEECs appear to be weakening in recent years: short-term loans have rapidly grown after 1994, asset markets are becoming more developed, especially with the looming EU accession; and credit relative to GDP is increasing. None of these trends has to spell financial market instabilities *per se*, unless the real sector is slowing down, which may be the case if exports or domestic demand are weakening. Export demand may decline should importers of products from the transition economies, particularly in the EU, experience a recession. In particular, Germany is the most important trading partner for the region: Poland, Hungary, and the Czech Republic sent well above 30% of its exports to Germany in 1996, or 1997, while Slovenia exported close to 30% there, and Slovakia still more than 20% (ECE, 1999). As signs of a slower than expected recovery in the EU emerge, it may contribute to a slower real growth in the CEECs. However, growing domestic demand could compensate a decline in export demand. Yet, unemployment remains above 10% for the region, and average wages decline in 1997, after several years of growth from 1991 to 1996 (Table 5). For example, in Slovenia, wage growth slowed in 1997 and early 1998, such that wage increases lagged behind productivity gains (ECE, 1998h). Put differently, the fact that banking instabilities have not emerged yet appears to be a result of a unique confluence of economic trends at the right time and right place, which are unlikely to be repeated.

4. CONCLUSION

The stability of the banking systems in CEECs in the wake of the South East Asian and Russian financial crises appears to be attributable to a lack of speculative financing, and a more long-term outlook by international investors. In particular, a growing real sector has experienced increasing financial constraints until 1996, when credit began to expand again in most economies. Also, the fact that capital markets are largely underdeveloped appears to have been a blessing since, even where market speculation existed, real consequences of sharp stock market drops have been limited. Finally, a greater emphasis on FDI flows and the growing share of long-term loans have helped to insulate the CEECs from the consequences of large outflows of short-term capital.

We have looked at the question as to why the transition economies in Central and Eastern Europe have not been caught up in the recent financial turmoil, which has spanned from South East Asia to Russia to Brazil. We find that a unique constellation of economic fundamentals, rather than deliberate policies have helped to insulate transition economies. While policies, such as capital controls, may have had a stabilizing impact in the early transition phase, they have recently been reduced or eliminated. Instead, we find that reductions in credit relative to GDP, despite real expansion, the lack of asset market speculation, and a growing importance of more long-term capital inflows appear to have had a stabilizing effect during the recent global financial turmoil. However, as most trends show signs of reversing themselves in

1997, the recent insulation from the fall-out of the South East Asian and Russian crises appears to have been unique. In other words, the CEECs may not withstand another financial crisis of South East Asian proportions without seeing their own financial systems failing.

REFERENCES

Abel, Istvan, Pierre L. Siklos, and Istvan Szekely (1998), *Money and Finance in the Transition to a Market Economy*, Northampton MA: Edward Elgar.

Balino, Tomas and V. Sundararajan (1991), *Banking Crises: Cases and Issues*, Washington DC: International Monetary Fund.

Balczerowicz, Leszek, Barbara Blaszczyk and Marek Dabrowski (1997), "The Polish Way to the Market Economy 1989-1995", in W.T. Woo, S. Parker and J. Sachs, eds., *Economies in Transition*, Cambridge MA: MIT Press.

Banerjee, Biswajit, Vincent Koen, Thomas Krueger, Mark S. Lutz, Michael Marrese, and Tapio O. Saavalainen (1995), *Road Maps of the Transition: The Baltics, the Czech Republic, Hungary, and Russia*, Occasional Paper #127, Washington DC: IMF.

Bank for International Settlements (BIS) (1998a), *International Banking and Financial Market Developments*, Basle: Bank for International Settlements.

Bank for International Settlements (BIS) (1999), *Consolidated International Banking Statistics for End-1997*, Basle: Bank for International Settlements.

Bank for International Settlements (BIS) (1997), *Financial Stability in Emerging Market Economies, Report of the Working Party on Financial Stability in Emerging Market Economies*, Basle: Bank for International Settlements.

Bank of Slovenia (BOS) (1998), *Foreign Exchange Regime in Slovenia*, updated October 16, 1998, http://www.bsi.si/html/eng/laws_regulations/foreign_exchange.html

Benink, Harald (1995), *Coping with Financial Fragility and Systemic Risk*, Financial and Monetary Policy Studies, Vol. 30, Boston: Kluwer Academic Publishers.

Benink, Harald and David Llewellyn (1994a), "Deregulation and Financial Fragility: A Case Study of the UK and Scandinavia", in D. Fair and R. Raymond, eds., *The Competitiveness of Financial Institutions and Centres in Europe*, Financial and Monetary Policy Studies, Vol. 28. Dordrecht and Boston: Kluwer Academic.

Benink, Harald and David Llewellyn (1994b), "Fragile Banking in Norway, Sweden and Finland: An Empirical Analysis", *Journal of International Financial Markets, Institutions and Money*, Vol. 4, 3-4: 5-19, 1994.

Bonin, John P., Kalman Miszei, Istvan P. Szekely and Paul Wachtel (1998), *Banking in Transition Economies*, Brookfield VT: Edward Elgar.

Bruno, Michael (1993), *Crisis, Stabilization, and Economic Reform: Therapy by Consensus*, Oxford: Clarendon Press.

Calvo, Guillermo and Fabrizio Corricelli (1993), "Output Collapse in Eastern Europe: The Role of Credit", *IMF Staff Papers*, March.

Calvo, Guillermo and Fabrizio Corricelli (1992), "Stabilizing a Previously Centrally Planned Economy: Poland 1990", *Economic Policy*, 14: 176-208, 213-226, April.

Czech National Bank (CNB) (1995), *Foreign Exchange Act of 26 September 1995*, Prague: CNB.

Demirgüc-Kunt, Asli and Enrica Detragiache (1997), "The Determinants of Banking Crises: Evidence from Developed and Developing Countries", *Policy Research Working Paper* #1828, Washington DC: World Bank.

Drusic, Ivo (1997), "Regional Dispersion of Foreign Direct Investment in Eastern Europe", in S. Sharma, ed., *Restructuring Eastern Europe: The Microeconomics of the Transition Process*, Lyme NH: Edward Elgar.

Economic Commission for Europe (ECE), *Trends in Europe and North America*, 1998 Statistical Yearbook of the UN Economic Commission for Europe.

European Commission (1998a), Regular Report from the Commission on the Czech Republic's Progress towards Accession, Brussels: European Commission, Nov. 04.

European Commission (1998b), Regular Report from the Commission on the Estonia's Progress towards Accession, Brussels: European Commission, Nov. 04.

European Commission (1998c), Regular Report from the Commission on Hungary's Progress towards Accession, Brussels: European Commission, Nov. 04.

European Commission (1998d), Regular Report from the Commission on Latvia's Progress towards Accession, Brussels: European Commission, Nov. 04.

European Commission (1998e), Regular Report from the Commission on Lithuania's Progress towards Accession, Brussels: European Commission, Nov. 04.

European Commission (1998f), Regular Report from the Commission on Poland's Progress towards Accession, Brussels: European Commission, Nov. 04.

European Commission (1998g), Regular Report from the Commission on Slovakia's Progress towards Accession, Brussels: European Commission, Nov. 04.

European Commission (1998h), Regular Report from the Commission on Slovenia's Progress towards Accession, Brussels: European Commission, Nov. 04.

Faruqi, Shakil (1994), *Financial Sector Reforms, Economic Growth, and Stability*, Washington DC: World Bank.

Fleming, Alex and Samuel Talley (1996), *The Latvian Banking Crisis: Lessons Learned*, Policy Research Working Paper No. 1590, Washington DC: World Bank.

Garber, Peter M. (1996) "Managing Risk to Financial Markets from Volatile Capital Flows: The Role of Prudential Regulation", *International Journal of Finance and Economics*, 1:183-195.

Goldstein, Morris and Philip Turner (1996) "Banking Crises in Emerging Economies: Origins and Policy Options", *BIS Economic Papers* #46, October 1996, Basle: Bank for International Settlements.

Haavisto, Tarmo (1997), *The Transition to a Market Economy: Transformation and Reform in the Baltic States*, Brookfield VT: Edward Elgar.

Hardy, Daniel C. and Ashok Kumar Lahiri (1992), *Bank Insolvency and Stabilization in Eastern Europe*, IMF Staff Papers 39, 4:778-800 (September 1992).

Hoen, Herman W. (1998), *The Transformation of Economic Systems in Central Europe*, Northampton MA: Edward Elgar.

Horvath, Julius (1998), *Exchange Rate Regimes in the Transition Economies: Case Study of the Czech Republic: 1990-1997*, ZEI Working Paper B11, 1998, Bonn, Germany.

International Monetary Fund, various years, Exchange Arrangements and Restrictions, Washington DC: IMF.

Kaminsky, Graciela and Carmen M. Reinhart (1996), "The Twin Crises: The Causes of Banking and Balance-of-Payments Problems", *International Finance Discussion Papers* #544, Washington DC: Board of Governors of the Federal Reserve System.

Lainela, Seija and Pekka Sutela (1997), "Introducing New Currencies in the Baltic Countries", in T. Haavisto, ed., *The Transition to a Market Economy: Transformation and Reform in the Baltic States*, Brookfield VT: Edward Elgar.

Lindgren, Carl-Johan, Gillian Garcia and Matthew Saal (1996), *Bank Soundness and Macroeconomic Policy*, Washington DC: International Monetary Fund.

Mygind, Niels (1997), "A Comparative Analysis of the Economic Transition in the Baltic Countries - Barriers, Strategies, Perspectives", in T. Haavisto, ed., *The Transition to a Market Economy*, Brookfield VT: Edward Elgar Publishing Co.

National Bank of the Slovak Republic (NBS), *Foreign Exchange Act of 20 September 1995*, Bratislava: NBS.

Norgard, Ole, D. Hindsgaul, L. Johanssen and H. Willumsen (1996), *The Baltic States after Independence*, Lyme NH: Edward Elgar.

OECD (1997), *OECD Economic Surveys - Slovenia*, Paris: OECD.

Polish Development Bank (in co-operation with the Ministry of Finance) (1992), *The Banking System in Poland 1991/92*, Warsaw: PBR.

Polish Development Bank (in co-operation with the Ministry of Finance) (1993), *The Banking System in Poland 1992/93*, Warsaw: PBR

Polish Development Bank (in co-operation with the Ministry of Finance) (1994), *The Financial System in Poland 1993/94*, Warsaw: PBR.

Radosevic, Dubravko (1997), "Capital Restrictions in Croatia", *National Bank of Croatia Working Paper*, March 1998, Zagreb: NBH

Radosevic, Slavo and David Dyker (1997), "Technological Integration and Global Marginalization of Central and East European Economies: The Role of FDI and Alliances", in S. Sharma, ed., Restructuring *Eastern Europe: The Microeconomics of the Transition Process*, Lyme NH: Edward Elgar.

Rybczinski, T.M. (1997), "Introducing New Currencies in the Baltic Countries: A Comment", in T. Haavisto, ed., *The Transition to a Market Economy*, Brookfield VT: Edward Elgar.

Sheng, Andrew (1996), *Bank Restructuring: Lessons from the 1980s*, Washington DC: World Bank.

Sharma, Soumitra (1997), *Restructuring Eastern Europe: The Microeconomics of the Transition Process*, Lyme NH: Edward Elgar.

Skreb, Marko (1997), "Banking Sector Reforms in Croatia: Problems and Prospects", in S. Sharma, ed., *Restructuring Eastern Europe: The Microeconomics of the Transition Process*, Lyme NH: Edward Elgar.

Toporowski, Jan (1997), "Financial Fragility in the Banking System of Transitional Economies in Eastern Europe", in S. Sharma, ed., *Restructuring Eastern Europe: The Microeconomics of the Transition Process*, Lyme NH: Edward Elgar.

United Nations (UN), *World Economic and Social Survey 1999*, New York NY: United Nations.

Weller, Christian (1999), *The Finance-Investment Link in a Transition Economy: Evidence for Poland from Panel Data*, ZEI Working Paper B4, March 1999, Bonn, Germany: ZEI.

Weller, Christian (2000), "Financial Liberalization, Multinational Banks and the Supply of Credit: The Case of Poland", *International Review of Applied Economics*, forthcoming.

Weller, Christian, and Morzuch, Bernard (1999), "Why are Eastern Europe's Banks not Failing When Everybody Else's Are?", *ZEI Working Paper B18*, September 1999, Bonn, Germany.

Weller, Christian, and Scher, Mark, 1999, Multinational Banks and Development Finance, ZEI Working Paper B16, September 1999, Bonn, Germany.

Weller, Christian, and von Hagen, Jürgen, 1999, Financial Fragility or What Went Right and What Could Go Wrong in Central European Banking?, ZEI Working Paper B13, June 1999, Bonn, Germany.

Table 1. Banking Sector Problems in CEECs

Country	Banking Sector Problems
Croatia	
1995	Banks accounting for 47% of bank credit have been found to be unsound.
Czech Republic	
1993	Several banks have been closed since 1993.
1994	In 1994-95, 38% of loans were nonperforming.
1998	By the end of the first half of 1998, 29% of loans have been classified as bad loans.
Estonia	
1992-1995	Banking crisis, where insolvent banks held 41% of banking system assets, the licenses of 5 banks have been revoked, 2 major banks were merged and nationalized, and 2 large banks were merged and converted to a loan recovery agency.
1998	Two small banks were closed in the wake of the Russian crisis.
Hungary	
since 1987	Eight banks, accounting for 25% of financial system assets, became insolvent.
1993	At the end of 1993, 23% of all loans were problematic
1997	A run on Postabank, the second largest retail bank, ensued in March 1997. The authorities intervened, and the bank was eventually nationalised.
Latvia	
1995	Banking crisis, where two thirds of audited banks recorded losses n 1994. Eight bank licenses were revoked in 1994, and 15 more were revoked during the first seven months of 1995. The subsequent closure of the largest bank (with 30% of deposits) and two other major banks triggered a banking crisis in the spring of 1995.
1998	Failure of Latvia's fifth largest bank, Rigas Komercbanka, in the wake of the Russian crisis.

Table 1. Banking Sector Problems in CEECs (Contd.)

Lithuania	
1995	Banking crisis, where of 25 banks, 12 small ones are being liquidated and 4 larger ones do not meet the capital adequacy requirements, the fourth largest bank was closed, and the operations of 2 banks, which accounted for 15% of deposits, were supported in 1995.
1997	Strengthened regulation triggered bankruptcy proceedings against one bank in the summer of 1997.
1998	Authorities decided to liquidate State Commercial Bank after repeatedly failing to find a buyer.
Poland	
1991	16% loans were classified as losses, 22% as doubtful, and 24% as substandard.
Slovakia	
1995	Loans classified as non-standard were high at the end of August 1995. All 5 major banks required government sponsored restructuring operations.
1997	IRB, the third largest bank, encountered serious liquidity problems, and had to be put under forced administration by the National Bank of Slovakia in December 1997.
1998	The proportion of bad loans in the three biggest banks reached 39% of loans in the first quarter of 1998.
Slovenia	
1992	Between 1992 and 1994, three banks with two thirds of banking system assets, were restructured.

Source: Lindgren, Garcia and Saal, 1996; European Commission, 1998; Reuters

Table 2. Money and Credit

Year	M1/GDP	M2/GDP	Credit/GDP	Discount Rate	Inflation
1990	24.56	43.51	80.98	34	203.33
1991	24.13	46.88	73.39	21.2	119
1992	26.88	50.51	68.47	330.9	444.67
1993	21.57	49	60.94	28.53	490.99
1994	20.7	47.63	57.61	11.32	29.45
1995	18.24	47.24	50.54	15.41	18.46
1996	17.63	54.33	51.52	11.5	11.86
1997	24.9	68.48	76.37	11.19	9.84

Note: All money and credit figures are GDP weighted averages, whereas discount rates and inflation rates are simple averages. In the case of Estonia, the interbank rate is used instead of the discount rate. All figures are reported in percent.

Table 3. Exchange Rate Changes

Time	Changes
Hungary	
06/1991	Legal markets for currencies which have not been officially quoted established. The National Bank of Hungary adjusts the official exchange rate to a basket of currencies weighted according to currency composition of foreign trade turnover.
12/1991	Change of the currency basket to determine Forint's external value from 11 currencies (weighted according to currency composition of foreign trade turnover) to 50 % ECU - 50% USD. Spot exchange rates now quoted on the basis of international markets' exchange rates of the same instead of previous business day. Banks allowed to freely set exchange rates for currency notes and traveler's checks if buying rate is not above and selling rate not below the official middle rate and margins for currency notes are the same around the commercial banks' middle rate for currency notes.
02-09/1993	Exchange rate depreciations in February, March, June, July, September by 1.9% to 4.5%.
06/1993	Widening of exchange rate margins within which banks allowed to quote interbank and customers' rates from 0.3% to 0.5%.
08/1993	ECU in currency basket for Forint pegging replaced by Deutsche Mark.
01-12/1994	Widening of official spot buying and selling rates> margins form +/- 0.3% to +/- 0.5% (January); to 1.25% (August); 2.25% (December).
01-12/1994	Exchange rate depreciations in Jan., Feb., May, Jun., Aug., Oct., Nov. by ca. 1.0% - 2.6%.
04-05/1994	Elimination of several restrictions on currency purchases for tourism and business travel.
05/1994	Changing of the currency pegging basket: 50%DEM, 50% USD to 70% ECU, 30% USD.
06/1994	Nonresidents allowed to convert Forints from foreign trade into foreign exchange.
03/1995	Devaluation of the exchange rate by 8.3 %; adjustment of the exchange rate peg according to preannounced rate of crawl.
04/1997	Monthly depreciation rate reduced from 1.2% to 1.1%
08/1997	Further adjustment of the monthly depreciation rate to 1.0%
01/1998	Reduction of the monthly depreciation rate to 0.9%

Table 3. Exchange Rate Changes (Contd.)

01/1998	Imports and exports of domestic currency allowed up to Ft 350,000 per trip .
Poland	
05/1991	Devaluation of the zloty. The National Bank of Poland adjusts the official zloty rate by pegging it to a basket consisting of five currencies.
10/1991	Introduction of crawling peg policy with depreciation by up to 1.8 % a month.
09-11/1994	Reduction of the monthly depreciation rate from 1.6% to 1.4%.
01/1995	Removing exchange restrictions on international transactions.
05/1995	External value of zloty allowed to fluctuate within margins of 7% around the central rate.
01/1996	Reduction of crawl rate by 1% a month.
Czech Republic	
02/1993	Introduction of the Czech koruna. The Czech National Bank adjusts the official koruna rate by pegging it to a basket consisting of five currencies.
05/1993	Reduction of currencies in basket to peg koruna to from five to DEM and USD.
01/1994	Maximum allowance for foreign travel raised to 12,000 koruna per year.
02/1994	Simplification and partial liberalization of permit procedures for enterprises to keep foreign currency accounts.
03/1994	Adjustment of koruna exchange rate against clearing ECU from 3% above the market cross rate to parity.
09/1994	Limit to import or export domestic currency increased to 5,000 koruny.
04/1995	Fee of 0.25% on banks' foreign exchange transactions with National Bank
02/1996	Widening of foreign exchange rate band of koruna fluctuation from 0.5% to 7.5% against the central rate.
05/1997	Canceling of foreign exchange rate band; introduction of new exchange arrangement based on managed floating system to stabilize koruna against the Deutsche Mark
Slovak Republic	
02/1993	Introduction of the Slovak koruna. The National Bank of Slovakia adjusts the official koruna rate by pegging it to a basket consisting of five currencies.
01/1994	Annual limit on foreign exchange allowance for tourists increased to Sk 9,000's equivalent.
07/1994	Change of exchange rate pegging basket from five currencies DEM and USD (60:40).

Table 3. Exchange Rate Changes (Contd.)

05-09/1995	Revaluation of the koruna under bilateral payments agreement with the Czech Republic by 4% (May) and 1% (September).
09/1995	Termination of bilateral payments agreement with Czech Republic.
10/1995	New Foreign Exchange Law: Koruna fully convertible for current international transactions.
01-10/1995	Further increase to annual limit on foreign exchange allowance for tourists to 16,000 Sk (January); 30,000 Sk (July), 60,000 Sk (October).
07/1996	Exchange rate margins widened to +/- 5%.
12/1996	Limits on exporting and importing of national and foreign currency abolished and partly replaced by declaration requirement.
01/1997	Margins of exchange rate band widened to +/- 7%
Estonia	
06/1992	Currency Board with a fixed exchange rate of 8 Estonian Kroons to 1 DM.
12/1993	Elimination of requirement that spread between buying and selling rates of foreign exchange by banks not exceed 7%.
03/1994	individuals permitted to open foreign exchange accounts with domestic banks
Latvia	
02/1994	Informal pegging to SDRs at 0.7997 Latvian Lats to 1 SDR.
Lithuania	
04/1994	Creation of a Currency Board with a fixed exchange rate of 1 Lithuanina Litas to 1 USD.
Croatia	
06/1991	Introduction of Croatian dinar. Foreign exchange rate pegged to a basket of currencies.
05/1994	Croatian dinar as national currency replaced by kuna at the ratio of 1 kuna :1000 dinars.
03/1997	Foreign juridical persons allowed to withdraw monthly foreign currency equivalent up to HRK 15,000 from deposit accounts

Table 3. Exchange Rate Changes (Contd.)

Slovenia	
06/1991	Introduction of Slovenian tolar. Exchange rate determined through a managed float.
07/1992	Foreign exchange transactions allowed.
02/1997	Cash withdrawals from foreign exchange accounts exceeding equivalent of SIT 250,000 per month are to be approved by BOS.

Source: IMF, Exchange Arrangements and Restrictions Annual Report.

Table 4. Changes in External Capital Controls

Time	Tighten/ loosen capital controls	Changes
Hungary		
01/1991	Tighten	Financial institutions' foreign borrowings to be approved by the NBH. Credits to foreigners by Hungarian financial institutions limited to maturities up to 6 months; exceptional cases with NBH authorization. Joint ventures generally without approval; exception: foreign participation of more than 10% of banks' & insurances' equities. Reglementation of joint ventures' taxation and further questions.
01/1991	Loosen	Abolition of the licensing requirement for joint ventures.
01/1996	Loosen	Elimination of capital account restrictions Foreigners allowed to buy securities with maturities longer than 1 year without extra NBH permission. Permission of outward equity investments if equity share of over 10% is acquired (canceled on March 20)
07/1996	Loosen	Liberalization of issue, placement and introduction of OECD government bonds and highly-rated OECD-based enterprises' bonds and shares. Extension of foreign exchange law's provisions on domestic securities to debt instruments with maturities of 1 year and more.
01/1997	Loosen	Liberalization of issue and introduction of bonds with maturities of more than 1 year and OECD-based enterprises' investment grade-rated shares. Limitation of banks' short-term lending to non-residents to 50% of total foreign exchange liabilities (from 50% of foreign exchange liabilities to foreigners). Liberalization of banks' futures and options transactions in foreign currencies.
01/1997	Loosen	No longer government approval for foreign participation in banks required.

Table 4. Changes in External Capital Controls (Contd.)

11/1997	Loosen	Liberalization of short-term lending to non-residents
01/1998	Loosen	Liberalization of issue and introduction of shares, other securities, bonds and other debt securities with a maturity of more then 1 year on domestic security market which are denominated in foreign exchange and issued by OECD-based enterprises B irrespective of credit rating. For residents: ability to purchase these securities without foreign exchange authorization.
01/1998	Loosen	Elimination of restrictions on investments in branches of foreign companies (in addition to investments in joint ventures and fully foreign-owned companies). Elimination of further, more specific criteria on these direct investments.
Poland		
07/1991	Loosen	New foreign investment law; all restrictions on transfers of profits and capital repatriation canceled
01/1995	Loosen	Removing exchange restrictions on international transactions
02/1997	Loosen	Liberalization of capital transactions: Limit for investment in publicly tradable securities issued in Poland by foreign entities raised to ECU 300,000,00 Residents allowed to purchase publicly traded securities in OECD countries ; purchases above ECU 50,000 needing 3 months' notice to NBP
03/1997	Loosen	Insurers permitted to purchase securities traded in OECD countries (minimum ratings required). Insurers allowed to invest abroad a maximum of 5% of funds covering their fund.
01/1998	Loosen	Controls on lending to nonresidents lifted.
Czech Republic		
09/1994	Loosen	Partial liberalization of foreign securities purchases by residents. Simplification of rules to acquire properties abroad. No longer import and export restrictions on securities denominated in koruny.

Table 4. Changes in External Capital Controls (Contd.)

08/1995	Tighten	Curtailment of borrowing abroad by banks by limiting open positions of National Bank towards nonresidents.
04/1997	Loosen	Foreign exchange permits no longer required for foreign securities issued, for the introduction of foreign securities in the domestic market and nonpublic trading.
Slovak Republic		
12/1996	Loosen	Limits on exporting and importing of national and foreign currency abolished and partly replaced by declaration requirement.
12/1996	Loosen	Liberalization of financial credits with a maturity of 5 years and above provided by Slovak residents to OECD residents. Liberalization of receipt and provision of trade credits for OECD trade. Liberalization of foreign borrowings by residents with a maturity of 3 years and above.
12/1996	Loosen	Liberalization of direct investments in OECD countries.
07/1997	Loosen	Foreign exchange permit longer required for the issue of securities when they are marketable in the main market of foreign stock exchanges
04/1998	Loosen	Permission no longer required for OECD residents when the securities are marketable in the main market of foreign stock exchanges Foreign bank branches were allowed to acquire real estate for pursuing bank activities, but only in the case of construction or reconstruction.
Latvia		
04/1996	Loosen	Elimination of cabinet approval requirement for foreign direct investment above $ 1 million.

Table 4. Changes in External Capital Controls (Contd.)

05/1997	Loosen	Persons registered in Latvia allowed to purchase urban land when more than one-half of the paid share capital of the company belongs to (1) the citizens of Latvia, (2) the citizens of countries with which Latvia has an agreement to promote foreign investment, (3) a group of the previous categories, and (4) a public joint stock company quoting shares on the stock exchange.
Croatia		
02/1996	Loosen	New trade law allows domestic juridical persons to do foreign direct investments.
03/1997	Loosen	Foreign juridical persons allowed to withdraw monthly foreign currency equivalent up to HRK 15,000 from deposit accounts.
Slovenia		
04/1992	Loosen	Ratios of foreign exchange deposits required to be held abroad by deposit money banks as cover against domestically held foreign exchange deposits changed to 5-90%, depending on deposits' maturity. Permission to commercial banks to extend foreign exchange credits to resident juridical persons.
02/1995	Tighten	40% of external borrowing with maturities of less than 5 years not immediately used for import financing to be deposited to a unremunerated Tolar bank account.
07/1996	Tighten	Extension of the maturity of loans borrowed abroad by residents subject to 40% interest-free deposit requirements from 5 to 7 years.
12/1996	Tighten	Introduction of 10% interest-free deposit requirement on loans borrowed abroad by residents with maturities of more than 7 years.
01/1997	Loosen	Domestic banks permitted to extend credits to nonresidents.

Table 4. Changes in External Capital Controls (Contd.)

02/1997	Tighten	Cash withdrawals from foreign exchange accounts exceeding equivalent of SIT 250,000 per month are to be approved by BOS.
		Nonresidents' portfolio investments in secondary market-traded securities and derivatives have to be performed through custody accounts at domestic banks.
05/1997	Loosen	Remove of interest-free deposit requirement for loans raised abroad for setting up company abroad, increasing capital or purchasing foreign companies' shares.
06/1997	Loosen	Domestic companies other than banks were granted permission to extend financial credits to affiliated companies.
07/1997	Loosen	Banks allowed to exempt from the balancing requirement the portfolio investments in shares acquired by nonresidents who undertake for the next 7 years not to sell, assign or dispose of securities to third parties except to other nonresidents who undertake the same commitment.
		Constitutional Amendment allowing nonresidents to acquire the right to own real estate pursuant to provisions of a law or an international agreement, under the condition of reciprocity.
11/1997	Loosen	The Slovenian Export Corporation was granted to extend financial credits to nonresidents in accordance with its business strategy.
		The interest-free deposit requirement for loans raised abroad by the Slovenian Export Corporation no longer applied if the proceeds from the loan were used for credits extended to nonresidents.

Source: IMF, Exchange Arrangements and Restrictions Annual Report, various years.

Table 5. Real Economic Variables

Year	GDP/Cap. (PPP $)	Δ GDP (%)[a]	Δ Ind. Prod. (%)[a]	Unemp. (%)[b]	Avg. Monthly Wage ($)[a]	Budget Def./Surplus (% of GDP)[s]	Δ Stock Market (%)[a]
1990	6627.59	-7.58	-15.93	5.54	279.57	1.27	NA
1991	5365.65	-10.63	-14.63	9.28	156.12	-4.19	NA
1992	5376.9	-1.72	-4.64	11.07	235.03	-4.97	NA
1993	5486.2	1.05	0.95	12.55	243.12	-2.86	NA
1994	5847.9	3.68	6.96	11.9	280.93	-2.87	4.98
1995	6256.5	5.59	7.11	11.67	345.79	-2.94	-8.09
1996	6717	4.73	5.12	10.87	416.2	-1.23	53.78
1997	6775.6	5.32	8.1	10.13	363.52	-1.47	-1.99

Note: All figures, except for GDP per capita, are GDP weighted averages. GDP per capita is a population weighted average. The data are taken from *Business Central Europe (BCE)'s* Key Data 1990-97, *IMF's* International Financial Statistics and DataStream.

Table 6. Stock Market Capitalization in CEEC's

	1992	1993	1994	1995	1996	1997	1998
Croatia	NA	NA	3.31	3.12	NA	22.48	15.05
Czech Republic	NA	NA	14.57	30.97	32.11	26.88	20.00
Estonia	NA	NA	NA	NA	NA	22.27	9.46
Hungary	1.59	2.28	4.12	5.84	12.37	35.81	29.49
Latvia	NA	NA	NA	0.21	3.00	6.22	5.90
Lithuania	NA	NA	0.98	2.61	11.42	17.80	10.05
Poland	0.31	3.73	3.54	3.90	6.61	9.62	13.80
Slovak Republic	NA	NA	7.76	7.08	12.09	9.75	9.70
Slovenia	NA	NA	4.08	2.92	3.65	9.35	12.11

Notes: All figures are in percent of GDP. Sources are the IFC, Emerging Stock Markets Factbook, and the BIS-IMF-OECD-World Bank statistics on external debt.

Table 7. International Economic Statistics

Year	Exports ($bn)	Imports ($bn)	Current Account ($bn)	Foreign Exchange Res. ($bn)	FDI Flows ($mn)	Total Outstanding Debt ($bn)	Short-term Outstanding Debt ($bn)	Long-term Outstanding debt ($bn)	MNB Loans ($mn)
1990	44	43	2.1	7.8	411	81.1	15.44	55.53	295
1991	40.9	47.3	-1.9	14.7	1747	84.9	12.38	62.52	505
1992	48.3	52.8	2.5	11.0[d]	2198.2	83.7	9.19	70.12	396
1993	54.3	62.4	-3.8	17.8	4037.6	88.9	7.62	67.18	767
1994	61.6	68.6	-0.2	25.3	2999.4	92.6	7.26	72.57	2763
1995	88.3	98.9	-0.436	50	9016.8	106	11.3	76.84	4213
1996	94.6	115.2	-11.9	54.1	7144.3	107.4	15.7	NA	9053
1997	103	127.1	-14.5	55.8	7675.5	106.9	19.5	NA	14168

Sources: *Business Central Europe (BCE)*, online, Key Data 1990-97; *IMF*, International Financial Statistics; *World Bank,* World Debt Tables; *BIS*, Consolidated International Banking Statistics.

Chapter 8

BOND MARKETS IN ADVANCED TRANSITION: A SYNOPSIS OF THE VISEGRÁD BOND MARKETS*

Katinka Barysch
Centre for European Economic Research, Mannheim (ZEW)

Friedrich Heinemann
Centre for European Economic Research, Mannheim (ZEW)

Max Steiger
Centre for European Economic Research, Mannheim (ZEW)

* Produced within the ACE-project "The Implications of Financial Innovation and Deregulation for Economies in Transition" (ACE 94-0715-R)

1. INTRODUCTION

Bond markets are a relatively recent phenomenon in central and eastern European countries. Neither fixed income investment instruments nor the institutional and legal structure for their issuance and exchange existed in centrally planned economies. The monolithic financial sector was designed and used to monitor and enforce planned industrial production and to maintain macroecononomic stability. It was the central plan rather than market forces which determined the allocation and distribution of financial resources. There was therefore no need for bond markets. Neither the treasury nor local government organs, let alone enterprises, issued bonds for households to invest in (Montias, 1994: 12). [1] While somewhat neglected during the early stages of transition, there is now universal consensus that the rapid development of efficient financial systems is a prerequisite for restructuring and economic development in

[1] Obligatory bonds sales took place in the Soviet Union during the Stalin period (Montias, 1994). Corporate and Municipal bonds were issued in Hungary in the 1980s, see below.

R. MacDonald and R. Cross (eds.), Central Europe Towards Monetary Union: Macroeconomic Underpinnings and Financial Reputation, 149–245.

central and eastern European economies (see, e.g., Bonin/Szekely, 1994; Griffith-Jones/Drábek, 1995). Bond markets form an integral part of more developed financial systems and they can be expected to play an increasingly important role in the reform countries of central and eastern Europe.

This paper will therefore analyse the potential role of bond markets in the process of economic development and the transition to a market economy. After discussing the case for efficient bond markets in section two, the actual progress already achieved in different bond market segments in the central and eastern European countries is examined in section three. The next section will concentrate on the legal and institutional framework for issuing and trading fixed income securities. Even well organised primary markets will not lead to the development of efficient bond markets in the absence of liquid secondary markets in which bond issues of several issuers and with different maturities can be traded freely. Section five will therefore lay out the institutional preconditions for efficient secondary markets for fixed income securities and measure the actual developments in the Visegrád countries against this yardstick. Increasing financial openness and the need to satisfy the demands of foreign investors have accelerated institutional reforms in secondary markets for securities. Section six will further explore the advantages and drawbacks of the process integrating the bond markets of the Visegrád countries into the international financial system. In the conclusion we will attempt to identify the most important impediments to the development of efficient bond markets in these countries. We will also offer some tentative advice as to how this process might be accelerated whilst avoiding distortions in the domestic financial markets.

The impressive speed of change in central and eastern European financial markets made it near to impossible to keep track of all current developments and reform efforts in the region. We therefore restricted ourselves to outlining the most important developments in these markets and their implications for the transition process more generally. More detailed accounts are provided for the regulatory and institutional frameworks of primary and secondary bond markets. However, even these seemingly stable frameworks are undergoing rapid change. The Visegrád countries are adjusting and readjusting the financial infrastructure to market imperatives and seek to bring their regulatory systems more in line with internationally accepted standards. The deadline for assimilating material for this paper was November 1996. Some information received at a later point time up to January 1997 was used where appropriate We also tried to include forecasts and information about upcoming reform in 1997.

Some other aspects of the financial systems in the east-central Europe, notable the banking sector and equity markets, have been extensively researched. Bond markets, on the other hand, have so far received scant attention. Most of this paper is therefore based on original research. Our sources of information included ZEW-questionnaires send out to the resident ACE-co-operation partners [2] as well as information provided directly by officials and market participants in the Visegrád countries. Moreover, we relied on statistics and analysis from local financial institutions and international banks active in the region. Obviously, most of this material is not conducive for providing a conventional system of quotations. We have nonetheless attempted give indication of the sources of information as far as possible.

2. THE CASE FOR EFFICIENT BOND MARKETS IN TRANSITION ECONOMIES

The development of bond markets in the transition economies cannot be studied in isolation from the broader topic of financial market reforms in these countries. The establishment of markets for debt instruments is not an end in itself but should help to make the emerging financial systems in eastern Europe more efficient and responsive to market forces. Bond markets will only accelerate the transition to a market-type economy and make a contribution to economic development and growth if a number of preconditions are fulfilled (see Bröker, 1993; Feldman and Kumar, 1995; Pardy, 1992):

A macro-economic and fiscal environment conducive to the supply of good quality securities and sufficient demand for them. In particular: inflation needs to be brought down to manageable levels, interest rates have to be liberalised, and a minimum of fiscal responsibility is necessary to free up financial resources in the economy.

A legal, regulatory and institutional infrastructure capable of supporting the efficient, fair, and stable operation of securities markets. These institutional requirements include certainty of property rights and contracts, transparency of trading, public disclosure by non-state borrowers, investor protection against unfair practices by intermediaries and insiders, and protection against financial failure of intermediaries and market institutions. Moreover, a properly functioning banking system and liquid interbank payment system are an important precondition for the development of securities markets (Blommstein/Spencer, 1993).

Considerable reform and development efforts are required for bond markets in the Visegrád countries to reach the desired goals of efficiency, transparency and stability. Mature securities markets in OECD countries can serve as a model for the central European reform process. However, there are limits on the extent to, and speed with, which Western institutions and practices can be introduced in the transition economies. Financial sector reform involves a time-consuming process of adaptation

---

[2] In particular, we acknowledge helpful support from Victória Múcková and Marián Nemec (National Bank of Slovakia), Josef Mervart (Czech National Bank), Jarek Neneman (University of Lodz) and Rita Bozzai (Financial Research Ltd., Budapest).

and learning and the gradual building up of market infrastructure. Although bond markets were non-existent in the central European economies prior to the start of reform, the idea of an institutional tabula rasa, on which some kind of "designer" securities markets can be build is misconceived. Institutional and behavioural legacies of the communist planning system limit the range of current possibilities and options in institutional innovation and the adoption of market-conforming practices (see Hausner/Jessop/Nielsen, 1995). Moreover, any across-the-board advice applicable to a large number of transition economies is likely to be unrealistic. Country-specific factors, in particular the historical, institutional, regulatory and political circumstances which have worked together in shaping a country's financial system, need to be taken into account. If these preconditions are fulfilled, bond markets can serve a number of important function in the transition process.

The most important function of capital markets in a market economy is to provide a mechanism to link deficit units with surplus units and thus help to achieve an efficient allocation of capital. Mature bond markets allow borrowers and investors to diversify sources of investment capital and spread investment risk. They facilitate financial deepening and, in the long term, lower the cost of capital and contribute to economic growth. Bond markets are suitable to serve medium- and long-term credit needs in the economy by channelling ultimate savings directly or indirectly, via financial intermediaries, into marketable debt instruments.

In the presence of public deficits government bonds are a noninflationary source of budget finance. Many economies in transition are burdened with a high stock of debt and relatively high deficits. An efficient bond market allows government to minimise borrowing costs and to restructure maturities to guarantee the sustainability of debt-servicing. If adequate instruments for financing the budget are lacking, for example because of problems with tax-collection, the central bank may be forced to finance the deficit through direct lending to the government. The inflationary consequences of budget financing through central bank credit are well documented. Efficient bond markets allow the government to resort to domestic savings to finance the deficit and thus facilitate the fight against inflation.

Mature bond markets are a precondition for a market-oriented conduct of monetary policy. With an active bond market monetary policy can be carried out through the issue and repurchase of government securities. In the absence of efficient securities and money markets, monetary policy has to rely on direct means such as credit ceilings and interest rate controls. These are likely to distort the allocation of capital in the economy (BIS, 1993). Moreover, issuance of central bank or treasury bills are important for the development of money markets as they facilitate interbank transactions and increase liquidity.

Bonds may be an important source of finance for the enterprise sector. Newly privatised enterprises in the region are in great need for long-term capital for restructuring and expansion. Supply of capital has so far come primarily from banks which are notoriously risk-averse. The issuance of debt securities is also attractive for firms because the costs for the financial intermediaries are saved. In recent years the degree of securitization has progressed far in the industrialised countries (OECD, 1995). Securitization may offer particular advantages for the transition economies where traditional intermediaries, such as banks and insurance companies, need further time to function properly.

Bonds offer a yielding investment opportunity for the household sector. Fairly priced bonds are an attractive investment for risk-averse private savers. Availability of bonds can thus stimulate private savings which are the most reliable source of capital. This is of particular importance in the transition economies where there is a large demand for capital for enterprise restructuring and infrastructure reform in combination with traditionally low private savings rates (EBRD, 1996: 78-86).

Domestic bond markets may also attract foreign investors. It is generally in the interest of reform countries to diversify the sources of foreign capital. Besides seeking credit from supranational organisations or foreign direct investment it is desirable to attract portfolio investment. Portfolio investment includes the purchase of securities such as company stocks or bonds. Among these, foreign borrowed capital is politically less controversial than ownership of domestic equity. Possibly foreign investment in fixed income securities is also more reliable than equity investment. A domestic bond market that is open to the world represents a link to world capital market. This is important for the efficient international allocation of capital.

Domestically, mature bond markets intensify competition in the financial markets: Bonds can be a substitute for financial intermediation and the provision of debt financing through the banking sector. Thus, a competitive bond market can impose pressure on the banking system to improve efficiency and the level of services, for example through a reduction of interest rate margins between borrowing and lending rates. This is of particular importance in the transition economies where reforms of the banking system are still lagging those in the production sector and where banking is highly concentrated on a regional and sectoral basis (EBRD, 1995: 153-170; Kern, 1996). Furthermore, bond markets may help central and eastern European banks to manage their balance sheets. Bank bonds are a suitable means for recapitalising financial institutions suffering from excessive bad loans. Well functioning securities markets allow banks to securitize their debt and better manage the maturity match and risk profile of their balance sheets (Pardy, 1992: 9).

Last but not least, the bond market is the market which decides the equilibrium interest rate. It is crucial for the intertemporal allocation of savings and investment that this market is efficient. In the reform countries where interest rates have been distorted first, by direct government and central bank controls, and second, by the monopolistic structure of the banking sector, this market process is of particular importance.

3. PRIMARY MARKETS: THE DEVELOPMENT OF THE DIFFERENT MARKET SECTIONS

The previous section highlighted several important functions that bond markets can fulfil in the transition process. However, these general considerations cannot easily be applied across the board to the central European economies. The Visegrád countries started the reform process with differing degrees of financial development as well as different legacies of the past. It is therefore necessary to look more closely at the financial and fiscal system in each country and to analyse the actual and potential role of bond markets in this specific environment. Moreover, different sectors of the bond markets play different roles in the financial systems of market economies. In OECD countries, the market for government bonds are in general more developed than markets for debt instruments issued by regional bodies and corporate entities. Usually, government bonds act as benchmark for the pricing in all bond market sections. This does not necessarily hold true for all central and eastern European countries.

Closer analysis of the developments in different bond market sections provides important clues about the overall reform process in each country, and the degree of enterprise and fiscal reform in particular. We have therefore divided our empirical and analytical framework not only with regard to countries but also with regard to different bond market sections.

Figure 1. Structure of Circulating Bonds by Issuer, End 1995 (in percent)

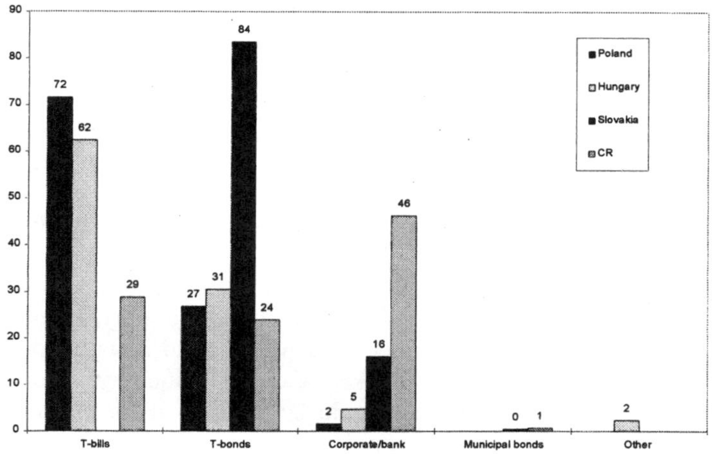

Source: ZEW questionnaire.

Table 1. Domestic Bond Markets at the End of 1996

	Poland	Hungary	Czech Republic
Bonds outstanding in USD bn	15.5	10.0	12.0
As share of GNP in %	11	21	24

Sources: Estimates of Dresdner Bank, no comparable data for Slovak Republic

4. GOVERNMENT SECURITIES

In the transition economies, as in more developed countries, the government bond sector is crucial for the development of other segments of the bond market. For reasons examined below, an early development of the non-state bond market was impeded by the structural legacies of the communist past. Government bonds had a special significance in the early stages of capital markets development because securities issued by the state were suitable to attract investors' confidence from the start and thus helped in the development of capital markets in general. The evolution of a market for government bonds also provided the infrastructure and regulatory framework for the private securities market (BIS, 1993). Deepening of securities markets requires a regular supply of standardised securities from prime issuers. In more developed capital markets government bonds usually act as a benchmark for risk-assessment and for pricing of non-state issues. This is crucial for the establishment of a well-defined yield curve, which cannot be done with lesser-rated credits.

In building an efficient state bond markets, the central European transition economies have been struggling to find the right equilibrium which is necessary to enhance rather than hinder the advancement of the bond market as a whole. On the one hand, a high volume of new issues in each period is crucial for providing market liquidity and facilitating the price finding process. If primary issues are lacking, government securities cannot provide a benchmark for the corporate and bank bond sector. On the other hand, if the market is swamped with low-risk, high yielding government paper for budgetary reasons, crowding out may prevent the development of non-government bond markets.

Supply side developments in the state bond sector reflect public borrowing requirements and the need to stabilise liquidity in the banking sector. High funding needs for infrastructure development and impending reforms of social securities systems as well as the need to roll over existing debt are apt to guarantee a continuous and sufficient supply of government debt instruments. On the other hand, central European countries are trying to decrease public spending for stabilisation purposes and, more generally, to reduce state involvement in the economy. If public borrowing needs are modest governments might decide to issue bonds to simply retain a presence in the market and help liquidity through consistent and regular issuance. This could be justified if the proceeds were used to finance long-term investment or infrastructure development programmes, for which fixed interest bonds with longer maturities are ideally suited.

During the early stages of reform, the issuance of government fixed income securities was hampered by relatively high inflation, in particular in Poland and Hungary. There was therefore a natural tendency to develop the short end of the market first and to issue floating rate or index-linked bonds rather then fixed coupon paper. [3] Up to 1993/4 bond markets basically consisted of short-term treasury securities with very few issues of medium-term bonds (Dresdner, 1994). Strengthened confidence in the reform process and successes in the fight against inflation were a precondition for the emergence of medium- to long-term securities. Maturities of state bonds in east-central Europe are gradually getting longer. However, as long as inflation and interest rates can be expected to continue to come down relatively rapidly governments will remain cautious in issuing long-term debt instruments with fixed coupon payment.

On the demand side, low private savings rates and the traditional pattern of investing savings in bank accounts rather than securities were the main impediments for the development of the government bond market. In most transition economies, local commercial banks still account for the bulk of investment in government securities. The intermediation performed by banks in channelling private savings into budget financing has not necessarily been beneficial for the transition process. By giving preference to low-risk government securities, banks often did not meet the high credit demand for enterprise restructuring and private investment. On the other hand, due to a general lack of alternative low-risk investment opportunities commercial banks as well as non-bank

[3] Index-linked bonds, which are common in some central and eastern European countries, might carry the risk of leading to institutionalised inflation. It would therefore be advisable for governments faced with high inflation rates to rely on short maturities. These, however, entail the requirement of continuous refinancing and the assocoitated risks (BIS, 1993).

entities had little alternatives to holding government paper. Once the privatisation process gathered momentum, demand for equity began to outpace demand for government bonds in most countries. Given the scarcity of capital in central European countries, demand for government bonds remained closely linked to stock market developments. This became particularly obvious in the second half of 1994 when the rapid fall in share prices translated into increased demand for alternative investment opportunities, in particular bonds and thus provided a boost for the fixed income market.

Table 2. Government Bonds (Excluding T-Bills) Outstanding at the End of Period

	1993	1994	1995	End June 1996
Poland PLN bn	1.41°	4.37°	11.10°	16.10°
Hungary HUF bn*	319.51*	465.21*	574.12*	615.41*
	778.23**	1,034.52**	1,221.02**	1,676.77
Czech Republic CZK bn	19.50	28.27	41.67	46.80
+	7.95	15.9	54.1	51.78

Sources: For Poland: MoF Poland, 1995, 1996c; for Hungary: AKK, 1996c; for the Czech Republic: CNB, 1996b; for Slovakia: ZEW Questionnaire, Statistics of the NBS.

* Bonds issued by the central government.

** Figures including Social Security Fund, Consolidation Bonds, and other special purpose issues

° Excluding non-negotiable Treasury securities

4.1 Czech Republic

In the Czechoslovak Republic the first bonds were issued in 1989, before the division of the country. These were traded in the so-called interim secondary market, an informal market organised by the Czech National Bank and domestic commercial banks. The legislative framework, which established the bond market in its present form, was in place by the end of 1992 (BV, 1995; Hein, 1994: 173-4). At the beginning of 1993 the Czech government began to finance the previous two years' budget deficits through issuing fixed coupon bonds with medium-term maturities. Financial and monetary stability provided a suitable framework for the establishment of a well-functioning securities market. However, the strong fiscal position of the central government made the development of a liquid market for state bonds extraordinarily difficult. Since 1993 the government has achieved budget surpluses.

As long as the budget remains balanced or even in surplus, new government bond issues are only replacing old debt and the market will remain thin and illiquid. The government continues to issue a modest amount of medium-term bonds four times a year in order to retain a presence in the market and to dampen rapid growth in the money supply. [4] Rapid growth of the market capitalisation of the Czech bond market -- in excess of 150% on a year to year basis since 1993 -- was mainly due to the increases in issuance volumes of corporate and bank bonds (Aspekt Financial Information).

[4] In 1995 and 1996 the Czech government issued a total of CZK 20 and 40 bn, respectively.

Not only in terms of volume but also with regard to maturity structure is the Czech corporate bond market more advanced than the state bond sector. While the longest available maturity of state bonds is still five years, enterprises and banks started issuing bonds with maturities of up to ten years. On the whole, however, the bond market is dominated by two to five year maturities and there is a lack of low-risk long-term paper in the Czech Republic. Some hopes are vested in the medium-term development of a more liquid market for mortgage securities (see below).

The Czech National Bank (CNB) issues its own bills to stabilise the liquidity of the banking system. In 1995, these were the main instruments used to sterilise large foreign capital inflows with an issuing volume that exceeded that of T-bills by a factor of ten. The National Property Fund also offers short-term bills on a regular basis. As these do not fall under tax preferences for government securities they usually yield about 6-7% more than comparable T-bills.

Figure 2. Bonds Outstanding, End of June 1996, CZK bn, Nominal Value

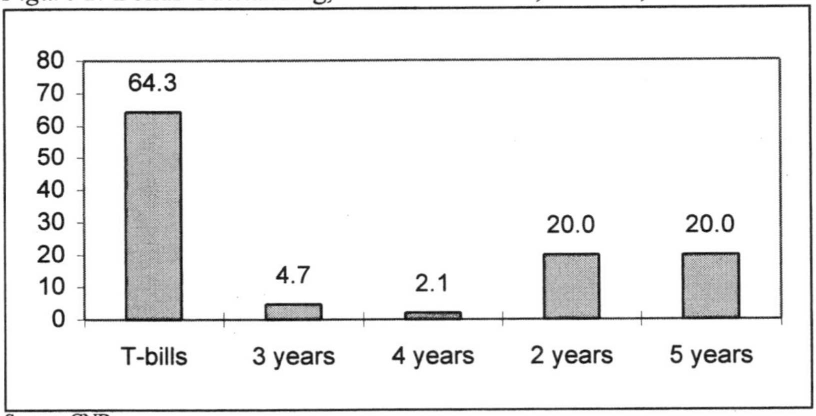

Source: CNB

4.2 Hungary

The establishment of the domestic state debt market dates back to 1988 when the government started issuing non-tradable three, six, and nine-months treasury notes. T-bill auctions were introduced in 1989 to facilitate monetary management. The issuance of fixed rate bonds with maturities longer than twelve months was originally impeded by high inflation and a lack of investor confidence due to previous problems with fixed rate instruments[5] (BIS, 1993). The domestic market for short-term government securities, on the other hand, developed very rapidly. Since 1991, the domestic bond market has been flooded with large volumes of government paper as a result of high and fluctuating demand for credit by the central government. The consequences for the reform process in Hungary were twofold. First, crowding out has impeded the development of the capital market. The budget deficit has resulted in a shortage of capital for enterprise restructuring and expansion. Investors and analysts criticise that the flood of government bonds has choked the fledgling markets for commercial bonds. Equity market development was hampered by the fact that, up to the end of 1995, the average return on shares were below the yields of less risky government paper. Banks held an increasing share of their assets in the form of low-risk, high-yielding government bonds which considerably decreased their propensity to lend to the private sector.

Second, under Hungarian central bank law the National Bank of Hungary (NBH) was obliged to purchase a pre-specified amount of treasury bonds and bills each year to help finance the budget deficit. Although this indirect way of budgetary finance is preferable to earlier ways of direct central bank credit, it nonetheless has negative consequences for monetary stability and the development of efficient monetary management (Kemme, 1994: 45 -6). The absorption of a large share of primary issues by the NBH also had negative implications for liquidity and pricing efficiency in the domestic bond market. First, the purchasing obligations of the central bank left the Ministry of Finance with the possibility to exert control over the issuing price. Second, large holdings of government securities by the central bank proved to be an obstacle to the development of a liquid secondary market.

Fiscal consolidation and impending reforms of the central bank law can be expected to help both monetary stability and the development of the bond market. The austerity package introduced in March 1995 established a ceiling for the budget deficit of six percent of GDP. This target figure has more or less been achieved due to solid revenues and tight control of expenditure, although the collection of social security contribution arrears still represents a considerable problem. Despite the fact that the social security deficit again exceeded the original target in 1996, the total fiscal deficit could be brought down further. On the monetary side, recent structural reforms seek to strengthen the central bank, and make public finance more transparent. This mainly concerns the transfer of responsibility for the central bank's 'devaluation debt' to the central state budget at the beginning of 1997 (European Commission, 1996; CS first Boston, 1997).

---

[5] Attempts to create a domestic capital markets started in the early 1980s with the issuance of corporate and municipal bonds. Most of these instruments carried fixed rate coupons. Rising inflation towards the end of the decade caused a collapse of bond prices. The aversion of Hungarian retail investors against long-term fixed rate instruments can be related to the damage done to investors' confidence during this period (BIS, 1993).

Considerable progress has already been achieved in reducing the role of the NBH in the government bond market. While in December 1994 it held 32.9% of all deficit financing government securities, its share was down to 8.03% in August 1996 (AKK, 1996c).

Hungary's relatively high inflation is also reflected by the fact that more than two thirds of outstanding treasury bonds are floating rate rather than fixed coupon. Moreover, the yield curve is underdeveloped with the government debt market being heavily concentrated in short maturities of less than twelve months and medium term notes. One of the main goals of Hungary's capital market policy has been to gradually shift supply to longer maturities. Up to the end of 1995, T-bills covered the largest share of the central government's borrowing needs. In 1996 only about one third of domestic net issues carried maturities of less than twelve months the remainder being medium-term bonds with maturities of one, two, and three years. There are a few issues of five-year bonds outstanding and only one long-term instrument with a maturity of ten years (NBH, 1996). [6]

Some analysts believe that relatively high inflation and the expectation of considerable interest rate reductions will prevent the development of the long-term bond market in the near future (Euromoney, 1996c). On the other hand, investors seem to be more confident with the government's determination to fight inflation and demand for government debt by domestic institutions has risen sharply in 1996. This resulted in a large supply-demand imbalance in the primary market with auctions of government bonds being heavily oversubscribed. As inflation is expected to continue to fall in the course of 1997 demand for longer-dated paper should increase further.

For 1997, the government faces massive redemption of outstanding issues which it plans to finance through further issues of bonds with maturities of two, three, seven, and perhaps five years. It is expected that net issuance volumes will approximately be the same as in 1996 but gross issuance will certainly increase (Forecasts of the Government Debt Management Agency). The market for Hungarian government paper could get a further boost in 1997 if tax and social security reforms are realised, institutional investors strengthen, and Hungary further enhances its standing in international markets.

[6] These figures concern bonds issued by the central government for budgetary reasons. Special-purpose issues to finance the Social Security Fund, the Higher Education and Housing Programmes usually have maturities of more than 10 years. These constitute a large part of all outstanding bonds but are not publicly traded (AKK, 1996c).

Figure 3. Hungarian Budget Financing Treasury Securities Outstanding at the End of August 1996, at Face Value, HUF bn

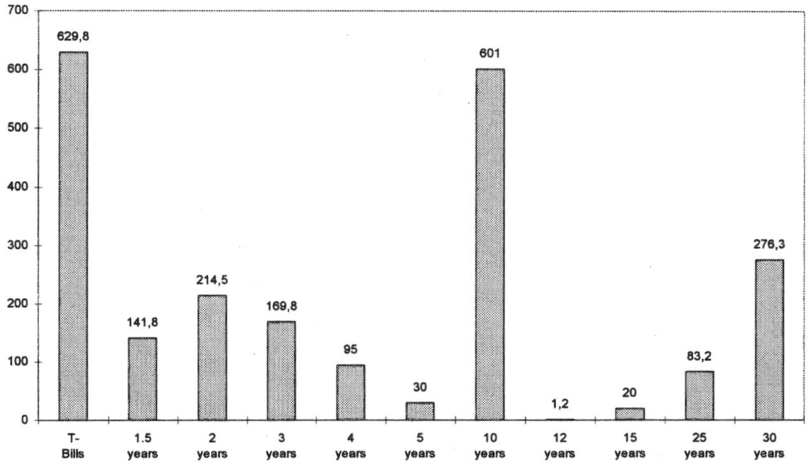

* Incl. Government Debt, non-marketable, only one issue listed at BSE
** Treasury
*** Government Debt
Excluding special purpose and government guaranteed bonds.
Source: AKK, 1996c.

4.3 Slovak Republic

Similar to Hungary, the state used to be by far the most important issuer on the Slovak bond market. Government paper accounted for 90% of the outstanding volume at the beginning of 1995. The national government bond market had a relatively slow start. In mid-1994, the National Council, the Slovak parliament, approved of the issuance of treasury debt securities for financing previous and current budget deficits. Issuing volumes of government securities grew rapidly in 1995, which had several positive effects on the process of fiscal and financial reform. Through the funds raised in the capital markets the government was able to fully repay the direct credit it had received from the Central Bank for covering the previous two years' budget deficits. Another positive aspect of government issuance activity was the reduction of excess liquidity in the banking system. Moreover, changes in the term structure of the state-paper primary market provided a useful indicator for private-sector issuers of fixed income securities (NBS, 1995).

Due to fiscal consolidation, starting in 1995, issuing volumes decreased significantly. Total issuance of government paper in 1996 was less than a quarter of the volume issued in the previous year. Rapid growth of primary issues in the non-state sector compensated for the decrease in supply of government paper to a certain extent. On the whole, however, total volumes of primary issues fell considerably and the overall size of the Slovak bond market remains small, even if compared to other central European markets. Fiscal prudence, a lack of alternative low-risk investment, and discriminatory taxation of non-state securities resulted in a marked demand-supply imbalance in the state bond market (VUB, 1996a; 1997a).

Most of the outstanding government debt is medium-term bonds rather than T-bills, a situation which is rather untypical for central and eastern Europe. The Slovak T-bill market remains illiquid and the amount outstanding is low (SKK 17.7 bn or USD 578 mio at the end of August 1996; ING Barings, 1996). The National Bank of Slovakia (NBS) issues its own bills on a regular basis with the aim to reduce excess liquidity in the banking sector. Increasing monetary stability allowed the government to issue fixed-coupon bonds from 1994 onwards and to gradually extent maturity structures. However, like in the Czech Republic the longest maturity for government bonds is still five years. Unlike in the neighbouring Republic, Slovak enterprises and banks have not stepped in to extend the yield curve which therefore remains underdeveloped.

On the demand side, the government bond market is entirely dominated by the banking sector. The share of government bonds held by commercial banks increased from 89% in 1994 to 95.9% in December 1996, mainly due to their purchasing activities in the primary market. Despite a reduction of the nominal value of government bonds to make the bond market more accessible for small investors, individual private investors still hold a mere 0.17% of outstanding treasury bonds in 1996 while foreign investors account for 0.02% of the market. The NBS does not hold government bonds but it occasionally purchases T-bills directly from the Ministry of Finance. According to Slovak Central Bank Law, the central government may resort to NBS credit for budget financing up to a limit of 5% of state revenue. In 1994, this limit was exceeded by a considerable amount. In 1996, the NBS purchased SKK 36.4 bn of a total of SKK 119.9 bn of T-bills directly from the Ministry of Finance. (NBS, 1995; supplementary information provided by NBS).

Figure 4. Slovak Treasury Securities at the End of December 1996, in SKK bn

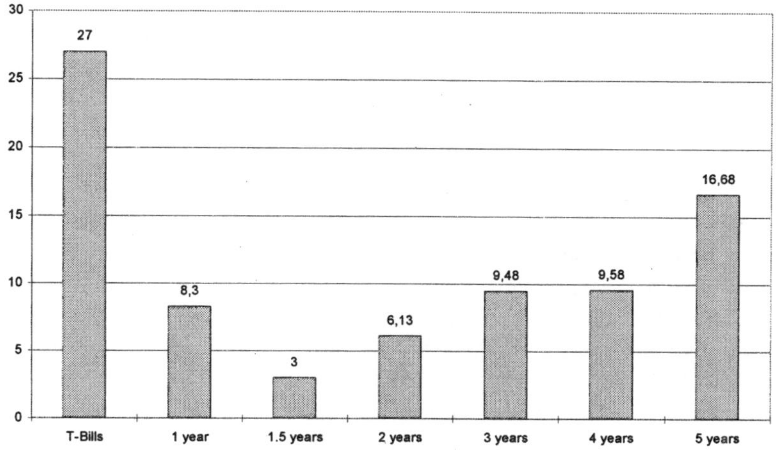

Source: NBS

Table 3. Issuance of Domestic Bonds in the Slovak Republic, in USD mio

	1993	1994	1995	1996
Government	100.83	253.62	1 290.73	354.26
Corporate	9.10	27.01	216.78	396.61
Banking	4.55	11.12	138.66	279.67
Municipal	3.03	3.97	8.96	21.63
Total	1117.51	295.72	1 655.13	1 052.18

Source: VUB, 1997b.

4.4 Poland

In Poland the supply side of the bond market is equally dominated by the government. Although Poland owes almost two thirds of its public debt to foreigners, internal debt is now growing considerably faster (by 17.4% in 1995 compared to a 4.4% increase in external public debt). This is in line with the government's attempt to reduce its dependence on external sources of finance and to improve its standing in international markets. The national deficit is largely financed through the issuance of Treasury securities. Because of the need for budgetary consolidation primary issuance since 1993 has been modest.

The Polish monetary authorities started issuing bonds as early as 1989. In addition to helping to finance the budget deficit (through so-called 60%-State Borrowing Bonds) early types of state securities were issued to speed up privatisation (bonds convertible into shares in privatised companies), to recapitalise ailing commercial banks (Reconstruction Bonds), and to cover state indebtedness to the central bank (Conversion Bonds). All these instruments were directly placed with the NBP and certain local commercial banks and are not tradable. A considerable share of these early issues was denominated in US dollars rather than zloty. These "passive" debt securities could therefore not form the basis for a liquid and efficient domestic bond market. Tradable government floating rate notes with a maturity of one and three years were first issued in 1992. Falling inflation and growing confidence in the reform process allowed the Ministry of Finance to introduce two- and five-year fixed coupon paper in 1994 and ten-year variable-rate bonds in 1995.

Floating rate notes, which used to dominate the primary and secondary bond markets in Poland, have now been overtaken by two- and five-year fixed rate bonds. Ten-year paper is particularly popular with domestic private investors, but its share in outstanding government bonds is relatively small. Growing confidence in economic stabilisation is also reflected by the fact that Poland has increasingly relied on bonds denominated in domestic currency. Whereas at the end of 1992 almost half of Poland's T-bonds were denominated in dollars, the share was down to 16.7% at the end of 1995 (MoF Poland, 1996a; 1996b; 1996c).

Similar to the Hungarian National Bank, the National Bank of Poland (NBP) used to play a dominant role in financing the government deficit through direct credits as well as purchases of government securities. The consequences for monetary stability and the development of the bond market were very similar to those observed in Hungary: an underdeveloped non-state bond market, problems with monetary management, and a distortion of market forces in the primary market. According to the NBP, the obligation of the Bank's obligation to purchase primary issues directly enabled the Ministry of Finance to manipulate the issuing price and interfere with the interest rate level on the market. During 1995, the Bank began to reduce its role in financing the public deficit. It diminished its holding of T-bills and non-negotiable bonds but remained nonetheless obliged to purchase government bonds directly to help finance the budget deficit[7]. The new Polish constitution, which is under preparation, will rule out any budget financing through the NBP and thus prepare the way to Poland's accession to the EU.

In the course of 1995 and 1996, the NBP already considerably reduced its holdings of domestic public debt (from 35.4% in 1994 to about 15% at the end of June 1996). This corresponded to a rapid increase of public indebtedness to the banking sector as the NBP sold on its holdings

---

[7] The Act on the National Bank of Poland obliges the central bank to buy government securities directly from the Ministry of Finance up to 2% of projected expenditures of the budget for a given year. In practice, the Parliament regularly suspends this obligation and lays down the limit for NBP purchases (in terms of purchasing price) in the budget law. In 1995, the Ministry of Finance sold only 50% of the stipulated amount of Treasury securities to the NBH. In 1996 the amount is expected to be even lower (Information form the Montery Policy and Credit Department of the NBP).

of T-bills to commercial banks through the interbank market.[8] As in other central European economies domestic banks are the most important investors in Treasury securities. In 1996 the banking sector holds about two thirds of all outstanding treasury securities. Private investors are more active in the bond market than is the case in other central and eastern European countries. The attractiveness of the state-bond market to retail investors is mainly due to tax incentives and the regular use of public offerings (MoF Poland, 1996c).

Figure 5. Polish Treasury Securities Outstanding at the End of June 1996, in PLN bn and Relative Figures

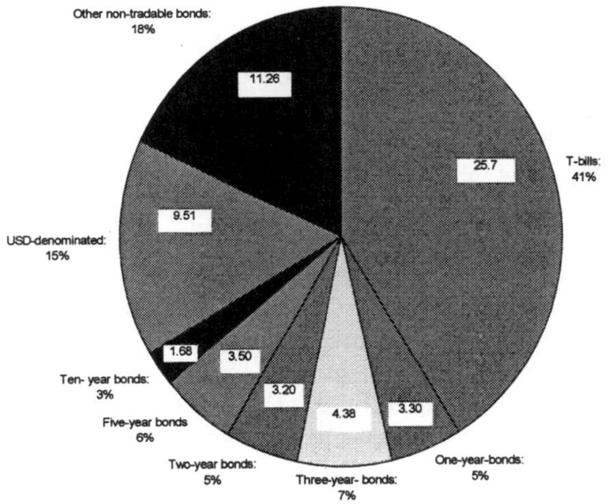

Source: MoF Poland, 1996c

While T-bills are used by the NBP to ensure efficient money market operations, they are primarily issued to provide a non-inflationary source of financing for the Polish budget deficit. The Ministry of Finance has already reduced the share of T-bills in public debt from 50.5% at the end of 1992 to 43.0% at the end of 1995 and pursues the objective of further reducing this percentage (MoF Poland, 1996a).

---

[8] These sales were mainly conducted in an attempt to sterilise the large capital inflows during 1995 and thus reduce inflationary pressures (see NBP Annual Report 1995). The NBP's holding of T-bills have been fluctuating in 1996 from zero at the beginning of the year to a high level over the summer when the NBP was once again obliged to purchase T-bills from the MoF to currently zero again (because the stock of T-bills in the NBP portfolio have matured). (**F.!** Possible consideration: Mr Osinski of the NBP pointed out that currently the NBP is very restricted in its OMOs because of the lack of an adequate securities portfolio..)

Table 4. Available Maturities for Treasuries in the Visegrád Countries

Poland: T-Bills: 8, 13, 26, 39, 52 weeks T-Bonds: 1 year (inflation rate + 3%) 3 years (13-weeks-T-bill + 10 %, reduced to 5% in 97) 2 and 5 year with fixed rates. 10 years (52-weeks-T-bill + 10%, 5-year call option)	*Slovak Republic:* T-Bills: 1, 3, 6, 12 months T-Bonds: 1-5 years, fixed rate
Czech Republic: T-Bills: 13, 26, 39, 52 weeks T-Bonds: 2, 5 years*, fixed rate	*Hungary:* T-Bills: 1,3, 6, 12-months, discount and interest bearing T-Bonds: 2- 5 and 10 years*, fixed and floating rate

Source: ZEW questionnaire.
* 1,5 years series discontinued in 1996

5. CORPORATE AND BANK BONDS

Corporate bonds have a potentially important role to play in the process industrial and financial sector reform in formerly planned economies. With the enforcement of hard budget constraints, newly privatised enterprises increasingly need to rely on their own funds to finance restructuring and new investment programmes. Banks need to raise fresh capital to clean up their balance sheets and comply with higher capital adequacy ratios. Fixed-income securities provide a suitable means of raising long-term funds for these project. However, newly privatised or commercialised enterprises in central and eastern Europe have been largely unwilling or unable to supplement equity and loans with long-term debt funding for several reasons. First, in the early stages of reform alternative sources of funding were mostly cheaper and more easily accessible than debt financing through the capital markets. Although lending rates in east-central Europe have decreased in recent years due to monetary stabilisation and increasing competition in the banking system short-term bank credit continues to be the main source of corporate funding in the region. Medium- to long-term credit is increasingly available to prime borrowers, inter alia in the international syndicated loan market. Equity markets have developed rapidly due to mass privatisation programmes and increasing sophistication of local exchanges.

Disinterest in the local bond market also reflected the structure of the economy after the start of reforms. In industrialised countries it is mainly large, well-established companies that issue bonds, because the issuing costs have to remain small relative to bond yields. For small and medium-sized companies, debt financing through the capital market is in general too expensive. However, it is exactly this sector of small and medium-sized enterprises which is the most dynamic in the transition economies. Central and eastern European states continue to hold relatively large stakes in the biggest enterprises and financial institutions which means that corporate funding is often directly or indirectly financed through the government budget. On the other hand, because of the uncertainty concerning profitability of former state-enterprises these cannot easily access capital markets in the absence of government guarantees. Development of the corporate bond market is therefore to a certain extent a function of the success of the privatisation programme (Dresdner, 1994).

High inflation constituted an additional obstacle to the issuance of corporate bonds. Equally important was that crowding out through large central budget deficit in Hungary and Poland. On the micro-level, debt funding was hindered by a lack of experience with issuing methods, the preparation of prospectuses, and the use of issuing syndicates. Due to the general lack of technical skills of employees in the finance area, corporates had to rely on outside sources for advice and financial management. However, while most banks established capital market departments early in the reform process there was no real experience in bond issues. In the early years of financial market development corporate bonds were therefore essentially disguised loans (Eichler, 1995).

For these reasons, corporate bond markets remained underdeveloped in the region, with the exception of the Czech Republic. Up to the end of 1994, only the most advanced companies relied on debt funding through the capital markets. The first corporate issuers were large domestic enterprises that were partly or wholly sold off to strategic foreign investors. The issue of CEZ, the Czech public electricity supplier, in June 1993 was widely considered as path-breaking for the development of corporate bond markets in the region (Eichler, 1995). In late 1994, when equity markets stagnated, many enterprises in central and eastern Europe sought alternative sources of corporate finance, in particular bonds and commercial paper. However, the renewed stock market boom in the Visegrád countries, the continued inflow of direct foreign investment, and the increasing availability of longer-term corporate loans seem to diminish the need for a rapid expansion of the corporate bond market.

On the demand side, the main problem of the non-state bond markets in the region remains the high degree of uncertainty concerning credit risk. Only a small number of the largest utility companies and banks have obtained ratings by one of the internationally recognised rating agencies. There are no domestic rating agencies in central and eastern Europe[9] and accounting and disclosure practices often fell short of western standards.

---

[9] The first central European rating agency, CERA (Centrum Ratingu i Analiz SA) was established in Poland in December 1996. The firm will rate investment risk of bonds and other debt instruments in accordance with the standards established by internationally recognised rating agencies and provide general analysis of the securities markets. It plans to extend its activities beyon, initially in the Polish domestic market but subsequently also in neighbouring central European countries (The Warsaw Voice,.2.2.1997; Handelsblatt, 30.1.1997).

Table 5. Corporate Debt Securities in the Visegrád Countries

	Poland	Hungary	Czech Republic	Slovak Republic
Amount outstanding end 1995	PLN 737,4 mio	HUF 69 bn	N/A,	SKK 10,4 bn
Maturities	Predominantly short-term commercial paper up to three months,	Short-term CP and promissory notes, very few longer maturities,	CP up to twelve months, corporate and bank bonds from two to ten years, but mainly in the range of two to five years	Commercial paper up to three months, Corporate and bank bonds from three to five years,
Number of corporate and bank bonds traded at the stock exchange in QIII 1996,	none	3	56	14 (+ 18 listed at the RM-S)

Sources: ZEW Questionnaire; Hypo-bank CZ, a,s,; BSSE, 1996b, September; RM-S.

5.1 Czech Republic

The Czech Republic has by far the most developed market for corporate bonds in the region. The market has expanded rapidly in volume terms since 1994 but it remains heavily concentrated in a few major issues mainly by the largest banks and public utility companies (CEZ, SPT Telecom, Skofin, Komercni Banka, and CHB). For industrial enterprises bank credit and equity remain the main sources of corporate finance. Some observers expect that the issuance of enterprise bonds will become a more important form of fund raising in line with the increasing sophistication of the Czech capital markets. The market for bank bonds proved to be even more dynamic than the enterprise sector. In 1995, banks overtook the central government as the most important issuers in the domestic market. At the end of August 1996, bank bonds represented 41% of the Czech bond market while government bonds accounted for 32% and enterprise bonds for 25% (Aspekt Financial Information). Bonds are issued not only by the biggest banks in the capital but also some provincial and even foreign institutions. The issues are mainly used to refinance lending activities and might thus help to create a sounder basis for Czech banking[10] (BV, 1995).

As a result of the active non-state primary market, the Czech Republic has the most developed yield curve in the region. The standard maturity of corporate bonds was three years up to 1994. Subsequently the five-years-plus segment expanded rapidly, mainly because of recurring

[10] The banking crisis in 1996 does not seem to have affected the market for bank bonds to any great extent. Bank failures were largely restricted to smaller private banks. The state continues to hold a significant stake in the five biggest financial institutions, which are also the main issuers in the bond market. This may entail an implicit state guarantee for outstanding bank bonds. Moreover, the Czech government proved its willingness to bail out bankrupt financial institutions to avoid a large-scale crisis of confidence in the Czech financial system.

benchmark issues of five year T-bonds. Few longer maturities of up to twelve years exist but there is no liquid market for these long-term bonds. The market for short-term corporate debt instruments developed in the course of 1995. A number of floating rate and convertible bonds further increase variety in the corporate bond market.

However, some problems remain in the Czech corporate bond market. A significant share of corporate bonds carry simple or often even multiple call options which has made them less attractive for foreign and domestic investors alike. Demand-growth for non-state bonds is also impeded by tax discrimination in favour of government bonds. The withholding tax on non-state bonds, in combination with relatively high inflation, resulted in negative real yields in many cases.

Czech enterprises and banks were the first eastern European non-state entities to raise money in the international bond markets in order to avoid the constraints of the relatively narrow domestic market.

5.2 Slovak Republic

After a slow start in 1993 and 1994, the Slovak non-state bond market began to develop at a fairly rapid pace with corporate and bank bond issues of some USD 353 million being floated in the course of 1995. Comparing the amount of medium- and long-term credit to enterprises in 1995 with the issuing volumes in the corporate bond market during the same period, it becomes obvious that the Slovak capital market has emerged as an alternative source of business finance. Comparisons of the loan interest rates and the "all-in" cost of funds raised through bond issues show that the capital market offers cheaper fund raising opportunities. The ratio of corporate bonds to long-term loans reached about 1:10 in 1996 (VUB, 1996b; 1997a).

Low inflation allowed a lengthening of maturities in 1996 but unlike in the Czech Republic, maturities in the corporate bond markets are in the narrow range from three to five years and do not exceed those of government bonds.[11] The lack of long-term government paper resulted in an undefined yield curve which makes the price finding process in the non-state primary market difficult. Whereas government, municipal, and bank bonds have been issued with fixed coupon rates since 1994, many corporates still carry variable interest rates.[12] A large share has been structured with call options. Coupons on corporate bonds are usually 1.5-3% higher than those of bank bonds reflecting higher risk and a lack of liquidity. There a few issues of convertible bonds outstanding.

[11] The only exception is a 7-year bond floated by Slovenské elektráme, the Slovak electricity company, in December 1996. VUB, one of the country's largest banks, plans a 7-year issue for early 1997 (VUB, 1997b).

[12] The spread over the discount rate has fallen by two thirds between 1993 and 1995 and reached 3-5% in early 1996. In late 1995 the first corporate bond with fixed coupon was issued and by the end of 1996 the ratio of fixed to variable coupon enterprise bonds was about 4:5.

Commercial paper is mainly issued with maturities of less than three months in the form of promissory note programmes on the Slovak money market. CP is regarded as a quick and easy means of short-term financing and rates compare favourably with the costs of short-term credit. However, demand for these instruments is low because the tax rate of 40% makes them rather uninteresting for domestic investors. Despite the popularity of corporate bonds in Slovakia the domestic market remains relatively small. Slovak companies therefore face the need to seek international placements and to borrow directly in international capital markets. After a number of corporate issues had been partly subscribed by foreign investors, VUB-bank floated the first bond in December 1996 which was entirely placed with an international syndicate. Two of the largest Slovak enterprises entered the international markets successfully through issuing Euro-bonds. (Figures provided by BSSE; Euromoney, 1996c; ZEW Questionnaire; VUB, 1997b)

Figure 6. Development of the Slovak Corporate Bond Market

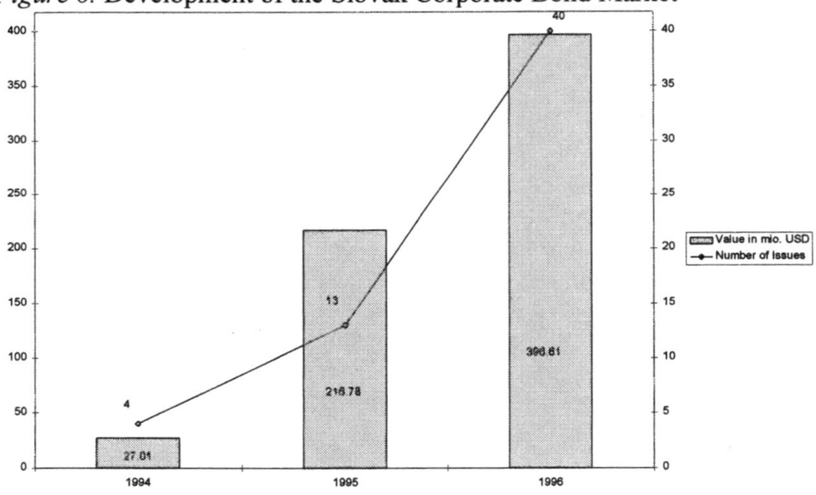

Source: VUB, 1997b.

5.3 Poland

In Poland high inflation and the availability of more attractive instruments for investment have prevented the development of a corporate bond market.[13] Up to the end of 1995, there had been three zloty-denominated bond issues, two by large multinational companies and one by a local brewery. It was hoped that the improvement of the legal framework through the Bonds Law of 1995 would create an environment more conducive to a rapid development of the non-state bond market. The law requires private issuers to disclose sufficient information and is thus

[13] Polish Analysts point to another inhibiting factor: insufficient knowledge about this alternative means of funding in Polish industry and a lack of awareness on the part of domestic investors.

designed to enhance confidence in the fledgling corporate debt market. [14] It also allows corporate entities to issue different types of debt instrument, such as convertible or asset-backed bonds, to increase the flexibility and attractiveness of debt funding in the Polish capital market.

However, by the end of 1996, the corporate bond market is still in its infancy. The market for "KWIT" commercial papers (promissory notes), which were originally issued through ING Bank, emerged as an alternative means of corporate finance in 1995. The first issues were placed by multinational enterprises but Polish companies are also increasingly using this facility. In addition, Bank Handlowy provides issuing and trading services for its own commercial paper programme. "Bony Handlowe", registered debt instruments with maturities from one week to twelve months, are issued through open tender or private placement. The issues are guaranteed by the issuing agent and borrowing enterprises are required to fulfil certain disclosure requirement, thus reducing the risk of investment in these debentures. Through its Capital Market Centre, Bank Handlowy furthermore organises secondary market trading and provides clearing and settlement services for CP (Bank Handlowy, 1995).

The market for commercial paper market has grown at a rapid pace during 1996 with foreign investors playing an increasingly important role (BV, Sept. 1996). It is estimated that corporate debt instruments amounted to some USD 550 mio in October 1996 (compared with USD 15 bn in government securities). However, the overwhelming majority of corporate issues still carry maturities of under three months. Poland's first medium-term corporate bonds with maturities of 12 and 18 months were issued in late 1995 by Elbrewery, the country's biggest brewery, and there is one convertible bond outstanding which was issued by a start-up computer company in the fall of 1996 (FT Finance Eastern Europe, Dec. 1 1995; FT, 30.10.1996).

Although these issues may be interpreted as encouraging signs for the Polish non-state bond market, there are several reasons why Polish enterprises are unlikely to rely on longer term debt financing through the capital markets in the near future. First, relatively high inflation and interest rate uncertainty make the issuance of long-term debt instruments unattractive. Financing through medium-term bonds is too expensive compared to medium-term credit, which has continuously become cheaper due to a high degree of liquidity and increasing competition in the Polish banking system. Moreover, placing bonds in the illiquid market is too cumbersome and time-consuming compared to the issuance of commercial paper. The lack of demand for corporate debt instruments represents another major obstacle. Investors prefer low-risk government bonds or high-yielding commercial paper. As long as there is no

[14] According to Creditanstalt Securities S.A. two corporate issuers defaulted on their issues of commercial paper up to 1996.

secondary market for non-state bonds (see section 5) this situation is unlikely to change. Higher demand for first issues is expected to come from institutional investors in the future, in particular pension funds and insurance companies. Analysts furthermore expect that the amounts of investment needed by the larger Polish corporations will soon exceed the volume of credit that can be provided through syndicated loans and that bond issues will increase as the only viable alternative (Information provided by Creditanstalt Securities S.A. and Raiffeisen Capital Polska S.A.).

Polish financial institutions have attempted to avoid the underdeveloped Polish non-state debt market through issuing bonds directly in international markets. Two of Poland's largest banks successfully issued Euro-bonds and have thus opened cheaper and more flexible sources of funding for Polish private sector borrowers.

5.4 Hungary

In Hungary, the high demand for low-risk government bonds effectively crowded out demand for riskier investment in private-sector bonds. Corporate borrowers rely instead on commercial paper, the markets for which developed in 1992/3 at the time of the credit crunch when many companies did not have access to the loan market. According to the NBH, gross issuing volumes of corporate debt instruments in the first half of 1996 rose threefold compared with the first half of 1995 although the number of issues remained almost constant. The vast majority of these issues is short-term with a maturities of up to three months (NBH, 1996). However, precise figures for the size of the Hungarian corporate bond market are not attainable and the size of the market may actually be underestimated. Corporate debt instruments are mainly issued through private placements and these do not have to be reported to the State Securities and Exchange Commission. The amendments to the Securities Law planned for 1997 will institute reporting requirement for private placements so that the situation in the Hungarian non-state bond market should become more transparent.

6. MUNICIPAL BONDS

Municipal bond markets in the Visegrád countries are lagging far behind the other bond market segments in terms of issuing volumes and liquidity. Nowhere do municipal bonds represent more than a small fraction of the domestic bond market. This can be expected to change in the medium run as bond markets offer a potentially important source of capital for urgently needed infrastructure investment and may help to bridge the gaps between tax revenue, investment expenditure, and proceeds of public investment. With the current trend towards decentralisation in central and eastern Europe, local authorities are required to assume growing responsibilities. On the other hand, less resources are being disbursed through the central government. Municipalities will therefore face the increased need to raise own funds through credit and debt instruments. On the demand side, municipal bonds may be an attractive investment opportunity for foreign and domestic investors alike because they usually offer higher yields than comparable T-bonds with manageable credit risk. However, in a 1996 report Moody's, the rating agency, warns that sub-national bond issues in central and eastern Europe are not free of default risk. Although the risk of ultimate default in the sense of legal bankruptcy is very remote, there is a real danger of municipalities getting behind on their debt payments. Even the strictest laws on territorial borrowing in the domestic capital market do not usually address the issue of the timing of actual disbursement. The risk may be regarded as lower in countries such as Poland where mechanisms for horizontal equalisation exist at the territorial level (Moody's, 1996).

After the Bond Law 1995 created the legal framework for the issuance of municipal bonds, *Poland*'s municipal bond market started to develop at a fairly rapid pace at the beginning of 1996. The first large municipal bond issues were floated by the City of Gdynia in January and May 1996. A number of other cities, including Lodz, Krakow and Lublin, entered the bond markets with issues between PLN 20 and 90 mio in the course of 1996. Taken together, Polish municipal authorities raised approximately PLN 500 mio in the capital markets in 1996. In the main the funds raised are to be spent on refurbishing urban mass transport systems and improvement of infrastructure (FT Finance East Europe 5.1.1996, 19.7.1996; Bank Handlowy, 1996a). In addition to financing needs, considerations of prestige were important for many larger cities -- and the large banks that placed the bonds. After this rapid start, the pace of new market entrants is expected to be lower next year. The larger, more well known cities already have issues outstanding and there is a limited number of quality municipalities left that can issue bonds. Demand for municipal bonds is modest because the of the tight spread over treasury securities and the lack of liquidity in the secondary markets (Euromoney, 1996c; Information provided by Raiffeisen Capital and Investment Poland).

Municipals issued in the *Czech Republic* amount to just 2% of the total bond market in 1996. The total amount outstanding at the end of June 1996 was CZK 9.74 bn with maturities ranging from five to seven years (CNB, 1996b). The municipal bond sector is the least liquid because investors tend to hold the bonds to maturity rather than trade them. Many of the smaller issues are collateralised with mortgages and a few have been fully guaranteed by the Czech Savings Bank (Euromoney, 1996c). In *Slovakia* the municipal bond market is at a similar stage of development as in the neighbouring Czech Republic. Whereas the number of issues launched is comparable to that of corporate bonds, the total principal outstanding is considerably lower. In the third quarter of 1996, some 22 issues of municipal bonds were outstanding with a market value of SKK

570 million (Figures supplied by BSSE). No municipal bonds were outstanding in *Hungary* at the end of 1996. Some of the larger eastern European cities acquired international ratings and could thus benefit from falling borrowing costs in the international markets. The City of Prague was one of the first local authorities raise funds in the Euromarkets and a number of other large municipalities from the region quickly followed. It is expected that international issued by sub-state entities from central and eastern Europe will increase significantly in 1997.

7. MORTGAGE-BACKED BONDS

In more developed countries, mortgage bond (or mortgage-backed bonds) are important to provide an adequate supply of long-term finance for real estate at attractive interest rates. In the Visegrád countries they might develop into a source of capital for urgently needed housing construction and urban development. With economic growth and large inflows of foreign direct investment came an increased demand for residential and commercial real estate and office space. It became apparent that building up an efficient system for long-term real estate financing is of great economic and political importance.

By passing a new mortgage law in July 1995 the *Czech Republic* was the first of the reform countries to introduce a legal framework for the issuance of mortgage bonds. The new law defines these bonds as debt securities (hypotécní zástavní list) the value of which is fully backed by property or eligible supplementary collateral. Czech mortgage bonds are comparable to the German "Pfandbriefe" in most respects. However, unlike in Germany, the Czech bonds can be issued by any bank that acquired a special license as part of its general banking license. The maximum loan-to-value ratio is 70%, which is 10% higher than the German equivalent. Interest-rate income from mortgage-backed bonds is tax-exempt for individual and corporate investors (Neubauer/Stöcker, 1995).

In July 1996, Vereinsbank CZ floated the first mortgage bond issue of CZK 100 mio with a maturity of five years. Demand for the issue by institutional investors was high but a lack of demand in the underlying Czech mortgage loan market is impeding the development of this new bond market segment. Mortgage costs tend to be higher than rents which are still heavily subsidised. The government is planning to extend subsidies to the loan markets to reduce the prohibitive costs of borrowing. Demand for further mortgage-backed bond issues is assured by the absence of low-risk, readily available, long-term paper in the Czech market. It is widely expected that the mortgage-backed sector will increase liquidity on the long end of the Czech bond market in the medium term (Business Central Europe, Nov. 1996). In *Poland*, the Bonds Law envisages the introduction of mortgage backed bonds but no issues took place in 1996. In *Hungary*, the need for a mortgage market arose after local governments began with mass sales of poorly maintained state-owned apartments in 1990. The legal framework for a mortgage market will be in place at the beginning of 1997. Additional legislation which will allow institutions to raise funds for mortgage loans by selling mortgage-backed bonds is expected to be passed in March 1997 (Bloomberg Columns). *Slovakia* also plans the introduction of mortgage-backed bonds for 1997 but no information was available in 1996.

8. THE INSTITUTIONAL AND LEGAL FRAMEWORK FOR AN EFFICIENT BOND MARKET

8.1 Feeding the Bond Market: Issuance and Placement Practices

For the development of a liquid and transparent bond market in emerging market economies, the way in which new issues are brought to the market is of great importance. Issuing and placement practices do not only determine pricing efficiency and transparency in the primary markets, they also influence liquidity in the secondary markets and the types of investors attracted to the bond market. For the organisation of the primary market, four techniques for issuing and distributing newly offered bonds shall be considered:

Auctions. Bonds are sold through either American-style auctions at which each investor pays the price he bids, or Dutch-style/uniform price auctions, at which each bidder pays the price of the last accepted bids. Auctions for treasury securities are held periodically by the central bank or special institutions set up by the Ministry of Finance. Direct participation is often reserved for the special group of authorised primary government dealers, approved annually by the Central Bank and/or the Ministry of Finance.

Private placements. Bonds are directly sold to a small number of selected financial institutions. Private placements are often not explicitly defined in securities legislation. Usually the term refers to all bonds aimed exclusively at institutional investors and therefore not seeking an initial stock exchange listing. Bonds issued by way of this cost-effective method are often eligible for listing at a later stage. Issuers usually opt for this step in the case of large volumes for reasons of prestige and to enhance liquidity in the secondary market.

Public offering. Bonds are sold to a wider investor base at a fixed price. This is usually done through a banking consortium either on a commission basis or with a placement guarantee (underwriting). Investors are registered as subscribers to the offered bonds during the subscription period.

Tap issues. Bonds of a given series are sold over a longer period either over the counters of designated financial institutions or through selling new issues directly into the secondary market.

In practice, these methods are often used in combination depending on a number of factors, including the general market environment, the size and reputation of the issuer, the planned volume and frequency of new issues, and the investor group to be targeted by the issue.

Particular problems exist in the eastern European countries of transition in the pricing process of new issues. In established bond markets, the process of issuing new bonds can be based on the information available on the secondary market of circulating paper. In a situation of illiquid or non-existent secondary markets, the task of pricing new issues on the primary market is more demanding. Market oriented auction systems should be installed that help to use all available information for price determination. The public sector can act as a pioneer in establishing issuing procedures and providing regular information about market conditions. In OECD countries market-oriented approaches to the management and the issuance of public debt have become increasingly popular during the last decade (OECD, 1994b). These may serve as a model for the improvement of primary markets in east-central Europe. The experience shows that pricing efficiency of primary markets for government debt can be increased through regular and frequent auctions of government securities with a large volume per issue,
- a balanced mixture of maturities,
- advance notification of auction details,
- participation of all relevant potential purchasers in the auction, and
- ex-post assessment of the auction results.

Table 6. Issuance Calendars for Government Securities

Poland defined in the Budget Law. T-bills every Monday 1-, 3-, and 10-year quarterly 2- and 5-year fixed coupon bonds monthly	Hungary T-Bonds once a month 1- and 3- months T-Bills weekly 6- and 12-months T-Bills every two weeks 1 year Private Investors Bills once a month 1 year Saving Bills continuously
Czech Republic preannounced for every fiscal year T-bonds in the first week of the 2nd month each quarter T-bills weekly	Slovak Republic no issuing calendar

Sources: ZEW Questionnaire, AKK, 1996c.

In general, the issuing techniques for government bonds in the Visegrád countries are in line with the move to market oriented approaches in OECD countries. American-style auctions are used in all four countries and the auction details are widely publicised. However, the efficiency of the primary markets still needs to be improved. Pricing problems in the government bond market in Slovakia emerged in the course of 1996. The Ministry of Finance and the NBS refused to pass on higher interest rates to auction participants through increased yields on short-term treasury and NBS bills as well as medium-term notes. The bids offered by the small number of commercial banks present at the auctions were rejected as "inadequately high" by the NBS. A large number of auctions in the third quarter were unsuccessful as a result (NBS, 1996). In Poland, a significant share of the banks and brokerage houses accepted as primary dealers in the state paper market did not fulfil their functions to the satisfaction of the issuers. The NBP therefore tightened the regulations for participation in the primary T-bond market to filter out the most active participants and announced a considerable reduction in the number of licensed market-makers for T-bills for 1997 (The Warsaw Voice, 5.1.1997). Considerable scope for improvements seems to exist in the private-sector primary markets. The large share of private placements constitutes a problem not only for the transparency of the market situation but also for the development of a liquid secondary market.

Table 7. Issuing Methods for Government Bonds

	Poland	Hungary	Czech Republic	Slovak Republic
Auctions	American style. Minimum bid PLN 1 mio, The Polish Ministry of Finance reserves the right to increase/reduce the amount of T-bills auctioned off per session,	American Style. Minimum bid HUF 1 mio, maximum bid HUF 100 mio, Competitive and non-competitive bids, The quantity of bonds issued can be changed by up to 25% after the bids have been received,	American style	American style
Issuing Agent	National Bank of Poland	Government Debt Management Agency of the Hungarian State Treasury(AKK)	Czech National Bank	National Bank of Slovakia
Auction Participants	Only banks and brokerage houses which have a proven record of activity in the primary markets, In particular, they are required to have purchased T-bonds worth at least 0,2% of total bond sales during the preceding three months,	Selected brokerage companies which act as primary dealers,	Authorised primary government dealers, approved annually by the CNB (for banks) and the MoF (for security dealers),	Restricted to licensed dealers (investment funds, brokers, banks) which act for their customers.

Table 7. Issuing Methods for Government Bonds (Contd.)

	Poland	Hungary	Czech Republic	Slovak Republic
Public Offerings. Subscription	Two-thirds of one-year floating rate bonds and also some three-year bonds series are sold through public offerings using Bank Pekao SA's service outlets throughout Poland. Subscription was introduced for one-year bonds in late 1996,	A significant share of T-bonds are issued through syndicates made up of brokerage houses, Since April 1996 subscriptions follow auctions for the same series and at a price 0,2% higher than the auction price,		
Private placement		Dominant issuing method for Social Security Fund and Consolidation Bonds, but also used for Central Government bonds, According to the AKK only auctions will be used from QIII 1996 onwards,	----	A small amount of T-bonds were sold directly but the NBS is now entirely relying on auctions,
Form of issued securities	Bearer in book-entry bonds only,[15]	Registered and bearer,	"Registered bearer", in fact name bonds,	Bearer

Table 8. Issuing Methods for T-bills

	Poland	Hungary	Czech Republic	Slovak Republic
Issuing method	American-style auctions on a discount basis, Min, bid PLN 100,000, Competitive and non-competitive bids,	American-style auction, Bids between HUF 1 mio and 10 mio, Competitive and non-competitive bids,	American-style auction,	American-style auctions, Volumes may or may not be fixed in advance,
Auction Participants	Domestic and foreign legal entities and individuals which have been accepted by the NBP as primary dealers,	Licensed primary dealers for interest-bearing T-bills, Domestic banks, financial institutions, brokerage houses, KELER, BSE, foreigners with NBH authorisation for discount T-bills,	Banks and brokerage houses, No fixed primary dealer contracts,	Domestic and foreign brokerage houses which are registered with the NBS,

[15] Under the Commercial Code investors are still entitled to obtain physical documents. The new securities legislation, to enter into force in 1997, will terminate this right, which is in practice already obsolete.

Table 8. Issuing Methods for T-bills (Contd.)

	Poland	Hungary	Czech Republic	Slovak Republic
Issued form	Book-entry form only through the Central Treasury Bill Register	Issued in book-entry form, transferable bearer instruments,*		

Table 9. Issuing Methods for Non-State Bonds

Poland	Hungary	Czech Republic	Slovak Republic
In accordance with the 1995 Bonds Law, non-state legal entities may issue bonds by way of public offerings and private placement where the number of targeted investors may not exceed 300, Public offerings are regarded as too expensive and time-consuming for non-state entities, Commercial paper as well as municipal bonds are privately placed with commercial banks and enterprises through the Polish Development Bank or the more active local and foreign investment banks,	Non-state bonds are almost exclusively issued through private placement, Only three issuers sought listing at the exchange.	Initial public offerings and listings are the exception, The reason for the popularity of private placement seems to be the cost advantage as well as the fact that official listing at PSE is regarded as too cumbersome, However, the trend is towards more centralisation and an increasing number of listings.	Corporate bonds are mainly privately placed through large domestic banks, Subsequent listing at the Bratislava Stock Exchange or the RM-S is compulsory for all publicly traded securities,

Sources: ZEW Questionnaire
For Hungary: AKK, 1996a, 1996b; NBH, 1996;
For Poland: NBP Annual Report 1995; International Securities Regulation Report May 1995, Information provided by the Monetary Policy and Credit Department of the NBP.
For CR: BV, Feb., 1995;
For Slovakia: ZEW Questionnaire.
* Discount T-bills are printed in the form of one global note.

9. STATUTORY FRAMEWORKS: A DELICATE TRADE-OFF

Since regulatory and legal frameworks for capital markets were non-existent in the centrally planned economy, they had to be build from scratch after the start of reform in order to meet new market requirements.[16] The regulatory regime for efficient and stable bond markets should focus on three main areas:

- the new issue market and related disclosure, accounting, and listing standards,
- secondary market trading activities, including market surveillance and enforcement, and
- supervision of market practitioners through registration and prudential standards (Chuppe/Atkin, 1992).

In devising an adequate legal framework for emerging capital markets, governments faced a trade-off between two major goals of regulatory policy. On the one hand, financial policies should be designed to increase the efficiency of financial markets. The reform process in the Visegrád countries started off with an array of government policies which impeded efficiency in securities markets, whether fiscal (preferential tax treatment), monetary (reserve requirements, credit ceilings), or institutional (preferential market access for the federal government for budget financing) (BIS, 1993). Therefore, improving functional efficiency of capital markets required, to a certain extent, the retreat of the state from the financial sector to give market forces greater scope in the allocation process. From this point of view, it could be argued that governments should limit regulations to the correction of market failures. On the other hand, building up confidence in fragile financial systems in the economies in transition requires prudent regulation and supervision. This includes the protection of investors and other market participants against losses due to fraud and other malpractices as well the minimisation of systemic risk.

After five years of economic reform, regulatory regimes for capital markets are in place in all the central European countries. The main problem in the regulation of security markets in the region does not seem to be legislation but law enforcement. The legal infrastructure in the formerly planned economies might be incapable of dealing with too complex regulatory systems. A clear and simple legal framework and an efficient enforcement mechanism should therefore be given priority in the regulatory process. In mature markets, areas not covered by laws are usually regulated by executive instructions, court decisions, customs, and self-regulatory rules of proper behaviour. This framework is only slowly emerging in central and eastern Europe. The number and capacity of commercial courts turned out to be inadequate and the procedures to solve conflicts related to capital market contracts is often too slow and costly. The regulatory agencies or administrations in these countries should therefore be granted the legal authority to act quickly and efficiently. They

[16] In the debate about an adequate regulatory framework for financial markets in central and eastern Europe, the focus was mainly on banking regulation. As the stock market crisis of 1987 demonstrated, confidence in the stability of the financial systems be undermined by shocks from any sector within the financial system. Therefore, prudential concerns should not be confined to banking but should cover all financial markets in the transition economies. After the emergence of irregularities in some central European stock markets more attention was given to the regulation of securities markets.

should also have the power to inflict punitive charges on market participants which violate rules of conduct or prudential regulations (Pohl et al., 1995: 25).

Moreover, regulatory authorities in transition economies with dynamically growing securities markets need to be alert to new regulatory issues generated by structural change, for example connected to advances in information technology or the increasing role of foreign financial institutions. It is therefore important that laws and regulations governing trading and the role of financial intermediaries allow for change rather than impede it. Supervisory authorities need to be given sufficient authority and discretion to interpret the law and promulgate new regulations in order to keep pace with developments (Pardy, 1992: 19).

Of particular importance for the development of emerging bond markets are the rules governing access to the primary market. Administrative supervision in this respect is all the more important as there are no domestic rating agencies operating in the Visegrád countries and the large international rating houses have so far only evaluated a small number of the largest enterprises and banks. In order to build up and maintain confidence in emerging bond markets it is important that only bonds of a minimum quality are admitted to the market in the initial stages. For reasons of systemic stability, a clear definition of access for non-state borrowers in the national bond markets should be laid down in securities laws. The admission of bonds of lesser quality might be envisaged at a later stage when investors have gained more experience.

In order to enable investor to make reasoned investment decision, effective disclosure standards need to be specified and enforced for all private sector borrowers issuing securities to the public. However, disclosure requirements may be insufficient to ensure investor protection in the early stages of bond market development. First, most of the potential corporate borrowers are newly privatised enterprises which cannot provide audited financial reports for more than a few years. Second, local investors often lack experience and sophistication and should not be expected to assess the creditworthiness of borrowers on the basis of scant information available. Disclosure requirements may be supplemented by quality controls and standardisation requirements. In defining the criteria for market access, the central and eastern European countries might consider international guidelines such as those laid down by the IOSCO for international borrowers or those used internationally operating rating agencies. The task of monitoring and enforcing market access rules can be entrusted either to the Ministry of Finance or a specialised agency like the securities commission (see Bröker, 1993: 18-9).

In the initial stages of development regulations concerning the issuance and trading of bonds tended to differ substantially in the four

Visegrád countries. Two forces might work into the direction of greater harmonisation: First, rapid improvement in the regulatory systems in central and eastern Europe and their adaptation to international standards is an important precondition for attracting foreign portfolio investment. Unclear legal frameworks or intransparent market practices may deter potential foreign investors or may have to be paid for by higher premia to cover additional risk. Second, in the view of the prospective accession to the European Union early in the next century, the Visegrád countries will be required to bring their regulatory systems more in line with relevant EU legislation. The four central European countries under consideration have embarked on this process of harmonisation with different degrees of success. The following short survey about securities laws and market supervision will show that the Visegrád countries have tested different solutions to trade-off between systemic stability and efficiency in securities market regulation.

9.1 Poland

The Polish securities market is widely regarded as the best regulated in the region. On the other hand, some of the requirements related to the issuance and public trading of securities are regarded as too strenuous and there have been calls for simplification and more flexibility (The Warsaw Voice, 22-29.12.1996). The foundations of the regulatory regime were laid down in the Law on Public Trading in Securities and Trust Funds of 1991. It provided for the establishment of the Warsaw Stock Exchange as well as Polish Securities Commission (PSC) and it covers the issuance of bonds and bills through the central government. The Bonds Law of 1995 created a general framework for the issuance of corporate and municipal bonds. Only legal entities that have prepared financial statements for at least three years and meet stringent capital requirements may issue unsecured bonds. Strict disclosure and information requirements have to be fulfilled by corporate issuers if they use private placements or publicly offer bonds which are not to be publicly traded. In the case of public offerings, the issuer has to conclude a contract with a bank which subsequently represents the rights of the bond holders and keeps them informed about the financial standing of the issuer. There is no obligation to consult the issuance of bonds with the central bank nor are there restrictions with regard to minimum issuing volumes. Minimum requirements for the issuance of fixed income securities only apply to listings at the Warsaw Stock Exchange.

The Polish Securities Commission, which was modelled after the US Securities and Exchange Commission, is the main regulatory and supervisory body for the Polish capital markets. The Commission is an independent government agency which directly reports to the Prime Minister. Its role is to protect investors by ensuring that rules of fair trading and competition are observed in the public trading of securities, and that the securities markets operate in an orderly and efficient manner.

Among other things, the Commission has authority over all public offerings of securities, reporting requirements, and operating practices. It is also responsible for providing licenses and supervision for brokerage houses, through which public trading in securities exclusively takes place. The Securities Commission's authority has been further enhanced by its ability to enforce punitive charges in the case of misconduct or misinformation. Regulatory policy is established by the Commission's President and a three-member board including the Minister of Finance, the Minister of Privatisation and the President of the Anti-Monopoly Office. (MoF Poland, 1996a; PSC, 1993).

The Law on Public Trading in Securities as well as the Stock Exchange Regulations are under review in late 1996. The amendments to the Securities Act aim to make Polish capital markets more responsive to market developments and to harmonise the Polish legal framework with OECD agreements and EU directives. The amended Law will also create the legal framework for the operation of the Polish over-the-counter market and bring it under the supervision of the PSC. Market participants have been granted an important role in reforming the legal framework (Bank Handlowy, 1996a).

9.2 Hungary

The Securities Act of 1990 (Act VI) established the legal framework for the Hungarian capital market. It defines the rules governing the public offering of securities and the rights and obligations of market participants. The Securities Act also constituted the basis for the establishment of the Budapest Stock Exchange (BSE) and the State Securities and Exchange Commission (SSEC), the main regulatory and supervisory body for the Hungarian capital market. The SSEC itself operates under the supervision of the Ministry of Finance and its head is appointed by the Council of Ministers. Its main task is to monitor stock exchange trading and ensure investor protection. Furthermore, the SSEC is entrusted with the approval of prospectuses which are required for the public offering of securities. In the case of bonds, the issuer has to be in operation for at least a full calendar year, submit all required documentation including the issuing prospectus in accordance with relevant regulations, and has to entrust a broker with the public offering (except when the issuer is a financial institution). However, the Securities Act does not cover the private placement of bonds which has led to a significant degree of intransparency in the Hungarian non-state bond market.

Securities trading at the stock exchange is governed by the Charter of the BSE, which has been enacted by the General Assembly of the BSE in accordance with the minimum requirements contained in the Securities Act. The approval of the SSEC is required for any amendment to BSE regulations concerning listing, trading and settlement. Entities involved in securities trading need to obtain a license from the SSEC. Following the Anglo-American system of specialised financial institutions, the Hungarian Securities Act allows trading of securities only as an exclusive activity so that only brokerage houses can become BSE members. The BSE Membership Regulations of January 1995 establishes the framework for membership and admission rules as well as continuous requirements for BSE members. Special requirements have to be fulfilled by BSE members to become active in the government securities market (BSE, 1995b).

The amendments to the Securities Act, which will enter into force at the beginning of 1997, will bring Hungarian regulations more in line with OECD requirements as well as regulations and practices in the EU. The new Act envisages the admission of commercial banks to securities trading as well as the incorporation of investment banks. It will thus broaden access to the Hungarian bond market while at the same time raising equity requirements for capital market participants. Private placement of securities, which have so far taken place outside the legal framework of the Securities Act, will be brought under the supervision of the SSEC. The Securities Act will therefore, for the first time, contain reporting requirements for non-state bond issuers. It also institutes an "obligation" to publicly offer securities if the par value of the series exceeds a certain limit. (BSE, 1996c; Information supplied by the AKK).

9.3 Czech Republic

The Czech government has traditionally pursued a free-market oriented approach to financial market regulation. A minimum of regulation was regarded as desirable to safeguard systemic stability whilst allowing for a high degree of market efficiency. While other central and eastern European countries have entrusted securities market regulation and supervision to independent agencies, in the Czech Republic these tasks are assumed by a department of Ministry of Finance. The Czech National Bank plays a subordinate role in the regulatory process. In Accordance with the 1991 Bonds Law, the Ministry's permission is required for all new non-state bond issues. Upon submission of the relevant documents the Ministry of Finance will assess the financial capacity of the issuer to meet the interest and principal obligations attaching to the debt over its full life. This authorisation process was introduced because it was felt that many issuers would lack the financial expertise necessary to evaluate their financial standing. There are no minimum requirements for new issues, except for securities listed at the Prague Stock Exchange (PSE).

The Ministry of Finance is equally responsible for the regulation and supervision of secondary market trading in securities. Stock exchange dealers have to obtain a license from the Ministry of Finance, or the Czech National Bank in case the applicant is a commercial bank. Specific capital and other requirements for securities dealers and brokers are laid down in the Stock Exchange Membership Rules. Supervision of exchange trading is exercised by the Exchange Commissioner, who is appointed by the Minister of Finance (PSE, 1996a). Supervision only covers the official exchanges. Off-exchange transactions largely take place outside the regulatory and supervisory framework.

In 1996, the free-market approach of the Czech government increasingly attracted criticism from domestic as well as foreign observer and market participants. In particular, the absence of an independent supervision and enforcement agency for the capital market resulted in frequent complaints about irregularities and a lack of official oversight on the Prague Stock Exchange. The perceived inadequacy of securities market supervision in combination with intransparent practices of some Czech investment funds led to a retreat of foreign investors from the Czech capital market in 1996 (Business Central Europe, December 1996).

After prolonged political controversies, the government decided in late 1996 to establish an independent supervisory body, modelled after the US Securities and Exchange Commission (SEC) and the French Securities Commission (COB). The new Czech Securities Commission (SECOM) is expected to start operating in mid-1997. It will issue and enforce its own regulations, settle disputes and devolve parts of its authority to self-regulatory bodies. It will be responsible for licensing market participants in accordance to stricter rules, to authorise all public issues of securities, and to regulate and monitor securities trading, including OTC trading (PSE, 1996c).

9.4 Slovak Republic

As the regulatory and institutional foundations for the Slovak capital market were created before the division of the Czechoslovak Republic, the legal framework is similar to the one in the Czech Republic. In accordance with the 1992 Act on Securities, the Ministry of Finance acts as the supreme regulatory and supervisory body for the securities market. Its supervisory role includes the issuance of publicly traded securities, secondary market trading, and the activities of the Securities Centre of Slovakia. Applications for new bond issues together with the issuer prospectus have to be submitted to the Ministry of Finance which then has to make a decision about authorising the issue within 60 days. Members of the Bratislava Stock Exchange (BSSE) and individual brokers also need to obtain their license from the Ministry of Finance. Any publicly traded security issued in compliance with the relevant regulations can be registered at the BSSE Free Market. Higher listing requirements exist for the Secondary and Main Market (ZEW Questionnaire).

On the whole, the regulatory and supervisory framework in the Slovak Republic seems underdeveloped in comparison with other emerging markets, in particular neighbouring Hungary and Poland. There have been complaints that laws and regulations concerning capital markets and the stock exchange are often unclear and contradictory. A clear legal framework for the supervisory role of the state over the stock exchange is still missing. Rumours of insider trading and fraud at the BSSE have emerged occasionally (Handelsblatt, 12.11.1996). The prevailing insecurity with regard to capital market supervision was exacerbated in the fall of 1997 through the political controversies surrounding the seventh amendment to the Securities Law (see below section 5.1.).

10. SECURITY: SUFFICIENT STANDARD OF THE SETTLEMENT SYSTEMS

Efficient clearing and settlement systems are a precondition for well-functioning bond markets. The ultimate goal should be simultaneous, secure and irrevocable exchange of cash for title, preferably computerised, rather than paper based. Although clearing and settlement may appear to be merely administrative or accounting procedures, problems can arise if one party to the deal does not live up to the agreement. Because of the need to ensure the performance of the two parties, there is often a close relationship between the clearing and settlement organisation and the stock exchange. In Poland and the Czech Republic, the exchanges or its larger members own and operate the organisation while in Slovakia the settlement centre is owned and controlled by the Ministry of Finance. In Hungary, it is owned jointly by the BSE, the Budapest Commodity Exchange (BCE), and the National Bank of Hungary.

Trading is hindered without the assistance of the clearing and settlement organisation because each party must independently verify the creditworthiness of the other. The clearing and settlement organisation in co-operation with the exchange may reduce counter-party risk in the following ways:

It might require that both parties provide securities and cash in advance of executing the trade. This is essentially what is done by the RM-S exchanges in the Czech and Slovak Republics because these deal with many small investors who do not trade through brokers.

Participation may be restricted by, for example, requiring that brokers meet certain capital standards. This usually means that the clearing and settlement organisation limits membership to the most reputable and creditworthy brokers, dealers, and market participants. The members must then ensure the creditworthiness of the non-members.

The third way is to organise a mutual guarantee system whereby all members of the clearing and settlement organisation agree to collectively stand behind the performance of members (Pohl et al., 1995: 14-15).

Finally, the stock exchange might become a counter-party in each sale or purchase transaction.

It is also important that clearing and settlement is closely integrated with a country's banking and payment system. Sufficient progress in banking reform and the establishment of liquid interbank markets were therefore preconditions for the development of securities markets in central and eastern Europe. In building up their clearing and settlement systems, the Visegrád countries have largely followed the unofficial standard of the Group of Thirty as well as recommendations from the International Society of Securities Administrators (ISSA) and the International Federation of Stock Exchanges (FIBV). These include:

Establishment of a centralised depository system for securities operating on the book entry principle.

Netting of transactions, which means that the clearing and settlement organisation should function as the counterparty in each deal so that bilateral credit and counterparty risks can be reduced.

Final settlement should occur within three days of the trade (T+3).

Settlement should be "delivery versus payment"; i.e. that securities and payment are transferred simultaneously.

The high degree of computerisation and the move to book-entry securities instead of physical securities has facilitated the development of quick and secure clearing and settlement in the Visegrád countries. However, some problems remained and there have been occasional complaints about delays and irregularities in the settlement process [17], although outright default of one of the counterparties do not seem to have occurred.

---

[17] For example, the settlement of trades through the Czech Central Registry of Securities has been criticized for involving long delays. According to Hypo-Bank CZ a.s., settlement of primary trading in T-bonds takes up to ten days. Therefore, a reform measures are to be carried out in 1997 to make the system more efficient.

Table 9. Settlement of Bond Transactions Conducted through the Stock Exchange

	WSE	BSE	PSE	BSSE
Clearing and Settlement Centre	The clearing, settlement, safekeeping and custody of securities traded on the WSE is handled by the National Depository of Securities (NDS), Only WSE members are members of the NDS,	Clearing and settlement of all publicly traded securities proceeds through the Central Clearing House and Depository (KELER), For trades conducted on the BSE a two-tier clearing system was introduced in Nov, 1996 to reduce the counterparty risk by limiting direct access of smaller and riskier investors to the clearing system[18],	All PSE transactions are settled through the Universal Settlement Centre (UNIVYC, previously the Stock Exchange Register of Securities), a joint stock company owned by PSE members,	Securities transactions are exclusively executed through the Slovak Securities Centre (SCP), which is fully owned and controlled by the Slovak Ministry of Finance,
Book-entry settlement	Since 1995, all government securities have been issued in book-entry form only, The entire clearing and settlement procedure is fully computerised,	About 95% of government securities are immobilised (but not dematerialised) and settled in book-entry form,[19]	Settlement through the Securities Centre is dematerialised,	Since October 1995 all stocks and bonds have been issued and traded in book-entry form only,
Central registry	All securities admitted to public trading must be stored in the NDS,	A subdivision of KELER acts as the central registry of publicly traded securities,	The Securities Centre is the central registry for all dematerialised securities,	The Slovak Securities Centre is the central registry for all book-entry securities,

[18] The rights granted to exchange members to trade in government securities and to clear and settle the resulting transactions have been separated. The latter is now limited to so-called "general" and "individual" clearing members who have to comply with certain requirements, including capital requirements (BSE, 1996c).

19 The number of physical withdrawals - although decreasing - remains high. During 1995 KELER's depository effected delivery of about 2.7 million pieces of securities and some 1.7 million physical withdrawals (KELER, 1996). The new Securities Act provides for a dematerialised rather than a paper-based system.

Table 9. Settlement of Bond Transactions Conducted through the Stock Exchange (Contd.)

	WSE	BSE	PSE	BSSE
Cash settlement	The NDS prepares and supervises money settlement for the members of the Exchange through the Clearing Bank (Bank Slaski), The member brokers settle the deal with the individual investors,	In 1995 KELER took over the exchange cash accounts of BSE members from the central bank while establishing a direct cash connection with the NBH and joining the GIRO system,	Financial settlement takes place through the Clearing Centre of the Czech National Bank, Non-banks settle through their custodian bank,	The BSSE sends instructions to the Bank Clearing Centre of Slovakia to effect money transfers between the clearing accounts of the members and the BSSE account with ING Banks Bratislava,
Guarantee fund	The NDS manages the Fund which guarantees all transactions concluded on the WSE,	The Stock Exchange Settlement Fund is run jointly by the members of the Exchange,	UNIVYC operates the Stock Exchange Guarantee Fund for the members of the PSE, Only transactions concluded in the central market are ensured,,	All members of the BSSE transfer collateral to the Guarantee Fund managed by ING Bank Bratislava, The Fund covers transactions in both listed and unlisted securities traded at the BSSE,
Settlement cycle	T+2 for continuous trading T+3 for single price auctions	T+2 for government securities* T+5 for other BSE trades	T+3 for anonymous PSE trades; T+2 - T+15 for direct trades registered at the PSE,	T+3 for BSSE transactions T for OTC/RM-S trades

*since September 1996

Table 10. Settlement of OTC Transactions

	Poland	Hungary	CR	Slovakia
Method	The NDS carries out all securities transfers between participants' accounts resulting from trading, corporate actions, off-market transactions, (including interbank bond trading) and free trades that lead to the movement of instruments from account to account,	Transactions conducted in the organised state paper OTC market are settled through KELER, No settlement rules exist for the unregulated OTC market but settlement also takes place through KELER for publicly listed securities,	UNIVYC provides clearing and settlement for both direct bloc trades registered at the Exchange and other kinds of OTC transactions which are subsequently entered into the PSE trading, Most OTC trading in bonds is executed and settled directly through the Securities Centre, Transactions through the RM-S system are automatically cleared through the RM-S clearing system,	Securities transactions are carried out exclusively through the securities accounts of the SCP, Transfers cannot be executed directly through the SCP but have to be conducted through either the BSSE or the RM-S,
Insurance of OTC deals	In 1996 the NDS was planning to establish a guarantee system for the new OTC market,		Direct trades at the PSE are not covered by the guarantee fund, nor are off-market transactions,	Only BSSE direct trades but not OTC trades are ensured by the Guarantee Fund,
Settlement cycle	As agreed between the participants but mainly T+0 for interbank bond transactions,	T+0 for the state paper market. As agreed between the participants in the unregulated market,	T+0 for transactions conducted through the Securities Centre	As agreed between the participants, T+0 for RM-S transactions ,

Sources:
Poland: Euromoney, 1995; The WSE, Organisation and Operation, July 1995; Bank Handlowy, 1996.
Hungary: BSE Annual Report 1994; Five Years of the Budapest Stock Exchange, June 1995; Euromoney bonds guide; Supplementary information by the BSE, KELER, 1995; 1996.
CR: PSE, 1995a; 1996a; 1996d; Euromoney, 1996c.
Slovakia: ZEW Questionnaire, BSSE Annual Report 1995, Central European Securities House May 1996.

11. IMPLICATIONS OF TAX-POLICIES FOR CAPITAL MARKET DEVELOPMENT

While it is conceivable that wide range of regulations impinge on the development of a national bond market (including banking laws, social security legislation, real estate and mortgage legislation, foreign exchange regulations, etc.) it is normally tax laws that have the greatest bearing on the bond primary and secondary markets. For instance, corporate bond issues might be impeded if enterprises are not allowed to deduct coupon payments from taxable corporate income. Issue taxes or stamp duties might make the offering of new bonds prohibitively costly. Stock exchange turnover tax can hinder the development of a liquid secondary market. Most importantly, withholding taxes on coupon payments as well as capital gains tax may be a particular obstacle to the development of a bond market, especially if competing investment outlets are not subject to such taxes (Bröker, 1994: 35).

Depending on the broader goals of financial policies, two different tax systems for fixed income securities have evolved in the Visegrád countries. While in the Czech and Slovak Republics the tax rate depends on the issuer of the bonds, in Poland and Hungary it is related to the status of the investor. Both types of taxational discrimination are likely to have distorting effects on bond market development. Moreover, differential tax rates on income or capital gains from different financial instruments distort capital raising and investment decisions. Borrowers and investors face incentives to structure capital raising and investment on the basis of tax considerations rather than on the fundamentals of value and risk. Tax discrimination between government securities and private-sector issues has been used widely to facilitate the development of the state-bond sector. This has usually led to an adjustment of yields so that coupons of corporate and bank bonds are often considerably higher to compensate investors for the "tax penalty". Practices of Tax policy has also been designed to influence the attractiveness of the bond market for particular investor groups. In Poland financial policy was designed to encourage long-term private investment in securities markets rather than bank deposits. Due to special tax preferences for individual savers, the Polish government bond market attracted a much broader retail investor base than was the case in the other central European countries. Trading patterns at the stock exchanges were also heavily influenced by taxation. In Poland, for example, the sums invested in T-bonds in the primary market used to be deductible from income tax for retail investors. The result was that T-bonds were traded at the exchange at a considerable discount (WSE, 1996a, No. 1). In the Czech Republic, tax policy prevents corporate investors from dealing in the secondary market for bonds. Trading in fixed income securities is regarded as "financial turnover " for tax reasons. As enterprises which generate high financial turnover risk losing their right to claim a refund on input taxes corporate investors are often unwilling to restructure their portfolios (Aspekt Financial Information).

Although foreign portfolio investment is mostly covered by double-taxation agreements and non-residents are therefore exempt from domestic withholding taxes, the tax regimes in the specific countries heavily influence the attractive of different securities market segments for international investors. The adjusted yields of Czech and Slovak non-state bonds have made the corporate bond market relatively attractive for foreign investors in comparison with the state bond sector. According to Czech analysts, the share of foreign investors in the secondary market for non-state bonds is further increased through widespread practices of "bond washing".[20] In most central and eastern European countries taxation of investment income from securities was under review in 1996 and significant changes are expected for 1997. The abolition of tax discrimination is desirable from an efficiency point of view. Moreover, external forces may have played an important role in shaping tax reforms in the Visegrád countries. Financial liberalisation has put central European securities markets in closer competition with funding opportunities in international and off-shore bond markets (see section five). Investment in the latter is mostly exempt from national withholding taxes and may therefore induce a degree of tax competition. There is a discernible trend towards abolition of withholding taxes in domestic bond markets in OECD countries (Benzie, 1992: 30-4).

Table 11. Taxation According to Issuer

Taxation of	Czech Republic	Slovak Republic
Government securities	Government securities issued after 1993 are tax-exempt[21],	T-bonds and T-bills are tax-exempt, NBS-bills are taxed at 15%,
Non-state bonds	Interest income from non-state bonds is subject to a 25% withholding tax, Capital gains are taxed at the investor's income tax rate, which range from 15% to 40% for natural persons and was 39% for legal entities in 1996, Capital gains are tax free for natural persons if the security was held for more than three months,	Corporate bonds are taxed at 15%, municipal bonds at 10%, and commercial paper at 40%,

Sources: For Slovakia: ZEW Questionnaire; Raiffeisen Zentralbank, 1995b; for the Czech Republic: PSE, 1996a.

[20] Bond washing is the practice of transforming taxable interest income and dividends into tax-free capital gains through selling the security before the payments of interest to (foreign) investors exempt from capital gains tax.

[21] According to the CNB, the tax prefenences for government securities will be abolished in 1997. The 25% withholding tax will than be levied on all fixed income securities irrespective of the issuer.

Table 12. Taxation According to Investor

Taxation of	Poland	Hungary
Individual private investors	For Polish natural persons income from the sale of Treasury bonds as well as interest rate income are exempt from income tax, provided that the bonds are not part of business assets, The discount on T-bills is also tax-exempt while capital gains are subject to the investor's income tax rate,[22] Discount on CP is taxed at 20% while capital gains from the sale of CP is subject to the investor's income tax rate,	Interest income as well as capital gains from publicly traded government securities is tax free for private investors, Individuals pay a capital gains tax of 10% if the gains were achieved in public trading,
Domestic legal entities	Polish legal persons pay the income tax rate of 40% on interest and capital gains from all kinds of securities (incl. T-bonds and bills, and CP), Interest income from government securities re-spent on the purchase of T-bonds is tax exempt and taxed at 20% if re-invested in T-bills,	For domestic banks/enterprises interest income and capital gains are taxed at the corporate tax rate of 18%,
Foreign legal persons	Capital gains are subject to a 40% income tax assessment; interest rate income is subject to a 20% withholding tax,,	Foreign subsidiaries are taxed at 18%, just like domestic legal entities, but pay an additional 23% supplementary tax on 65% of the tax base,

Sources: For Poland: MoF Poland, 1996a; Bank Handlowy, 1996b; for Hungary: Information provided by the AKK

12. SECONDARY MARKETS

Secondary markets for bonds should fulfil two essential functions: First, with continuous and high volumes of transactions in the secondary market bondholder are able to liquidate their holdings at any point in time prior to maturity. Bond markets thus mediate funds between different maturities on the side of lenders and borrowers. Issuers receive long term credits which they do not have to reimburse prior to maturity of the bond while investors may hold short-term funds in the form of bonds which can be sold on in secondary markets. A liquid secondary markets will increase the demand for issues in the primary markets and therefore decrease the cost of borrowing for new issuers. Second, liquid secondary markets are needed to establish market-based prices and yields. These can serve as a reference for an adequate pricing of new issues. They will also provide valuable signal functions for the economy more generally as they serve as

[22] The tax-exempt status of capital gains from T-bills and T-bonds will be terminated on the 31 December 1996.

a barometer of domestic economic conditions and give indication of the impact of anticipated moves in interest rates. In order to fulfil theses maturity-transformation and signal functions, secondary markets require a certain volume of marketable, standardised securities. In the initial stages of bond market development in transition economies these are most likely to be government bonds. In OECD countries, the government segment is usually the most liquid of the national bond markets.

In order to increase liquidity and transparency in the secondary markets, the Visegrád countries should therefore focus on improvement of the market infrastructure. In particular, a regular and transparent price discovery process, safe and reliable clearing and settlement systems and a good regulatory and supervisory framework must be installed. Development of efficient secondary markets is crucial not only because of the immediate needs of the market participants but also because the eastern European stock markets operate in an increasingly competitive environment. Financial opening and deregulation put each individual exchange into competition with foreign official exchanges as well as domestic and foreign over-the-counter markets for securities. This additional pressure has been one of the main driving forces for rapid improvements of stock market organisation in the central and eastern European countries. (see. e.g., Szabadföldi, 1996; BSE, 1995b; PSE, 1995c).

13. WHERE IS THE MARKET PLACE: CENTRALISED VERSUS DECENTRALISED STRUCTURE

Secondary trading of securities in transition economies is often heavily fragmented with a large number of transactions being conducted 'off-market' or 'over-the-counter' (OTC) [23]. A minimum turnover in the organised market, in particular at the official stock exchange, in relation to OTC trades is necessary for the transparency of the market situation. Government choices in this respect can be described in terms of a trade-off between consolidation and competition. On the one hand, it might be argued that the competitive effects of multiple exchanges will force exchanges to reduce transaction costs and improve the market infrastructure to enhance the efficiency of trading. On the other hand, multiple exchanges may have a detrimental effect on market quality, volumes of trade, and the price stability faced by individual traders.

What is more, informal markets have a number of weaknesses that might be particularly harmful in the fledgling capital markets of the Visegrád countries. First, informal markets often lack transparency

[23] Strictly speaking there is a significant difference between off-market transaction, i.e. deals conducted in informal markets, and over the counter trades. The latter may take place in organised OTC markets as is often the case in more developed capital markets. In central and eastern Europe, however, the two terms can be used interchangeably as the degree of organisation of OTC markets is still very low.

because formal reporting mechanisms for prices and volumes of transactions are largely absent. The result is an inefficient market where the same securities trade at different prices, offering arbitrage opportunities and free riding on official price determination. Second, informal markets usually operate outside the regulatory and supervisory framework installed for the organised exchanges. The lack of official oversight may provide greater scope for cheating with the consequence that professional and more sophisticated market participants may gain at the expense of inexperienced retail investors. It can be assumed that, in general, trading is more efficient and costs are lower if all buyers and sellers of a security are brought together in a single market.

Remarkable differences exist between the trading systems used for bond transactions in the four countries of east-central Europe. On a continuum that ranges from free competition between exchanges for capital and turnover to complete consolidation of all trading into one exchange the Czech Republic would be placed towards the free-competition end of the spectrum. Secondary market organisation in the Slovak Republic would be assigned to the other extreme of almost complete consolidation. The secondary markets in both Hungary and Poland can be allocated to the middle ground.

13.1 Czech Republic

For the Czech Republic, it is estimated that only 20-25% of domestic bond trading go through the Prague Stock Exchange. Bond trading mainly takes place through direct transactions at the counters of the Securities Centre (SC), the central registry of all dematerialised securities[24]. Professional investors, who prefer an organised market, have increasingly used the Prague Stock Exchange (PSE) in recent years. Unlike in the Slovak Republic, the RM-S Exchange, a computerised bourse which has grown out of the mass privatisation programme, is not used for trading fixed income securities. The fragmentation of the Czech market and the large share of off-market transactions generated complaints from domestic and foreign investors about a lack of price transparency and inefficient pricing in the Czech market (FT Finance Eastern Europe, 19.7.1996).

Similar to most central European regulatory authorities, the Czech Ministry of Finance was faced with the decision whether to suppress off-market dealing through amendments to the Securities Law. Several proposals were put forward in recent years to consolidate trading in order to improve the quality of pricing and prevent free-riding at the expense of market organisers. On the other hand, it was that penalising off-market dealing could be counter-productive because of the high share of institutional investors in the Czech secondary market and because trading

[24] Traders estimate that some 70% of all securities transactions go directly through the Securities Centre (FT Finance East Europe, 5.4.1996) while the Official Figure is closer to 50% (CNB, 1996a).

activity could be driven cross-border rather than on-market (Miller, 1994). In accordance with its liberal approach to capital market regulation the Ministry of Finance decided against using administrative means to encourage on-market trading. Competition rather than enforced centralisation will be relied upon to increase the transparency in the secondary market. In the first half of 1996 the Ministry granted a license to RTP group (Right Time Price) to set up a third Czech organised exchange with the aim of capturing a large share of OTC trading (FT, Finance East Europe, 5.4.1996). The new on-line trading system, which started operating at the end of 1996, will be used for trading shares as well as fixed income securities. The PSE also tries to attract a larger share of OTC transactions which are currently taking place at the Securities Centre. Reforms of the Universal Settlement Centre in 1996 were designed to facilitate OTC transactions using the PSE's information infrastructure and clearing and settlement facilities. In the new system, transactions conducted outside the PSE can subsequently be entered into the PSE electronic trading system and settled through the Universal Settlement Centre (PSE, 1996d).

13.2 Hungary

In Hungary, the share of OTC trading in fixed income securities is similar to the Czech Republic. Although all deficit-financing government bonds and T-bill are listed at the Budapest Stock Exchange (BSE) more than half of all T-bond transactions take place outside the official market. For T-bills the figure is even higher at 70-80% (BSE, 1996b; 1997). An organised OTC market for government securities has been managed by KELER, the Hungarian clearing and settlement organisation, since September 1994. KELER's state paper accounting system offers T-day settlement against the previous T+5 settlement cycle of the BSE as well as lower transaction costs. In this organised OTC market, the NBH, local commercial banks as well as brokerage houses may conclude prompt, repo, and repo extension transactions. It is also important for the government paper turnover at the BSE that in late 1992 banks had to quit the exchange in accordance with the Securities Act of 1990. Direct trades between commercial banks, which are an important investor group in the local bond market therefore take place outside the official exchange (BSE, 1995b, 1996a; KELER 1995).

Transparency of off-market dealing constitutes a significant problem as the Securities Act of 1990 does not cover OTC trading. Thus, broker companies operate in this market segment outside the supervision and regulations of the State Securities and Exchange Commission. The NBH (the most important investor in government bonds in the primary market and a net seller in the secondary market) has also been one of the most active traders in the OTC market with the justification of increasing liquidity in the secondary market (BIS, 1993).

13.3 Poland

The Warsaw Stock Exchange (WSE) puts much emphasis on the fact that securities trading is centralised in Poland, i.e. all transactions in publicly traded securities take place through the Exchange. The overall picture is not quite as clear, however. Treasury bonds are the only fixed income securities listed at the Warsaw Stock Exchange. There is no organised market for private sector issues and liquidity is reportedly very low. Commercial paper and municipal bonds, if traded at all, are exchanged in direct transactions between financial institutions. In addition to the organised exchange treasury bonds and notes are traded in the interbank market by brokerage houses which acquired a license from the Polish Securities Commission. According to the National Depository of Securities, off-market transactions in government bonds amounted to PLN 1.94 bn in the four months from July to end October 1996.

The absence of a secondary market for non-state bonds may be cited as one of the reasons for the underdevelopment of the non-state market segment. Considerable improvements may be expected in this respect in the course of 1997. A new decentralised exchange was established by the Polish Association of Brokerage Houses with the aim of providing an organised market for OTC trading. The new exchange, CeTO (Centralna Tabela Ofert), started operating in December 1996 and will mainly be used for shares of companies included in the new mass privatisation programme which do not fulfil the listing requirements of the WSE (Euromoney, 1995; The Warsaw Voice, 29.12.1996). According to the NDS, there are also plans to extend organised OTC trading to municipal and corporate bonds. Up to the end of 1996, only one sub-state issuer, Ostrów Wielkopolski, expressed interest in listing at the OTC exchange but it is expected that communal bonds will increasingly be traded there. It may in time also attract private-sector bonds as listing and trading at CeTO is cost-effective and information requirements are far less stringent than at the WSE. The Amendment of the Act on Public Trading of Securities at the start of 1997 will bring the new organised OTC market under the auspices of the Polish Securities Commission.

13.4 Slovak Republic

Slovakia is the only of the Visegrád countries that has effectively suppressed off-market trading by government regulation. It is estimated that until the sixth amendment of the Securities Law in August 1995 less than 20% of securities trading took place in the organised markets. The new law required that all transactions in publicly traded securities take place through the organised markets. The Slovak Securities Centre (SCP) only takes instructions for securities transfers from the official exchanges, i.e. the Bratislava Stock Exchange (BSSE) and the computerised retail exchange RM-S. The legislation was intended to increase liquidity and transparency in the secondary market and it led to a large number of new listings at the BSSE (VUB, 1996). Conflicting signals were given by the government of Prime Minister Meciar through the proposed seventh amendment of the Securities Law in November 1996. The new regulation would have allowed issuers to choose whether to issue securities in dematerialised or paper form. Only the former would require authorisation by the Ministry of Finance for trading on the public market while securities in paper form might again have been traded outside the public market where there are no reporting requirements (Trend, 13.11.1996). The amendment attracted considerable criticism from within the government as well as market participants and was finally vetoed by President Civic and returned to Parliament for reconsideration. It was subsequently decided that transactions in bonds and certain other publicly traded securities shall only take place in the organised capital markets in book-entry form (VUB, 1997a).

Unlike in the Czech Republic, where the RM-S retail exchange plays a subordinate role, a real competition between the two organised exchanges has developed in the Slovak Republic. In 1995 the RM-S exchange captured one third of all organised securities trading. During 1996 turnover on the Bratislava Stock Exchange grew considerably quicker and by the end of the year the volume of transactions carried out there is five times higher than trading through the RM-S. The coexistence of the two exchanges resulted in inefficient pricing and arbitrage opportunities until they were required to establish a single closing price. All proposals to consolidate the two markets through government degree have been frustrated by the strong opposition of the market organisers. The trend is towards more competition rather than less. For 1997 it is planned to transform the RM-S into a membership exchange and to introduce derivatives trading more or simultaneously at both exchanges.

Up to the end of 1996, competition was largely restricted to equity trading as organised bond trading almost exclusively took place at the BSSE. Although there were some 28 municipal and corporate bonds listed on the RM-S during 1996, only one corporate bond was actually traded. However, It is conceivable that in the near future the RM-S exchange will constitute more serious competition for the BSSE also in fixed income market. According to the market organisers, some technical difficulties which have impeded bond trading at the RM-S so far will be solved at the beginning of 1997. Competition between the two exchanges may be further invigorated by the government's decision that trading of the new National Property Fund Bonds should take place exclusively through the RM-S. Trading commenced in August 1996 but initially liquidity in this new market segment was poor as the massive sell orders were not met with any demand. Turnover increased considerably in the last months of 1996, with most transactions taking place in the segments for anonymous and direct transactions (Blick durch die Wirtschaft, 25.10.1996, RM-System Slovakia, 1996b).

Table 13. Share of Bonds Traded at the Stock Exchange

Poland: Only government bonds are traded at the WSE, Non-state bonds, if traded at all, are exchanged off-market, A considerable share of bonds is traded directly between authorised brokerage houses through the interbank market,	Czech Republic: Only some 20-25% of all securities transactions are conducted through the PSE, Direct transactions through the Securities Centre are the most popular form of trading,
Hungary: More than 50% of all bonds trades take place OTC, mainly through KELER's government securities accounting system, The figure for T-bills, which are also listed at the Exchange is even higher, at 70-80%,	Slovakia: Since the sixth amendment of the Securities Law in August 1995, all transactions have to take place in the public market, Possibly, the RM-S retail exchange will be increasingly used for fixed income trading in the near future,

Sources: See plain text

Transaction Fees

WSE, for T-bonds: 0.07% (reduced from 0.08% in Oct. 1996) (Bank Handlowy, 1996b)
BSSE: basic fee of 0.02% of the issue volume but maximum SKK 150,000
trading fees are 0.05% of the trading volume, maximum SKK 3,000.
direct transaction fees and Repo trades cleared by the BSSE are 0.3% of the trading volume, maximum SKK 3,000.
transfer and settlement fees for non-publicly traded securities: SKK 2,000.
(Slovak issuers pay 0.01% to the Ministry of Finance for authorising public trading, 0.05% to the Securities Centre for providing the ISIN, SKK 50,000 listing fee for listing at the BSSE, which is compulsory, plus other registration fees at the Securities Centre) (ZEW Questionnaire)
Admission fee for the *PSE* Main and Secondary Market is CZK 50,000. The annual transaction fee is 0.05% of the value of the issue but a maximum of CZK 200,000 for the Main Market and 75,000 for the Secondary Market. (PSE 1996a)

14. THE FURTHER PERSPECTIVE OF OTC

In the absence of administrative intervention, secondary bond trading that now takes place outside the official stock exchanges will only move to the organised markets if they offer advantages in terms of liquidity, transparency, lower transaction costs, and fair pricing. Issuers of eligible fixed income securities generally have lower incentives to seek a listing at the official stock exchange if unlisted securities are as vigorously traded as listed ones. Listings are then obtained not to reap additional benefits in terms of liquidity but for reasons of prestige, in particular to indicate to investors that the issuer is larger or more marketable and subject to more extensive disclosure requirements.

For investors in fixed income securities the preferences regarding the market place will to a considerable extent depend on transaction costs. The increasing use of modern telecommunication and information technology in securities trading has led to a continuous decline in variable transaction costs across the board. Thus, even small cost differentials may be sufficient to induce investors to shift their activities from one market to the other, and from the official stock exchange to the OTC market in particular. Transaction costs crucially depend on the liquidity of a market. It can therefore be expected that the most liquid market will attract the largest share of secondary market trading in the emerging capital markets of the Visegrád countries. A number of other factors may also determine investors' preferences for one market or another, including market transparency, the types of market participants, and the regulatory framework for market activities.

It can safely be assumed that the large share of OTC trading in the Visegrád countries is closely related to the remaining short-comings in the organisation and infrastructure of the official stock exchanges. A lack of liquidity at the official exchange, investors' desire for a maximum degree of anonymity, and the enhanced trading opportunities through computerisation tend to increase the attractiveness of OTC markets. This does not only hold true for the secondary markets in east-central Europe but is a universal trend observable in more mature markets in OECD countries. In Germany, for instance, the share of bond trading effected outside the official exchanges amounts to about 80%, although exact figures about the extend of off-market trading are unavailable here as in most other countries. Official stock exchanges and regulators all over the world have responded to the increasing popularity of OTC trading through improving information and communication channels, through reducing trading costs, and through the abolition of excessive or inefficient regulation. For the progress of capital markets in central Europe it is therefore of great importance to anticipate these global trends at an early stage in stock market development. Taking into account the experiences in other countries may enable these young stock exchanges to react more rapidly and flexibly than established western bourses to the changing needs of private and institutional investors, both domestic and international. The following section will highlight the wide variety of choices in organising an efficient market place.

15. ORGANISING THE MARKET: OPTIONS AND CHOICES FOR SECURITIES TRADING AT CENTRAL EUROPEAN STOCK EXCHANGES

Rapid structural change has characterised capital market development in recent years. Increasing globalisation, deregulation, automation as well as the growing involvement of professional investors have resulted in fierce competition among the national stock exchanges for international capital flows. The fledgling capital markets of the Visegrád countries will have to adapt to these broader currents if they wish to attract additional funds for corporate investment and public deficit financing. This is all the more important as competition for capital flows does not only take place between the official stock exchanges in different countries but increasingly, as shown in the previous section, between the official exchanges and OTC markets or so-called proprietary trading systems which are tailored to needs of institutional investors.

Questions which have to be answered in constructing an efficient exchange concern the following issues: market organisation (auction or market-maker system), the market frequency (periodic or continuous trading) and the segmentation of the market (Cohen et al., 1986: 1-14).

Given the relatively recent origins of the central European stock exchanges much progress has been achieved in making these markets more efficient. The official stock exchanges in the Visegrád countries are all based on the membership principle. Financial deregulation has allowed an increasing participation of foreign banks and brokerage houses. All four exchanges have rapidly followed the international trend towards computerisation of trading systems. The last market segment with open outcry was closed down at the Budapest Stock Exchange in the second half of 1996 so that trading is now fully electronic everywhere. Further improvements in the electronic trading systems will allow for remote access to the stock exchange enabling brokerage houses in foreign countries to directly take part in local trading. Computerisation has also facilitated the move towards real-time transmission of trading information through specialised information vendors such as Reuters and Telerate. As a result, current stock and bond market prices are now easily obtainable for investors all over the world. Increasing sophistication can also be observed in trading systems and market segmentation, as the following pages will show.

Table 14. Stock Exchanges in the Visegrád Countries

	WSE	BSE	PSE	BSSE
Start of Trading	1991	1990	1993	1993
Members in 1996	37 (June)	75 (Aug,)	109 (Oct,)	47 (Sept,)
Trading fully electronic?	Yes	yes	yes	yes
Trading five day a week?	Yes	yes	yes	yes
	11,00 - 14,30	10,15 - 13,15	11,00 - 14,00	10,30-14,00

Source: PSE, 1996a; 1996d; Ticker, January 1997.

The development of bond trading at the official exchanges has varied considerably from country to country, depending on the regulatory framework, placement practices, types of investors involved as well as the parallel development of the equity market. In the Czech Republic, for example, the market capitalisation of the bond market is still small compared to the equity market, which is mainly due to the mass privatisation process. The Budapest Stock Exchange was up to 1995 dominated by trading government securities. A significant share of Hungarian stocks was traded at foreign exchanges and the domestic equity market remained small and illiquid. Whereas financial institutions dominate most market segments at the exchanges in east-central Europe in Poland's bond market retail investors account for most transactions, at least in the single price auction system.

Table 15. Bond Trading as % of Total Turnover at the Exchange (incl. Free Market) II/1996

WSE	BSE (bonds + T-bills)	PSE	BSSE (QI+II)
31,87	63*	26,55	23

Sources: BSE, 1995a; WSE, 1996a, No, 2; PSE, 1996b, No,2; BSE, 1996a.
* figure for 1995

Table 16. Capitalisation of the Bond Market (at the Exchange)

	1993	1994	1995	1996
BSE* HUF bn	237,0	374,2	418,4	604,2 (Aug,)
PSE CZK bn	--	50,0	87,8	133,2 (Oct,)

Sources; BSE, 1996c; PSE, Online
*T-bonds only

16. MARKET ORGANISATION: AUCTION VERSUS MARKET-MAKER SYSTEM

Price determination in secondary markets can in principle be organised in two different ways. In a quote-driven or dealer market, trading is based on continuous quotation of bid/ask-prices by official market-makers or specialists who stand ready to deal specified amounts on both sides of the market. Alternatively, trading may be organised through an order matching system, where the price for one particular issue determined through an auction procedure and remains fixed over a certain period of time (Cohen et al., 1986: 15-47). Both types of trading systems involve advantages and drawbacks for the development of secondary trading in the Visegrád countries. Official market-makers or unofficial dealers can play a key role in the price discovery and stabilisation process. They actively buy and sell securities for their own account in response to expected short-term fluctuations in price or changes in supply and demand. In doing so they increase the stability and efficiency of capital markets. It has therefore been argued that central and eastern European regulatory authorities should encourage brokers to act as dealers or specialists in local securities markets (Pohl et al., 1995: 11). On the other hand, order-driven markets might be preferable in the early stages of stock market development. In thin and erratic markets, auction systems can provide a better price discovery mechanism and ensure that all orders interact. Efficient quote-driven systems can be difficult to achieve in emerging capital markets because the new brokers may not have adequate capital to act as dealers or market-makers, which would require them to hold inventories of securities (ibid.; OECD, 1991: 19, 50). Moreover, an efficient market-maker system requires a high degree of automation, both as regards trading and quotation procedures and the dissemination of market information, which may not be available in the early stages of secondary market development.

However, auction markets with low turnover may often be faced with the problem that in situations of substantial order imbalances the excess order amount cannot be executed. In this case, it might be desirable to combine the two systems in the sense that the central bank or designated financial institutions act as jobbers or market-makers to take "the other side" of the market (Bröker 1993, 32).

In OECD countries wholesale markets of all kinds, including foreign exchange markets, money markets and government securities markets, are usually organised through market-makers. Less liquid securities are commonly traded through auction markets [25]. Price matching might be appropriate for smaller and immature markets whereas in more sophisticated markets, it may impede the development of the market towards higher turnover and transaction size.

Initially, most trading of securities at the stock exchanges in the Visegrád countries took place through single-price auctions where orders were often accumulated over a number of days. In order to increase liquidity and smooth the price finding process, financial institutions such as banks and brokerage houses were assigned the role of specialists, in particular in government debt. However, in practice these systems did not necessarily work as ultimate demand and supply in secondary bond markets was simply too low to validate the system. With increasing trading activity, in particular in the government bond markets, market-makers started playing a more important role in the price finding process.

The members of the Warsaw Stock Exchange are required to appoint "specialists-brokers" for all publicly traded securities. These are expected to set daily quotations, to intervene to balance the market and support trading volume and market liquidity, and issue contract notes. For the bond market PKO SA is the only authorised specialist-broker. Government securities dealing in the interbank market is based on a system of market-markers. During 1996, 29 brokerage houses and banks had concluded special contracts with the NBP which obliged them to collect buy and sell orders, balance the market, and issue contract notes (Euromoney, 1995; MoF Poland, 1996a;).

At the beginning of 1996 a market-maker system for government securities was established in Hungary. Primary dealers are required to quote bid and ask prices for up to 25 securities they have been assigned. They are divided into two groups: those selling to institutional or wholesale investors and those trading in small lots via a network of branches. Their main functions include subscription of government bonds, accepting orders for purchasing discount T-bills at auctions, acting as a

[25] Market-maker systems are also often used in equity markets which include equities with low turnover. This might suggest that certain features of market-maker systems could also usefully be applied in emerging bond markets with relatively low trading volume (Bröker, 1993: 32).

site of disbursement, a back office and a custodian, and accepting order at the stock exchange (NBH, 1995).

17. MARKET FREQUENCY: PERIODIC VERSUS CONTINUOUS TRADING

Auction markets can be organised in two different ways. In a call market buy and sell orders are accumulated over a specific period and executed simultaneously when a market clearing price is established. In a continuous market orders can be executed whenever bid prices and asking prices cross. The main advantage of call markets is their simplicity of price discovery and the ease of dissemination of information. The timing of an order in a call market is not important because all orders brought to the market before call time are treated equally (Lucas/Schwartz, 1989: 23-4). This was important for markets in central and eastern Europe while communication systems were still being build up.

Continuous markets allow traders to learn and adjust to current market conditions from observation of incoming orders, bid and ask quotations, and volume of transactions. As a result, decisions better reflect current market conditions. Continuous markets also guarantee execution of orders at the market price and trading without delay (Schwartz, 1991: 185-6). Continuous markets enable market participants to execute transactions at any point in time during a trading session. However, higher frequency of trading might result in decreasing market liquidity and thus higher more volatile prices. The accumulation of buy and sell orders over a period in call markets will generally lead to more price stability (Lucas/Schwartz, 1989: 24).

In order to preserve price stability with higher auction frequency, stock exchange may use so-called circuit-breakers, i.e. specific percentage limits on the fluctuation of prices from session to session (Greenwald/Stein, 1988). Central European stock markets have extensively relied on such price limits, which range from 5% to 20%. Such limits, however, should not attempt to prevent fundamental changes in the market clearing price as long as these are not related to panic selling or computer-based trading programmes.

Thin trading and price instability have led most central and eastern European countries to adopt call auctions rather than continuous trading in most market segments. Continuous trading is increasingly being used for the most liquid securities at the exchanges. A stable system of continuous trading is also an important precondition for the introduction of standardised derivatives which is already under way or being envisaged by all four exchanges.

Table 16. Trading Systems at the Stock Exchanges

Poland	Hungary	Czech Republic	Slovak Republic
T-bonds are traded in a single price auction for retail investors and in continuous auctions for institutional investors and banks in which bonds in round lots of PLN 10 000 face value are traded, Continuous trading was computerised in 1995,	Continuous trading was organised by the BSE since its inception in the system of automatic order matching, This system now comprises all securities traded at the Exchange,	Continuous trading, in the so-called KOBOS system, has been established in March 1996 for a small number of liquid securities, The majority of PSE trading takes place through fixed-price auctions but the PSE plans to include more and more securities in KOBOS,	The BSSE organises anonymous trading through both continuous and single price auctions.

18. INTERMEDIATION: DIRECT VERSUS ANONYMOUS TRADING (OTC TRADING AT THE EXCHANGE)

A further consideration that is important in building up secondary trading systems concerns the type of investors which are likely to be active in secondary bond markets. Retail investors, which usually place small orders, have different requirements in terms of market organisation than institutional investors or banks which tend to trade in large blocs of securities. Anonymous auction trading is suitable to match a large number of small orders either through passing them directly through the price-determination process or through pooling small orders at a specified reference price. Institutional investors, on the other hand, often prefer to deal directly with each other to avoid the execution and price risk related to auction trading. In the less developed capital markets of the Visegrád countries, where retail investors are often underrepresented, there exists the danger institutional investors distort prices through their block orders because there may be a lack of sufficient counter-orders. Most of the central European exchanges established special trading sections to separate small transactions from large block trades and direct trading. The latter seem to be vastly more popular, which is a sign for the predominant role of banks and investment funds at central European bond markets.

Table 17. Bond Turnover According to Trading Methods as % of Total Bond Turnover in the Main Market, for 1995

	WSE	BSE	PSE	BSSE
Anonym, auctions	2	100	0,2	0,6
Direct Trades	79	*	97,2	99,4
Block Trades	19		2,6	**

Sources: BSE, 1995a; BSSE, 1995; PSE, 1995a; WSE, 1995a

* Direct trades in Hungary are conducted off-market and not recorded at the BSE.

** Block trading was introduced on the BSSE at the end of 1995.

18.1 Czech Republic

The division of trading into distinct trading groups and methods has gone furthest at the PSE. Securities are traded in three different groups and with five different types of trading: Daily fixing, which is the most widely used method for equity trading, is hardly used for fixed income securities. Following the daily fixing there is the possibility to trade after-session at fixed prices. Bond trading almost exclusively takes place through direct transactions. These can be conducted between the members of the Exchange for blocs of securities larger than CZK 200,000. The participants agree bilaterally about price and volumes which are then registered at the Exchange. The prices agreed are not quoted as the official price of the bond and there are no limit on price fluctuations. Moreover, blocs worth more than CZK 500,000 can also be exchanged in the system of automated block trades. Here anonymous auctions are used to match buy and sell orders. Again, the prices used are not related to the official price. The most recent trading method is continuous trading at variable prices (KOBOS) which is currently used for only a small number of securities. (PSE, 1995b; 1996a; 1996d). Fixed-price auctions, direct trades and bloc trades are used in the listed as well as the free market segments.

Table 18. Bond Trading at the PSE 1996 in CZK mio According to Trading Method

	Q I	Q II	Q III
Central Market	22,7	31,2	23,6
Direct Trades	19 655,5	23 166,8	35 123,6
Bloc Trades	699,7	1 027,8	251,8

Main, Secondary and Free Market
Source: PSE, 1996b.

18.2 Poland

At the WSE the segmentation into direct and anonymous trading is equally important. T-bonds are traded in three different markets. Firstly, on the main market of the WSE in the single-price auction system used for equities. Secondly, on the so-called bond block market where lots of PLN 10,000 are traded continuously at variable prices. And thirdly, bloc trading in off-session transactions by authorised brokers dealing directly with each other. From the introduction of bond trading at the WSE the continuous bloc market was vastly more popular than the single price segment. From 1995 onwards, off-session transactions became the most widely used trading method for government bonds which was largely due to lower commission. In 1995 and 1996 the WSE made additional changes to facilitate off-session bloc trades. The size of blocks were reduced and the limits on price changes were extended (WSE, 1994, 1995; 1995b; Bank Handlowy, 1996b).

Table 19. Bond Trading at the WSE 1996 According to Trading Method in PLN million (*Double Counted)

	QI	QII	QIII
Single price auction	339	456	430
Continuous bloc	732*	667*	2 190
Off-session bloc	1 961*	2 589*	4 552

Source: WSE, 1996a, 1996b.

18.3 Slovak Republic

Trading at the BSSE takes place in three subsystems: Apart from single-price auctions and continuous trading at variable prices, members can execute direct bloc trades using the BSSE electronic trading system. The offers received for bloc trades are not matched automatically but by means of address orders and the prices may vary during the course of the trading session. These systems are used in both the listed and the unlisted markets, (BSSE, 1995).

Table 20. Trading Methods at the BSSE 1996, Listed and Unlisted Bonds, in mio SKK

	Q I	Q II	Q III
Anonymous trades	1 619,2	1 28,0	3 575,8
Direct trades	3 016,0	5 51,5	5 411,3

Sources: BSSE 1996a; 1996b.

18.4 Market Segments: Main Versus Parallel Market

Different markets are not only used to satisfy the needs of particular investor groups but also to facilitate the classification of securities into separate groups in accordance with certain qualitative characteristics. In accordance with certain pre-specified quality criteria the same type of security may be traded in different market segments, for example main market, parallel market and free market.

Different listing requirements, for example with regard to disclosure requirements, capital, and auditing of company accounts, for the respective market segments can reduce uncertainty about the quality of the issue and mitigate distortions related to information asymmetries. Through differentiated listing requirements the stock exchange can thus fulfil an important function of quality certification in order to signal a certain minimum quality of the investment (Gerke, 1991: 2). The admission of securities to the higher market segments will usually depend on:

- a minimum threshold for the prospective market value of the issue,
- the ability of the issuer to provide audited yearly accounts for a certain number of years,
- a minimum percentage of the nominal value of the issue has to be floated through public offering,

- publication of all relevant information in the issuance prospectus, including company status, financial information etc.,
- additional continuous disclosure requirements are to be satisfied through quarterly or semi-annually reports business activities and ad-hoc publication of any new information which may be relevant for the evaluation of the issue.

The specific requirements for admission to the free or unlisted market segment are not usually included in the securities laws but left to self-regulatory bodies, such as the listing committees of the stock exchange or brokerage associations. Usually, the obligations of the issuer are less stringent for the lower market segments in order to attract smaller issues and issues of lesser quality to the stock exchange.

The Visegrád countries have largely followed the conventional segmentation found at Western European bourses into main, parallel and free market. At the *BSE*, the listed market is also called category A while the free or "traded" segment was named category B. This distinction is only relevant for equity trading as all bonds listed at the BSE are included in the listed market. For 1997 the BSE plans the introduction of a horizontal segmentation for equities, government securities, and derivatives with different trading techniques and methods of settlement used in each segment. At the *PSE*, segmentation underwent a fundamental reform in 1995. The previous "listed" market was subdivided into a „main“ and a „secondary“ market. While listing requirements for the main market were raised and a relatively high liquidity threshold was introduced, admission to the secondary market was facilitated. Applications are accepted through a quasi-automatic procedure as long as all required documentation is attached and no member of the PSE Listing Committee raises any objections. The preconditions for registration in the free market are limited to the submission of basic information about the issuer and the permission of the Ministry of Finance to publicly trade the securities (PSE, 1996a). In May 1996 the members of the *WSE* decided upon the introduction of a free market segment in combination with a tightening of the listing criteria for the top markets. There are, however, concerns that the unlisted market segment might not be an attractive place for securities trading due to the absence of issuers' profitability requirements and short accountancy period (The Warsaw Voice, 16.6.1996). Strong competition can be expected from the new organised OTC market. The *BSSE* has operated with three market segments from its inception. In the second tier of the listed category bonds are underrepresented while the unlisted market is the main venue for trading in non-state bonds (BSE, 1995).

Government securities are traded everywhere in the highest market segment and the listing requirements do not usually apply. Special conditions also often exist for municipal bonds. The number of listings of non-state bonds in the higher market segments remains low or zero, apart from the Czech Republic, where the largest issuers applied for listing for prestige reasons.

Table 21. Market Segmentation at the Visegrád Exchanges

	Poland	Hungary	Czech Republic	Slovak Republic
Market segmentation	Main, Parallel and Free Market, Government securities are exclusively traded in the Main Market, No other bonds had been admitted to WSE at the end of 1996,	All fixed income securities are listed in one segment in the spot market, Stocks are divided into the categories A and B, depending on share distribution, capitalisation, and reporting requirements,	Main, Secondary and Free Market, Bonds are mainly traded in the first and third tiers,	Senior and Junior Markets for listed securities, Registered Market for unlisted ones, All newly admitted securities are first traded in the Junior market, Transfer is possible after six months,
Min, issue size	For securities other than shares: PLN 12, 6, 2 million for the Main, Parallel and Free Market, respectively			The minimum volume for both listed segments is SKK 100 mio,
Min, share in public offer	For securities other than shares: 20% for the Main and 10% for the Parallel Market or a minimum of PLN 6,2 (2,2) million,		For issues included in the Main Market a min, of CZK 200 mio, or 20% subject to public offer, CZK 100 mio, or 15% for the Secondary Market, 10% for the Free Market,	
Liquidity threshold	Adequate liquidity and proper course of stock market trading must be ensured,		For the main market: CZK 3000,000 average trading per session in the last five months,	

Table 21. Market Segmentation at the Visegrád Exchanges (Contd.)

	Poland	Hungary	Czech Republic	Slovak Republic
Continuous disclosure requirements			Quarterly reports on business operations for the Main Market, semi-annually for the Secondary Market, No disclosure requirements for the Free Market,	
Financial statements	Issuers applying for listing on the Main Market must disclose audited financial reports for the last three years, For the Parallel and Free Market, the requirement is reduced to two and one year, respectively,			Audited financial statements for the last three years for listing on the Senior Market, or at least one year in the case of the Junior Market,

Sources:
Czech Republic: PSE 1995b, 1996a;
Hungary: FT Finance East Europe, 22 Sept, 1995
Poland: Bank Handlowe, 1996b.
Slovakia: ZEW Questionnaire.

Table 22. Number of Issues Traded at the Exchange (Listed and Free Market) End 1995

	BSE	PSE		WSE		BSSE	
	listed	listed	free	listed	free	listed	free
T-bonds	34 (+50 T-bills)	8		39		15	
Municipal bonds						15	
Corporate bonds	3	12	28			10	15
Shares	42	68	1,648	53	13	19	790
Inv, funds etc,	37					2	

BSE, 1995a; BSSE, 1995; PSE, 1995b; WSE, 1995a.

Table 23. Number of Issues Traded at the Different Segments in 1996

	BSE listed	PSE Main	Sec,	Free	WSE Main	Paral.	BSSE Listed		Unlisted
T-bonds	37 (+ 47 T-bills)	11			35		8		
Municipal bonds		1		11					
Corporate bonds	2	5	1	40			4		15
Shares	44	42	51	1,554	62	13	11	7	921
Inv, funds, Units etc,	31 (investment notes + 1 compensation notes)	2 (Units)	1	39	?				2

Sources:
PSE, October 1996 : PSE 1996c; Information provided by Hypo-Bank CZ a,s.
BSE: 31 August 1996, BSE, 1996c.
BSSE: 31 Sept, 1996
WSE: 31 June 1996, WSE, 1996a, No, 2.

Table 24. Turnover of Bond Trading in the Different Market Sections in 1995 and September 1996 (added in brackets are the number of transactions over the stated period)

	For the whole of 1995	Monthly turnover Sept, 1996
WSE in mio PLN		
continuous trading	3 734,57 (1 115)	1 622,68 (168)
block trades	15 121,74 (1 170)	2 571,51 (64)
single price auction	417,21	215,23 (19 49 7)
PSE in mio, CZK		
Main Market	57 957	18,54**
Secondary Market:	0	0,23
Free Market	11 789	5,10
BSSE in mio, SKK		
Listed Bonds	12 067, 60 (401)	2 101,12 (47)
Unlisted Bonds	270,70 (293)	772,23 (56)
BSE spot market in mio, HUF		
Bonds	77 210* (450)	34 579* (67)
T-bills	81 110* (1 412)	9 436* (49)

Sources: WSE, 1995a; 1996b; BSE 1995a, 1996b; PSE, 1999b; 1996c; BSSE, 1995; 1996b, Sept.
* double counted
** October 1996

19. AVAILABILITY OF INTEREST RATE DERIVATIVES

Derivatives on fixed income underlyings are indispensable instruments for bond portfolio managers in the fixed income markets of OECD countries. In these sophisticated markets interest rate derivatives are used

- as a cost-efficient hedge of bond portfolios against interest rate changes,
- to speculate on the future interest rate, and
- to create synthetic bonds and thus filling gaps in the term structure of circulating bonds.

It is important to differentiate between OTC non-standardised derivative products and highly liquid and standardised derivative contracts that are traded at an exchange, for example at LIFFE in London or DTB in Frankfurt. OTC interest rate swaps are already used in a number of central and eastern European. Nevertheless, the absence of standardised interest rate derivatives remains one of the major differences between the emerging bond markets in east-central Europe and more mature fixed income markets. At the end of 1996, there is an organised market for interest rate futures only at the Budapest Stock Exchange.

Derivatives on Eastern European stocks are more developed than interest rate derivatives. Standardised products on central European share indices are now traded at ÖTOB in Vienna and will be introduced at the local exchanges in central and eastern Europe in the course of 1997. The increasing use of continuous trading methods was an important precondition for derivatives trading as it allows for real-time input of prices. However, as the turnover figures provided above indicate, underlying bond markets are not sufficiently liquid to allow for the development of the kind of highly efficient derivatives markets found in Western countries.

Table 25. Derivatives Trading in the Visegrád Countries

Poland	Hungary	Czech Republic	Slovakia
The amendment to the Polish Securities law of July 1996 opens the way to trading in derivatives, For 1997 the WSE plans to start trading in futures on WIG 20 index and dollar and D-mark exchange rates, No plans exist for the introduction of interest rate derivatives in the near future,	Standardised derivatives have been traded at the BSE since 1995 including futures for three months T-bills and, since Sept, 1996 the BSE added future contracts on the 12-months T-bill, Options trading is planned for the 1st quarter of 1997,	OTC interest rates swaps as well as currency swaps and forwards are available on the Czech market but no standardised derivatives, The PSE plans to introduce trading in options on share titles and the index as well as in interest futures in the first half of 1997,	The Bratislava Options Exchange was closed down by the MoF in 1995, It turned out that the only instruments traded there were one-day forward contracts, The BOB had developed into a direct competitor of the spot market. It is now planned to introduce derivatives trading at the BSSE as well as the RM-S in 1997,

Sources:
For Poland: FT Finance Eastern Europe, WSE Information
For Hungary: BSE Handbook of Futures Trading 1995, Information from BSE, Handelsblatt 27,06,1996.
For CR: PSE Information
For Slovakia: ZEW sources, Handelsblatt 12,11,1996

20. EVALUATION: TRANSPARENCY AND LIQUIDITY

The choices concerning the system of market organisation in the Visegrád countries have to be evaluated in terms of transparency and liquidity.

Price and volume information on bond trading at the exchanges in the Visegrád countries is available through Exchange bulletins, newspapers, television, and partly in real-time through specialised communication systems such as Reuters. In general, the high degree of computerisation of securities trading has facilitated the emanation of trading information and enhanced transparency of the organised market.

The problem with transparency is not so much trading in the official market but the large share of deals conducted in informal markets with limited reporting requirements. In these markets individual transactions may entail significant search costs and may be out of line with prevailing prices. Intransparency in OTC markets in the Visegrád countries has often led to inefficiencies in the price finding process and a lack of reliable information about supply and demand conditions as well as transactions completed. This raises the risk for investors and it may create opportunities for "insiders", i.e. sophisticated traders and dealers who have better access to information, to manipulate trading and earn substantial profits at the expense of less sophisticated and less-informed investors. As secondary markets are essentially markets in information, regulation can improve them by increasing the amount of information they receive, process and disseminate among actual and potential investors (Sylla, 1995).This can be done improving the infrastructure for reporting details on transactions and through instituting reporting requirements for off-market trading.

Concerning the evaluation in terms of liquidity the results are less positive. The existence of at least one liquid bond market sector is crucial for providing reliable pricing information over the whole term structure. In the central and eastern European countries only a small number of bonds are sufficiently liquid to fulfil this function. A large share of outstanding issues are hardly traded. Low liquidity might result form the small volume of bonds outstanding, a small population of investors, or widespread buy-and-hold strategies, i.e. the desire of investors to keep bonds to maturity rather than trade them. Regulators and market organisers may consider supporting liquidity through such measures as improving the dissemination of price information and encouraging market-makers or dealers. Some kind of 'forced' consolidation might also be justified in fragmented markets in the Czech Republic of Hungary. This can be done by integrating sub-markets, requiring notification of the official exchange about off-exchange transitions (put-throughs), and by establishing a centralised depository of securities (Pohl et al., 1995: 2, 8-10).

20.1 Slovak Republic

Transparency in the Slovak bond market is ensured through requirement that all trading takes place in the public market. Market developments are thus easier to monitor than in Hungary and the Czech

Republic where a large proportion of trade takes place off-market. The introduction of the Slovak Bond Index[26] (SDX) in October 1996 should further increase transparency and enable investors to better follow developments in the market. The main impediment to the development of the fixed income market in Slovakia is the lack of liquidity. This is due in part to a lack of primary offerings (see above) and the lack in the choice of bonds. Thus bond-holders (mainly commercial banks), who might otherwise be inclined to restructure their assets, prefer to hold their portfolio to maturity rather than trading it (VUB, 1996b).

Activity in the Slovak secondary market started picking up in 1995 when an increased demand in both primary and secondary market was met by higher number of new issues. Bond trading at the BSSE used to be heavily dominated by government bonds, the share of which in total bond trading reached 92.4% in 1995. Yearly or quarterly turnover figures conceal a high degree of volatility in secondary trading volumes. During 1995, secondary trading in government bonds was characterised by large fluctuations in response to issuance activity in the primary market, the level of liquidity in the banking sector, interest rates on the interbank market, as well as legal changes (in particular the new law requiring centralisation of trading). Four transactions conducted in December 1995 in one government bond issue accounted for almost half of the yearly turnover (NBS, 1995).

Trading in corporates, and in particular the issues of VUB-bank and the steel conglomerate CSZ has increased significantly during 1996 but turnover of other non-state bonds remains modest. Since the beginning of 1996 the rise in bond trading at the BSSE has surpassed growth in equity trading which was initially due to growth in transactions involving unlisted bonds. Subsequently, the listed segment reported higher turnover caused by more active trading in a small number of government bonds.

Table 26. Trading in Government Bonds on the BSSE in 1995 in mio. SKK

Jan.	Feb.	Mar.	Apr.	May	Jun.	Jul.	Aug.	Sep.	Oct.	Nov.	Dec.
3	0,5	1 556	2 200	67	22	21	360	649	1 001	249	4 916

Source: NBS, 1995

Table 27. Bond Trading at the BSSE in 1996, Anonymous Trades

	Jan.	Feb.	Mar.	Apr.	May	Jun.	Jul.	Aug.	Sep.
listed	189,2	839,1	210,2	183,6	388,4	542,7	625,9	633,9	1 343,8
No, of tr,	*9*	*11*	*20*	*14*	*24*	*22*	*21*	*22*	*25*
unlisted	68,9	226,6	32,5	121,5	58,4	196,9	57,9	272,8	181,8
No, of tr,	*10*	*6*	*14*	*18*	*20*	*10*	*19*	*18*	*15*

Sources: BSSE, 1996a ; 1996b.

[26] The index comprises all government and other bonds traded on the listed market and a selected number of bonds from the registered market. The values for government and non-state bonds are calculated seperately. SDX is compounded of current prices pulus accrued interes and the cumulative interest payments starting from a certain reference date (VUB, 1996b).

Table 28. Bond Turnover at the BSSE in 1996, Listed and Unlisted Bonds, mio SKK

	July	August	September
government bonds	826,7	1 407,2	1 713,8
non-state bonds	2 272,6	1 607,0	1 728,9

BSSE, 1996b.

Table 29. Volume of Bond Trades in the Secondary Market, in USD mio.

	1995	1996
Government	377,00	322,64
Corporate	111,11	389,95
Banking	26,33	252,43
Municipal	4,27	6,49
Total	518,72	971,51

Source: VUB, 1997b.

20.2 Czech Republic

The PSE is slowly developing into a more actively used market for bond trading. Until the end of the year 1995, daily prices were quoted at the PSE only for some of the T-bonds and one corporate bonds. Illiquidity in most segments resulted in relatively large price movements in response to small orders. During 1996 liquidity - especially in corporate bond trading - has been increasing rapidly and daily direct trades [27] registered at the stock exchange exceed $ 10 million at the end of the year. The value of bonds traded rose from about CZK 70 bn in 1995 to CZK 114 bn in the first eleven months of 1996. However, the fact that bonds are almost exclusively traded directly between investors means that pre-trade transparency is low. Foreign investors were active participants in the secondary bond markets in 1996 whereas among domestic investors, in particular investment funds and local banks, buy-and-hold strategies are widespread (Euromoney, 1996c). At the PSE turnover remains heavily concentrated in a few corporate and bank bonds. In the third quarter of 1996, the titles of CEZ, Komercni Banka, and CSOB accounted for over half of total turnover in bonds trading in the Main and Secondary Markets.

The main problem of the Czech market does not seem to be liquidity but a lack of transparency due to the fragmentation of the market and the widely-criticised deficiencies in official oversight. [28] The large share of direct trades outside the PSE without reporting requirements has often led to inefficient pricing with multiple prices for the same instruments. The Securities Centre, where most trading takes place, does not continuously report information on prices, buyers and sellers but only publishes weekly average prices of OTC deals.

---

[27] As indicated above, the share of transactions carried out in automated trading is negligible so that it can be said that bond trading only takes place through direct trades.

[28] Note that fragmentation and irregular practices mainly affect the equity market. Here the division of trading activity between PSE, PM-S, OTC and the grey market and the dominace of investment funds has resulted in a loss of trust on the part of domestic and forein investors (see, e.g. FT 6.12.1996; BCE Dec. 1996).

Improvements in terms of transparency and stability in the Czech capital are to be expected in the course of 1997 due to reforms in the institutional and regulatory framework of the securities market. Polish rules and regulations and practices at the WSE are partly used as a model as the Polish capital market is widely regarded as the best regulated in the region. An independent Securities Commission will take over from the Ministry of Finance as the mains regulatory and supervisory body for the Czech capital market in mid-1997. The new agency will inter alia be responsible for regulating and monitoring the OTC market. In the interim period a Securities Office will be operating to monitor capital market development and to gradually decrease the role of the Ministry of finance in the Czech securities market. Moreover, transparency of OTC trading will be increased when from the first of February onwards the prices of all transactions conducted off-exchange through the Securities Centre will be reported (PSE, 1996c; PSE on-line; Neue Züricher Zeitung 17.12.1996).

Table 30. Bond Trading at the PSE 1996 in CZK mio (rounded figures), Main, Secondary and Free Market

Jan.	Feb.	Mar.	Apr.	May	Jun.	Jul.	Aug.	Sep.	Oct.	Nov.
6 758	6 047	7 131	7130	9 341	7 755	9 486	13 309	12 604	23 864	17 522

Source: Figures supplied by PSE.

20.3 Hungary

In Hungary, secondary trading takes place almost exclusively in government bonds as there are no markets for private sector debt instruments[29]. Although Hungary's primary state paper market is liquid with a large amount of government paper issued on a regular basis, secondary trading is concentrated in short maturities and remains thin at the longer end of the market. Liquidity in the government bond market has increased considerably during 1996 which was partly due to the new system of primary dealers. Average daily turnover in government bonds at the BSE increased from HUF 310 million in 1995 to HUF 1.69 billion in 1996. According to the statistics of the government debt primary dealers, financial institutions, brokers and institutional investors account for the large majority of transactions. In the third quarter of 1996, private and foreign investors made up 3% and 1% of government securities turnover, respectively (AKK, 1996c).

Trading in the secondary market for government securities more or less follows tendencies in the primary markets as the amounts of bids rejected at the auctions translate into demand on the secondary market. Turnover is also dependent on the performance of the stock market. The spectacular rise of the Hungarian stock market during 1996, combined with a significant decrease in the yields on government securities, drove

[29] Only three transactions took place in the non-state bond section of the BSE in the course of 1996 (BSE, 1997).

both small and large investors from the bond to the equity market (NBH, 1995; Euromoney, 1996c).

Up-to-date information about BSE trading is easily available through the BSE Information Systems, Teletext as well as real time information vendors and weekly and monthly publications. The publication of the T-bill index, DWIX, allows investors to monitor the development of the short-end of the market. DWIX usually moves in response to the liquidity position and the lending opportunities of commercial banks and shows strong correlation with the movements in the foreign exchange markets (NBH, 1995). In terms of transparency, the large share of transactions conducted outside the BSE represents a problem as there are no official reporting requirements. The situation is likely to change in the short to medium for two reasons. First, improvements in the BSE trading environment, in particular the shortening of the settlement period and the introduction of a special segment for bond trading, might attract a significant share of bond transactions back to the official stock exchange. Second, the amended Securities Law, which will enter into force the 1st January 1997, envisages the re-admission of banks to securities trading at the BSE, which should result in greater use of the public market for transactions among this important investor group. The amendment will also require all issuers of public bonds offered after the 31st December 1997 to apply for listing at the BSE.

Table 31. Bond Trading at the BSE in 1996, Turnover on Market Value in HUF million (Double Counted)

	Apr.	May	Jun.	Jul.	Aug.	Sept.
T-bonds	16 236	10 762	27 976	27 976	7 688	34 579
Corporates	41	0	531	531	0	0
T-bills	1 307	3 840	5 131	5 131	6 208	9 436

Source: BSE, 1996b.

Table 32. Cash Turnover at Market Value, HUF billion (Double Counted)

	1991	1992	1993	1994	1995	1996, Jan-Aug,
T-bonds	0,30	12,36	73,38	53,89	77,16	178,91
Corporates	0	0	0	0,01	0,05	0,57
T-bills		15,06	85,00	81,22	81,11	36,39

Source: BSE, 1996c.

20.4 Poland

In the Polish secondary market for government paper only the short-term maturities are liquid. Apparently the jobber system for government bonds does not work in practice but there are market-makers active in the short-term T-bill market. (Euromoney, 1996c). A shortage of alternative instruments induces Polish banks, the most important local investor group, to hold bonds to maturity rather than trade them. Development of a liquid secondary market for treasury bonds was originally hindered by the fact that a large proportion of T-bonds issued in the early years of reform were non-marketable. The share of the these non-negotiable instruments in total outstanding treasury securities has slowly diminished from 45.6% at the end of 1992 to 35.6% at the end of 1995. Treasury bills are still dominant in the marketable section and they are not listed at the WSE but are traded through the interbank market. Only some 20% of all treasury securities were therefore tradable at the WSE in 1995. As these bonds are concentrated mainly in the portfolio of large banks, the infrequent transactions are usually concluded for large blocks. Erratic changes in turnover have therefore characterised the Polish secondary market. Moreover, the largest share is traded in off-session and interbank transaction which further reduces the transparency of the market situation. Liquidity in the market for non-state paper remains close to zero due to the absence of a organised secondary market, a lack of choice of tradable instruments, and the predominance of private placements. CP is regarded as an attractive short-term investment opportunity and is usually held to maturity. Municipal bonds are privately placed and prices are only quoted by the issuing agent, if at all.

Significant changes can be expected in the course of 1997 which are suitable to increase transparency and liquidity in the Polish bond market. It is expected that the organisation of the OTC market will create the possibility to trade non-state debt instruments which are not listed on the WSE. The WSE itself plans to improve its information infrastructure by introducing real-time price information through Reuters and Telerate before the end of 1998.

Table 33. Bond Turnover Value WSE 1996, PLN million

Jan.	Feb.	Mar.	Apr.	May	Jun.	Jul.	Aug.	Sept.
661	636	233	1 112	640	481	838	1 928	4 409

Sources: WSE 1996a ; 1996b.

21. INTEGRATION OF CENTRAL EUROPEAN BOND MARKETS INTO THE INTERNATIONAL CAPITAL MARKET

The general trend toward the internationalisation and integration of capital markets started to extend to non-OECD countries in the late 1980s. The Visegrád countries are following this international trend through facilitating access for foreign investors to their domestic capital markets as well as issuing securities in international bond markets. The relatively rapid integration into international capital markets entails clear advantages for financial market reform and the transition process more generally.

International investors provide an additional source of budget and corporate financing which is desirable as long as domestic debt markets are thin.

The integration of the domestic bond markets into international capital markets links domestic interest rates to international interest rates and it increases the efficiency of the international allocation of resources.

Foreign investors can bring liquidity and expertise to domestic bond markets in central and eastern Europe. It can also be argued that the views of foreign investors are the best test of the performance of an emerging market because of their wide experience and high standards.

Moreover, external capital inflows can initiate a virtuous cycle when the involvement of foreign financial institutions enhances the efficiency and sophistication of the domestic market. The improved market environment as well as increasing familiarity with these markets can, in turn, attract additional investment flows (Feldmann/Kumar, 1995: 189).

International and Euro-bond issues may serve as a yardstick to measure the judgement of international markets and investors, not only with regard to the functioning of domestic securities markets but about the transition process more general. International bond market are more liquid and transparent than the fledgling markets of the Visegrád countries and may thus react more quickly to changes in the creditworthiness of central European borrowers.

On the other hand, foreign portfolio investment in the transition economies of central and eastern Europe entails certain risks that need to be balanced against actual and potential benefits. The problems associated with excessive reliance on external debt financing have become painfully obvious in the aftermath of the Mexican debt crisis. Portfolio capital is, by its nature, more liquid than foreign direct investment. Portfolio capital flows may thus put considerable stress on foreign exchange reserves because investors are able to sell securities rapidly in large volumes and repatriate capital. Securities markets may also rapidly transmit external shocks which simply reflect the mood in international capital markets and are not related to the domestic economy of the receiving country. Shifts in the portfolios of industrialised countries, even if small from the perspective of the investing country, may result in inflows and outflows that are large in relation to the size of the recipients capital market. Abrupt changes in market sentiment can induce a large-scale reversal of capital inflows and lead to sharp corrections in market prices. These may have serious implications for systemic stability of the financial system and the real economy. As experience in several industrialised countries has shown, a sharp downturn in asset prices can have significant adverse effects on the banking sector and, through negative effects on wealth and confidence, can lead to a retrenchment in consumption and investment spending (Feldmann/Kumar, 1995; Pardy, 1992).

22. FOREIGN PARTICIPATION IN DOMESTIC BOND MARKETS

The attractiveness of central and eastern European bond markets for international investors depends on a variety of factors that do not only include financial returns but encompass the whole spectrum of political, economic and financial reforms and related matters of market efficiency as well as legal and political stability. The specific factors that determine the relative attractiveness of central European securities markets for international investors can be divided into three groups:

Institutional efficiency. The organisation and functioning of the market infrastructure should meet the standards required by international investors. This includes the reliability of order handling and execution, custodian services as well as the clearing and settlement process. (Pohl et al., 1995: 18; Bröker, 1993: 26).

Financial benefits. Yields on domestic bonds should be sufficiently attractive as compared with those attainable in other internationally accessible bond markets. Potential gains from portfolio diversification will also be taken into account.

Market environment. This relates to the broader environment in which the investment takes place and includes all aspects of sovereign risk, including the political and legal framework. of the receiving country. Likewise, the macroeconomic environment, including inflation, GDP growth, and exchange rate stability weighs heavily in investors' decisions to commit funds to emerging market economies. Of particular importance are issues of taxation as well as foreign exchange rules and restrictions on capital and profit repatriation.

The problems of creating an *efficient market infrastructure* have been extensively discussed in the preceeding sections. As far as *financial benefits* are concerned, the attractiveness of central European bonds does not only depend on the macroeconomic environment in the respective countries and the risk premia which have to be paid by individual issuers but also on economic conditions in world markets and developments in other industrialised countries as well as emerging markets. Changes in international interest rates have been found to be an important factor determining capital inflows to emerging markets (Dooley et al., 1996). In this respect central and eastern European markets have benefited from the slow-growth, low-inflation environment in the OECD countries during 1995 as institutional investors were looking for high yielding securities. This dependence on the external environment implies the danger of a sudden drying up of capital should interest rates in the major industrialised countries start rising again with a new business cycle upturn. However, it seems that the inverse correlation between the level of interest rates in major industrialised countries and the demand for emerging market debt is no longer a close one. US interest rate increases in the first quarter of 1996 failed to have a major impact on issuing volumes from emerging markets (BIS, 1996: 23).

Furthermore, portfolio investment in central and eastern Europe crucially depends on strategies of diversification of large institutional investors. Diversification away from Latin American assets after the Mexican debt crisis has re-directed significant capital flows towards eastern Europe. Fixed income securities from the region suitable instruments for the diversification of global portfolios, in particular for US investors because central and eastern European fixed income markets are not highly correlated with American bond markets (ING Barings, 1996).

To discuss all the factors subsumed under the heading of *market environment* would be beyond the framework of the present paper. A few issues shall be highlighted which seem of particular importance for foreign investors. Traditionally, administrative restrictions and capital controls have been the most important obstacle to foreign portfolio investment in many emerging market economies. The dangers of premature capital account liberalisation in the face of structural impediments to market efficiencies have been widely discussed. The lessons to be learnt from the financial crises experienced by other emerging market economies in Latin America and South East Asia include that financial liberalisation can have destabilising consequences if structural problems in the financial sector remain unresolved (Fanelli/McMahon, 1996; Verbeek, 1996; Vos, 1995). Central and eastern European countries have originally adopted a cautious approach with regard to capital account liberalisation and international portfolio investment.

Foreign access to national bond markets was restricted for three reasons: First, despite liberal rhetoric, aversion against foreign capital inflows and surrendering market control and profits to foreign banks is still widespread in central and eastern Europe. Second, monetary authorities in the Visegrád countries are wary of short-term "speculative" capital inflows and their consequences for internal price stability and exchange rates. Third, those countries already burdened with a high stock of external debt were reluctant to allow further increases in external borrowing. The move away from external debtors is seen as crucial in order to enhance the standing in international markets and reduce debt servicing and borrowing costs. On the other hand, convertibility of the domestic currency and, more generally, a liberalised financial environment is a precondition for attracting foreign capital, and foreign portfolio investment in particular. All four Visegrád countries have therefore already introduced full currency convertibility in accordance with Article VIII of the IMF statutes and have gradually liberalised access to their domestic capital markets. [30] The move towards capital account liberalisation should also be seen in the context of accession to the OECD which entailed a pledge on the part of the new members to remove all remaining restrictions on capital account transactions before the end of the century in compliance with the OECD Codes of Liberalisation.

In 1996, foreign investment in bond markets is almost completely liberalised in all four countries. Some restrictions remain for foreign investment in Hungarian short-term securities for the above-mentioned reasons. Apart from administrative restrictions, a lack of reliable custodian services seems to have been a major obstacle to foreign portfolio investment in the earlier stages of reform (Pohl et al, 1995: 18). Consequently, the accessibility of domestic bond markets was closely related to reforms of the banking system and the rules governing foreign banking activities in the countries of the region. Through sufficient progress in banking reform and especially the increasing role of foreign financial institutions in the financial systems of the Visegrád countries foreign investors can now rely on a system of efficient custodian services in these financial markets. The free repatriation of profits, another precondition for foreign portfolio investment, is guaranteed in all four Visegrád countries.

Taxation of investment income hardly affects potential foreign investors directly since the Visegrád countries have concluded double taxation agreements with a large number of industrialised countries. Domestic tax systems do, however, indirectly affect the attractiveness of different bond market sections for non-residents. The most striking examples are the underrepresentation of foreign investors in the Czech and Slovak markets for tax-free government bonds and widespread practices of "bond washing" involving foreign investors in the taxable section (see section 4.4).

[30] Compared to other emerging makets, particularly in South East Asia, the Visegrád countries were amazingly quick in opening their domestic bond markets to foreign investors (Compare Euromoney, February 1995, and OECD, 1993 for the strategies of the Asian NICs).

Table 34. Convertibility of Central and Eastern European Currencies

	Poland	Hungary	Czech Republic	Slovak Republic
Convertibility in accordance with Art. VII of the IMF Statutes and capital account liberalisation,	Since 10 Dec, 1995**, Some capital account restrictions remain, Full convertibility until 2000,	Since January 1996,* investment, Capital account restrictions remain for residents,	Since 1 October 1995**; complete liberalisation of capital account planned until 2000,	Since 1 October 1995, Restrictions remain for capital transactions with foreign countries,
Remaining restrictions on foreign portfolio investment in domestic bond markets,	Foreign investors can purchase all debt securities without restrictions[31],	Foreign investors can purchase Treasury securities with an initial maturity of more than one year through participation in primary or secondary markets, The market for non-state debt instruments (currently basically commercial paper) is not yet open to foreign investors[32],	There are no restrictions on the quantity or value of securities that can be held by foreigners,	There are no restrictions on foreign investment and trading in the Slovak bond market,

Sources: Euromoney, 1996b.
Information provided by the NBP; NBH; NBS.
* Full convertibility of CA transactions before that date for non-residents and portfolio investment.
** High degree of de-facto liberalisation prior to that date.

The unstable macro-economic environment was a major obstacle to foreign portfolio investment in the early stages of reform. Initially, high inflation rates did not allow issuance of long-term fixed coupon bonds. The risk of depreciation of the local currency had to be balanced against nominal high interest rates of domestic assets. Moreover, for investors of hard currency countries, effective yields were too volatile to render investment in central European bonds viable (Dresdner, 1994). Exchange rate regimes and internal stability in the Visegrád countries have become more suitable to attract foreign portfolio investment. All the Visegrád countries utilise the exchange rate as an external anchor to speed up disinflation and strengthen confidence in the stabilisation process. The high share of D-mark and US dollar in the currency baskets guarantees a certain degree of stability for Western European and US investors. On the

[31] One-year bonds issued through NBP auctions were only made available to foreign investors in May 1996.

[32] In 1997 foreigners will be allowed to purchase bonds issued by investment grade non-state entities (Euromoney, 1996c).

other hand, exchange rate fluctuations between dollar and D-mark can entail currency risk for these investor groups. Due to continuous domestic price increases (partly exacerbated through large capital inflows since 1994/5) all countries have experienced real appreciation of their currencies. Given the fact that the central European countries all face growing trade deficits, the costs of the exchange rate regime are sometimes regarded as too high. The central banks of the Czech Republic, Slovakia, and Poland have attempted to discourage short-term capital inflows by widening the fluctuation bands of their respective currencies in 1996. These measures also had more or less temporary effects on the attractiveness of domestic bond markets. [33]

Table 35. Exchange Rate Regimes in the Visegrád Countries

	Poland	Hungary	Czech Republic	Slovakia
Exchange Rate Regime	Crawling peg with a monthly devaluation rate of 1% which is likely to be reduced to 0,7 - 0,8% in 1997,	Crawling peg with a monthly devaluation of 1,2%(to be reduced to 1% around mid-1997)	Pegged,	Pegged,
Basket	35%D-Mark, 45% US-dollar, 20% French franc, Swiss franc, pound sterling,	30% US-dollar and 70 % ECU, to be replaced by D-mark 1 January 1997,	65% D-Mark and 35% US-dollar,	60% D-Mark and 40% US-dollar,
Fluctuation Band	+/- 7%	+/- 2,25 %	+/- 7,5%	+/- 5%, widened to +/- 7% 1,1,1997

Sources: Euromoney, 1996b; VUB, 1997a.

A certain pattern can be distinguished in the way emerging markets attract overseas capital. The first step is often privatisation of large enterprises. Depending on the rules governing foreign direct investment, this is a suitable way to attract both international equity investment and project finance from foreign banks. The development of a domestic stock market is the next step, accompanied by the sale of equity or equity-linked financial instruments abroad. Finally, the opening up of domestic capital markets and wider access to the international debt markets mark the full integration into international capital markets (FT, 13.11.1991). Similarly, a country that wants to attract foreign capital typically has to progress through several tiers of investors (OECD, 1994a). Diversification of the sources of foreign capital is closely related to the country's standing in international markets as measured by country

[33] In the Czech Republic, for instance, the widening of the fluctuation bands of the crown in February 1996 had considerable impact on the domestic bond market while the market for equity was largely unaffected. The interbank market recorded a decline, especially for bonds with shorter maturities as investors tried to shed these assets from their portfolios. Spreads of quoted bonds widened temporarily which expressed widespread uncertainty about future prices and a diminishing interest in fixed coupon securities. State bonds were affected relatively little by the price decline because there are in general not held by foreign investors (CNB, 1996a).

ratings. The first international investors to show an interest in reform countries are normally specialised emerging market funds or high yield bond funds. These specialised institutions are apt to accept a considerable share of high-yield, high-risk paper for speculative purposes. Conventional institutional investors are usually restricted in the amount of non-investment grade paper they can hold in their portfolios. Since it is in the interest of the Visegrád countries to move fast to the attraction of more traditional investors with a longer time horizon, obtaining an investment grade rating from one of the internationally recognised rating agencies was an important step. Such an award equally important as a precondition for issuing bonds in the Euro-markets.

Table 36. Country Ratings in November 1996

Ratings	S&P	Moody's	IBCA
Czech R,	A	Baa1	A-
Poland	BBB-	Baa3	BBB
Slovakia	BBB-	Baa3	BBB-
Hungary	BB+	Baa3	BBB-

Source: Business Central Europe, November 1996.

Table 37. Ratings of Long-term Foreign Currency Debt, December 1996

	S&P	Moody's	IBCA
Czech R,	A (stable)	Baa1	A-
Poland	BBB- (stable)	Baa3	BBB
Slovakia	BBB-	Baa3	
Hungary	BBB- (stable)	Baa3	BBB

Source: Raiffeisen Zentralbank, 1996c.

Rapid success in monetary stabilisation and the establishment of a capital market infrastructure in conformity with western standards have increased the attractiveness of the Visegrád bond markets. As explained above, the international environment was also conducive at the time when the these countries began opening their capital markets to foreigners. On the whole, however, foreign portfolio investment in central and eastern European bond markets has remained modest. Booming stock markets in the regions have attracted the bulk of foreign portfolio investment as they offer higher returns, liquidity and transparency through widely published stock market indices. For fixed income investors, Brady bonds and the international bond issues of Latin American borrowers were more attractive for similar reasons.

22.1 Czech Republic

Discriminatory tax policy has made the government bond market rather unattractive to foreigners. Access to the potentially more interesting market for short-term T-bills used to be restricted for monetary policy reasons. Foreign investors are active participants in the corporate bond markets. In particular bank bonds proved attractive to foreigners because of high yields and sufficient liquidity in the secondary market. The Czech banking crisis of 1996 has to a certain extent undermined confidence in this market sector. The issues of the five largest banks are still in high demand by foreigners but caution prevails with regard to bonds issued by smaller financial institutions [34]. Corporate bonds issued by the largest Czech enterprises are also popular with foreign investors, in particular because they partly offer higher returns than bank bonds to compensate investors for a lack of liquidity. The bills issued by the National Property Fund are an attractive alternative to T-bills at the liquid short end of the market as they traditionally offer higher returns than the short-term securities offered by the Ministry of Finance or the CNB. At the close of September 1996, foreigners held CZK 23.9 bn worth of Czech securities, of which 65% were shares, 19% enterprise bonds, and 16% state bonds.

The Czech Republic encountered problems with large scale foreign capital inflows in 1995. Of USD 8.4 bn which flowed in during 1995, USD 1.5 bn were accounted for by portfolio investment and speculative inflows (Euromoney, 1996b). The inflows were welcome from the point of view of financing the current account deficit and they are regarded as politically uncontroversial due to the low level of external indebtedness. However, rapidly increasing foreign exchange reserves increased pressure on the internal money supply and thus forced the central bank and the Ministry of Finance to issue some expensive short-term debt instruments to reduce liquidity in the banking system. Revaluation pressure on the Czech crown is considered problematic given the growing current account deficit of the Czech Republic. Existing restrictions on short-term foreign investment were partly undermined by capital inflows shifting from short to medium and long-term investments. The attractiveness of short-term investment in the Czech koruna was diminished through the central bank's decision to widen the fluctuation band of the currency from +/- 0.5% to +/- 7.5%. It can be expected that the Czech domestic bond market will remain attractive for foreign investors in 1997 because Czech bonds have proved the least volatile in the region while offering good returns with low sovereign risk.

22.2 Hungary

Under the Hungarian Act on the Investment of Foreigners portfolio investment has been gradually liberalised but some restrictions on foreign access remain in 1996. Foreign investors only have access to the market for Treasury security, they are not allowed to purchase non-state debt instruments. Given Hungary's relatively high stock of external indebtedness the NBH is unwilling to see private sector borrowers raise additional funds abroad. Moreover, as the monetary authorities seek to limit the amount of speculative capital entering the country, there are restrictions on foreign purchases of T-bills with an initial maturity of less

[34] Due to the high share the government still holds in the largest financial instittutions it is widely assumed that these enjoy an implicit state guarantee. The Czech financial market remains heavily concentrated with the largest banks accounting for the majority of financial assets. Fierce compeition for market shares among smaller banks induced them to take undue credit risk.

than one year. The government is trying to channel both domestic and foreign demand into longer maturities and to make the domestic bond market generally more attractive to foreign investors. Special bond issues were reserved for foreign investors while others were only accessible for Hungarian residents. The latter would normally carry more favourable interest rates. Although Hungary is the main recipient of foreign direct investment in the region and has an impeccable debt servicing record, foreign investors are still largely uninterested in the domestic bond market. This lack of demand was partly due to the fact that the country up to the end of 1996 lacked an investment grade rating by one of the major international rating agencies. However, low yields and the exchange rate policy of continuous depreciation also played a part in rendering the Hungarian market relatively unattractive. At the end of 1995, foreign investors held 3.13% of all outstanding deficit financing government securities; by August 1996, their share had fallen to 2.47% (AKK, 1996c).

In connection with Hungary's admission to the OECD the government has liberalised long-term capital transactions with OECD countries. The Securities Law will be amended again in 1997 to bring it in line with EU legislation. Foreign investors' participation in the domestic bonds markets will then be facilitated while foreign participation in Hungarian enterprises through share-holdings would be restricted. Corporate bonds with investment grade ratings will be accessible for foreigners in 1997 (Euromoney, 1996b, 1996c).

22.3 Poland

Polish short-term government securities have attracted considerable attention from international investors since 1994 due to high returns and the relative external stability of the zloty. Foreigners bought 7.9% of all T-bills on the primary market in 1995 (NBP, 1995). The increased demand for zloty paper highlighted growing confidence in the stability of the Polish financial system, the Polish currency as well as the political development of this emerging market. However, the surge in capital inflows added to the NPB's foreign exchange reserves, which had already reached record levels, and increased the zloty money supply and thus inflationary pressure. (Handelsblatt 4.6.1996, FAZ 20.2.1996). There were concerns in 1996 that access to the zloty T-bill market might be restricted to safeguard monetary stability. The NBP regards administrative controls on foreign portfolio investment as a last-resort device but would not rule out their use altogether. In general, it is in line with the process of financial deregulation that central banks in eastern Europe have relied on market-oriented measures, such as the widening of fluctuation band rather than capital account restrictions.

Like other central banks in the region the NBP faces a dilemma with regard to its monetary policy stance. Although high internal inflation make a raising of interest rates seem desirable this is ruled out by the danger of attracting significant short-term capital flows. The resulting strengthening of the currency would entail competitive disadvantages for the export sector. Similar to the monetary authorities in the neighbouring countries the NBP uses reserve requirements as a tool for tightening monetary policy in addition to interest rate policy.

Excess demand for zloty-bills resulted in a sharp increase in T-bill prices and a drop in yields, which has reduced the attractiveness of this investment. The widening of the fluctuation band also contributed to making investment in short-term debt securities less attractive. According to the Ministry of Finance, the share of foreign investors in the domestic market for Treasury securities fell back to less than one per cent towards the end of 1996. The planned reduction in devaluation rates from 12.7% in 1996 to about 9% in 1997 would again increase the attractiveness of the Polish bond market with the possible result of a resurgence of speculative capital flows.

22.4 Slovak Republic

Foreigners are allowed to purchase and sell securities denominated in Slovak crowns under the provisions of the country's Foreign Exchange Act. On the primary market for government paper foreigners need to be represented by one of the licensed institutions. In the case of non-state issues the lead-managing bank can acquire bonds for foreigners. In the secondary market, buy and sell orders have to be executed by a member of the BSSE. Each foreign investor needs to open an account with the Slovak Securities Centre to effect transfer of securities and cash settlement. Despite the openness of the Slovak bond market, foreign involvement in the market has remained modest in 1996, partly because of widespread concerns about intransparency in the market and political risk. Compared to other emerging bond markets in the region, the Slovak bond market is regarded as too small and insufficiently liquid to attract much attention from foreign investors. As in the Czech Republic, the discriminatory tax treatment has made the government debt market unattractive to foreign investors. According to the NBS, foreigners held a mere 0.02 % of government bonds outstanding in December 1996. Foreign portfolio investment in the bank and enterprise sector is more active but privatisation insecurity turned out to be an impeding factor.

Table 38. Foreign Investment in the Slovak Enterprise Sector

	1995 mio, SKK mio, USD	1996 (Jan. - Sept,) mio, SKK mio, USD
Foreign direct investment	4 281142	2 937 96,4
Portfolio investment in equity	2 58086,7	0
Portfolio investment in fixed income securities	662,2	2056,7

Source: National Bank of Slovakia

23. INTERNATIONAL BOND MARKETS: GREATER CHOICE AND ENHANCED COMPETITION

As long as foreign demand for domestic bond issues remains modest, access to international capital markets is an important source of refinancing for east-central European borrowers. In addition to syndicated loans, Euro-bonds and EMTNs (Euro medium term notes) can offer access to international funding. Euro-bonds are typically debt instruments denominated in a major international currency which are issued outside the borrowers home country through an international syndicate of financial institutions. Although Euro-bonds are, for technical reasons, listed at the stock exchanges in Luxembourg or London, they are mainly traded over the counter with settlement taking place through one of the large specialised clearing houses (CEDEL, Euroclear).

For capital raisers in the Visegrád countries, the international bond markets may bring a number of advantages as supplements or even substitutes of domestic capital markets:

As long as governments and corporate entities in central and eastern Europe do not have access to broad and liquid bond markets, the Euro-bond markets offer a real alternative for raising funds for investment and restructuring.

Governments may benefit from cheaper funding through the Euro-markets if they are faced with high interest rates in domestic capital markets due to a lack of credibility.

Lower borrowing costs in international markets allow government to restructure existing external debt and thus reduce debt servicing costs.

The Euromarkets offer a high degree of liquidity and flexibility. Euro-bonds allow issuing agents to easily vary the terms of the issue, such as currency of denomination and structure. Rigidities in domestic markets as well as administrative restrictions on financial contracts and taxation, including withholding taxes, stamp duties etc., are most easily avoided by launching an issue in a different market (Benzi, 1992: 19-20).

It could thus be said that the opportunity for central European borrowers to raise funds in off-shore markets is beneficial not only because these provide additional sources of capital but also because they introduce an important element of competition for domestic bond markets. On the other hand, the threats to financial and monetary stability which emanate from large foreign investment in domestic securities markets may be exacerbated through large-scale use of the more volatile international bond markets. In more advanced capital markets there is an increasing degree of substitutability between domestic, international and Euro-bond markets due to financial liberalisation and enhanced swap facilities. It may therefore become more difficult for national monetary authorities to regulate and manage domestic securities markets.

The Visegrád countries (apart from Hungary which has been present since the 70s, see below) entered the Euromarkets at a time of record demand for emerging market debt when international investors had regained confidence after the 1995 Mexican peso crisis. The underlying reasons for this resurgence of demand were a mixture of improving economic fundamentals and international liquidity. Against the background of low interest rates, low growth and stable inflation rates in OECD countries, international investors' interest in higher yields offered by emerging market assets revived. Demand for central and eastern European bonds increased rapidly as international investors were trying to diversify their portfolio away form Latin American debt securities. The more fundamental reasons for the popularity of eastern European bonds were the reform successes during 1996, rapidly improving credit ratings and the prospect of eventual entry into the European Union. Developments in western Europe also benefited demand for central and eastern European debt. The prospects of accession to the European Monetary Union resulted in the decline of interest rates of many traditional higher-yield currencies such as the Italian lira. The convergence of European currency yields induced investors to shift funds to the next level of possibly converging economies in central Europe (FT, 31.1.1997).

Despite high demand for emerging market debt, the Visegrád countries have adopted a cautious approach to borrowing in international markets. Large national foreign exchange reserves and cheaper alternative sources of debt funding, in particular in the international syndicated loan market, made resort to international bond markets largely obsolete. Euro-bond issues by sovereign borrowers were often based on considerations of prestige rather than funding requirements. Sovereign issues are a preferred way to test the judgement of international investors about progress in economic reforms and the standing of the capital raiser in international markets. Sovereign issues are also important to establish a benchmark for subsequent non-state issues. Although Euro-bond issues from central and eastern Europe have become more frequent in 1996 [35], it is unlikely that the transition economies will rely on international bond markets to any great extent in the near future. Government borrowing in most countries in the region is limited by fiscal consolidation and central European central banks have been wary to see external indebtedness increase. Due to the demand-supply imbalance and rapid economic successes in 1996, yields on outstanding Euro-bonds from central Europe have fallen drastically. Lower borrowing costs allow sovereign issuers to partly avoid higher funding costs in domestic market and it enables those countries that

---

[35] According to Capital Data Bondware, central and eastern European issuers borrowed a total of USD 4.4 bn in Euro- and international markets (FT, 31.1.1997).

already have a relatively high level of external debt to reduce debt servicing costs through debt restructuring.

A growing number of non-state borrowers from the region are also taking advantage of decreased borrowing costs in international markets. Flexible and streamlined issuing procedures in the Euro-markets allow central European entities to access funds more quickly, avoiding the often cumbersome issuing requirements in domestic bond markets. As in the case of sovereign borrowers, considerations of prestige have been an important factor for banks, enterprises and municipalities in accessing the Euro-markets. High yields and low credit risk through explicit or implicit guarantees made the first corporate Euro-bond issues from the region a series of success stories. Most of the issues were heavily oversubscribed and spreads were often tighter than predicted even by the most optimistic analysts. In the course of 1996 spreads on outstanding bonds have tightened further and many of the initial issuers are planning to return to the market in 1997 to take advantage of improved funding opportunities.

The successes of the first Euro-bond issues from private sector issuers should not detract from the fact that risks remain on both sides of the market. Up to the end of 1996, foreign borrowing by private-sector entities has either been covered by a government guarantee and/or has been limited to blue-chip companies. As the number of corporate borrowers increases, central European governments are increasingly unwilling to extend such guarantees. Smaller entities mostly lack credit ratings, which implies higher, if not unacceptable, credit risk. Large banks and utilities, which are still predominantly state-owned, may benefit from an implicit government guarantee. However, the uncertainty connected to the future consolidation and/or privatisation of such state-owned entities may also prove an obstacle to borrowing abroad. The case of Polish Bank Handlowy's Euro-bond debut shows that privatisation uncertainty can be an important factor in raising capital in international markets (Euromoney Magazine, June 1996).

For the issuing company, the Euro-market debut also contains risks. Higher currency risk as a result of increased foreign borrowing may be problematic for financial managers who lack experience in managing currency risk. Moreover, there are no good hedging instruments available to cover long-term currency risk. It is widely expected that corporate bond issues in the Euro-markets will increase further in the course of 1997. However, the number of large issuers with acceptable credit risk is limited and funding needs of smaller private enterprises are mostly too modest to warrant accessing international capital markets.

23.1 Hungary

Hungary, which has been an active participant in international capital markets since 1971, is the only of the Visegrád countries which consistently relied on borrowing in the international markets. According to BIS statistics, Hungary accounted for 81% of a total of USD 18.4 bn of outstanding issues of international debt securities from the whole of eastern Europe in the first quarter of 1996 (BIS, 1996). By October 1996, the Hungarian National Bank[36] had floated almost 100 issues in 14 different currencies. According to the NBH, the amount of external debt outstanding is about USD 13 bn the largest share of which is medium and long-term and carries fixed interest rates. Hungary is also an exception in that it has repeatedly issued bonds in international markets without having obtained an investment grade rating. Although Hungary has never defaulted on its external debt it faced higher borrowing costs than Poland or the Czech Republic because of its sub-investment grade rating.

Hungary is expected to reduce its activities in the international markets in 1997 because gains through privatisation and high foreign direct investment allowed the Hungarian government to build up considerable foreign exchange reserves. The NBH will nonetheless continue to issue Euro-bonds because first, Hungary is still restructuring its external debt to reduce debt servicing costs; and second, the NBH seeks to remain present in the market and to test the general judgement of Hungary as a debtor (Handelsblatt, 16.4.1996). Only two Hungarian banks have launched international bonds but the NBH expects a larger number of private sector issues and some issuing activity by municipalities for 1997.

Table 39. International Bond Issues 1993-1996

Issuer	Date	Amount	Maturity	Coupon
NBH	January 1993	JPY 30 billion	5 years	6,80%
	January 1993	DEM 600 million	7 years	10,00%
	February 1993	JPY 40 billion	5 years	6,50 %
	March 1993	JPY 50 billion	7 years	6,45%
	June 1993	CHF 100 million	7 years	7,25%
	June 1993	USD 150 million	5 years	8,00%
	July 1993	JPY 50 billion	6 years	6,45%
	August 1993	GBP 100 million	10 years	10,00%
	Sept, 1993	DEM 1 billion	10 years	8,75%
	Oct, 1993	ATS 1 billion	7 years	8,50%
	Oct, 1993	USD 50 million	5 years	8,00%
	Nov, 1993	USD 200 million	10 years	7,95%
	Nov, 1993	FRF 1 billion	6 years	8,00%
	Nov, 1993	USD 200 million	20 years	8,875%
	Dec, 1993	CHF 200 million	6 years	6,75%

[36] As the state budget is financed from internal sources only, there are no Euro-bonds outstanding in the name of the Republic of Hungary.

Table 39. International Bond Issues 1993-1996 (Contd.)

Issuer	Date	Amount	Maturity	Coupon
	January 1994	DEM 1 billion	10 years	8,00%
	January 1994	EPS 10 billion	5 years	10,30%
	January 1994	JPY 50 billion	10 years	5,45 %
	April 1994	LFR 2,5 billion	7 years	8,875%
	June 1994	ATS 1,25 billion	7 years	9,00%
	July 1994	NLG 150 million	5 years	8,75%
	August 1994	JPY 15 billion	3 years	5,00%
	August 1994	JPY 15 billion	6 years	6,15%
	August 1994	USD 250 million	5 years	LIBOR +
	Oct, 1994	CHF 150 million	5 years	1,5%
	Nov, 1994	DEM 500 million	7 years	8,25%
	Nov, 1994	JPY 30 billion	8 years	9,75%
				6,65%
	January 1995	ATS 750 million	7 years	9,625%
	February 1995	JPY 25 billion	10 years	6,75%
	April 1995	JPY 15 billion	3 years	3,70%
	April 1995	JPY 15 billion	15 years	6,90%
	June 1995	JPY 30 billion	12 years	6,00%
	June 1995	DEM 500 million	6 years	9,00%
	June 1995	DEM 250 million	6 years	9,00%
	July 1995	JPY 25 billion	10 years	5,20%
	Sept, 1995	JPY 30 billion	10 years	5,00%
	Oct, 1995	CHF 200 million	5 years	6,75%
	Oct, 1995	JPY 10 billion	20 years	6,00%
	Oct, 1995	JPY 30 billion	12 years	5,00%
	Nov, 1995	JPY 25 billion	13 years	5,00%
	January 1996	JPY 40 billion	15 years	5,20%
	May 1996	DEM 500 mio	6 years	LIBOR + 0,9

Source: NBH, 1996.

23.2 Poland

The relatively high level of existing external indebtedness and fiscal prudence has made Poland cautious to use the new borrowing facilities in the Euro-bond markets. Poland issued its first dollar-denominated Euro-bond in 1995 despite the trend away from reliance on external creditors. The issue came as a surprise insofar as Poland had only one year earlier rescheduled its external debt through a London Club agreement. The main rationale of the bond issue was, according to the Ministry of Finance, to establish a presence in the market, to move away from the emerging market image connected to Poland's outstanding Brady bonds, and to establish a benchmark for potential private sector issues. The second Polish Euro-bond issue followed in July 1996, this time in the D-mark sector. Given Poland's strong foreign exchange reserves at the time of the issue, the purpose was again to accustom foreign lenders to the country's presence in international capital markets. The remaining restrictions of the capital account represent an obstacle for Euro-bond issues by private sector and sub-state entities. Up to the end of 1996, only two non-state entities, two of the country's largest banks, had entered the Euro-bond markets.

Poland issued about USD 8 bn in Brady Bonds in 1994 as part of its debt rescheduling agreement. These were mainly held by the banks that made the original loans and a narrow range of specialised funds. In January 1996, Moody's decided to award an investment grade rating to Polish Brady bond issues. This was the first time the credit rating agency has rated the credit of any Brady bond issue at this level. The upgrade allowed a broader range of investors to hold the debt instruments and resulted in a gradual decrease of yields of Polish Brady bonds towards levels of Polish Euro-bonds.

Table 40. Polish Euro-Bond Issues

Issuer	Date	Amount	Maturity	Coupon/spread at issue
Republic of Poland	July 1996	DEM 250 million	5 years	6,125%, 65 bp over Bobl
Republic of Poland	June 1995	USD 250 million	5 years	7,75%,185 bp over 5% US 1999 Treasuries
BRE	April 1996	USD 100 million	3 years	6,625 %, 1,0% over 6-months dollar LIBOR
Bank Handlowy Warsawie	April 1996	USD 100 million	3 years	7,0 %, 88 bp over US treasuries

Source: Ministry of Finance, Foreign Department

23.3 Czech Republic

Czechoslovakia entered the Euromarkets soon after the start of reforms with a USD 200 mio issue in 1991. This first issue was followed by a prolonged break in international issuing activity during the break-up of the country. Due to the sound fiscal position of the Czech central government, no further Euro-bond issues have taken place in the name of the Czech Republic. Czech corporates and banks, on the other hand, acted as pioneers in the international bond markets. CEZ, the Czech Republic's largest electricity supplier, was the first central European corporate to receive an international rating (investment grade). It subsequently entered the Euromarkets with USD 150 mio issue at the end of 1994. The success of this early issue was not only its relatively tight spread (110 bp over US treasuries) but also the wide distribution, both geographically and by type of investors. An interesting problem in placing the issue was that the company already positioned itself beyond the emerging market investors, which require very high returns, and investors in frequent issues who had not heard of CEZ and did not expect to find an investment grade utility in Eastern Europe (Eichler, 1995). Komercni Banka was the first Czech bank which issued Euro-bonds in April 1996.

Table 41. Selected Euro-Bond Issues out of the Czech(oslowak) Republic

Issuer	Date	Amount	Maturity	Spread/coupon
National Bank of Czechoslovakia	November 1991	USD 200 million	3 years	300 bp over US Treasuries
CEZ	1994	USD 150 mio	5 years	110 bp over US treasuries
Komercní Banka	April 1996	USD 250 mio	5 years	78 bp over US Treasuries
Pivovar Radegast	July 1996	DM 70 mio	5 years	

23.4 Slovakia

The National Bank of Slovakia entered the international bond market in 1993 at a time when the domestic bond market was still in its infancy. The Republic of Slovakia has not itself issued in the international market. It has, however, provided unconditional guarantees for all three corporate Euro-bond issues outstanding at the end of 1996 and thus facilitated access to international markets for Slovak companies. A novelty was introduced by VUB, the largest Slovak bank, in December 1996. The bank placed SKK 1.5 bn worth of domestic bonds entirely with foreign banks. The issue was in accordance with domestic law as well as international standards. Further issuance activity by Slovak entities will depend on whether private sector borrowers and local government can obtain international ratings. At the end of 1996, only three non-state entities had been subject to ratings from international rating agencies (the City of Bratislava, JCRA: BBB; Amylum Group, S&P: aa; Vodohospodárska výstavba, S&P: BBB-) (Information provided by NBS; VUB, 1996b).

Table 42. Slovak Euro-Bond Issues

Issuer	Date	Amount	Maturity	Coupon/Spread at issue
NBS	Sept, 1993	JPY 25 billion	5/7 years	7,75/8,00%
Calex, a,s.	Dec, 1993	USD 21 million	3 years	7,88%
Calex, a,s	July 1994	JPY 700 million	3 years	5,60%
City of Bratislava	Nov, 1995	JPY 6,5 billion	5 years	4,10%
Vodohospodárska výstavba, s,p,	Dec, 1996	USD 200 million	10 years	7,25%, 115 bp over US Treasuries

Sources: ZEW Questionnaire; NBS, Debt Management Department

24. CHECK AND SLOVAK CROWN ESTABLISHED AS NEW EURO-CURRENCIES

Central and eastern European borrowers have been expanding their investor base through accessing a widening array of currencies. According to the BIS (1996: 25), this diversification of issuance is the most important recent trend in emerging market finance. As the tables above indicate, deutschmark and yen denominated issues are increasingly popular with central European borrowers. More remarkable still is that central European currencies themselves are used to establish new benchmark sections in the Euromarkets. Originally, Euro-medium term notes or bonds denominated in Czech or Slovak korunas provided a profitable swap opportunity for large international borrowers with good credit standing. The involvement of foreign issuers, mainly international financial institutions such as the EBRD, the IFC or the World Bank, brought credibility to the local market and, to a certain extent, may have introduced new investors to the fledgling local currency markets in Eastern Europe. These local currency bonds usually have a triple-A rating and safe settlement through Cedel or Euroclear. Hence they allow more traditional institutional investors, which could not take the credit and settlement risk of domestic central European bonds, to enter these markets.

The *Czech koruna* market is the most sophisticated of the central European Euro-markets. It has grown very rapidly since the end of 1995 and by September 1996 more than 25 koruna-denominated issues in the form of Euro-bonds as well as EMTNs had taken place. The typical issue would have a volume of CZK 1 bn to CZK 2.5 bn and maturities range from one to five years. The bank that acts as lead-manager would typically try to involve an international institution with first class rating in the issuance. In most of the cases the korunas raised through the issue were then swapped into dollar or D-marks. At the end of 1996 the trend is for borrowers to hold on to the korunas or lend them on in the domestic market. Whereas the early Euro-bond issues in CZK were mainly bought by private-banking departments of large international banks, more recent issues also appealed to foreign institutional investors such as pension and emerging market funds mainly because of their higher coupon, but also because of the increased confidence in the Czech reform process. On the domestic side, demand for Euro-bonds denominated in the local currency seems to be thin, however. In the Czech Republic this is mainly due to unfavourable tax treatment: Whereas income from domestic bonds is subject to a withholding tax of 25%, the interest from international bonds is taxed at the normal corporate tax rate of 39%. Recently, Czech institutional investors have shown increased interest in the koruna sector of the Euromarkets, mainly because the tight monetary policy of the CNB has resulted in more appealing coupon yields. The Euro-bond market is connected to the Czech money market through the frequent swaps related to Euro-bond issues (Handelsblatt, 9.10.1996).

Remaining restrictions on the Polish capital account have prevented Euro-bond issues in *Polish zloty*. In order to satisfy international investors' desire for greater exposure to Poland's economic success, international investors created synthetic zloty-linked bonds. The EBRD was the first issuer to offer USD denominated global bonds linked to the PLN-USD exchange rate. The IFC and a number of large multinational corporations have also borrowed through these instrument. Zloty-linked bonds offer investors the high yields available on domestic Polish securities while carrying a much lower credit risk than Polish Government debt. According to the Ministry of Finance, Poland is currently discussing the issuance of zloty-denominated and settled bonds in the domestic Polish market as well as the Euromarket with a number of international financial institutions. The Ministry regards the tax immunity and the limit of ECU 300 mio. for foreign public issues in the Polish domestic market as the biggest obstacles for further issues in 1997.

The first Euro-*Slovak koruna* public bond was issued by the EBRD in August 1996, followed by an issue of three-year bonds trough the IFC. In October, the General Electric Capital Corporation (GECC) issued SKK 2 bn. worth of one-year Euro-bonds with a 11.625% coupon, i.e. 87.5 bp. lower than the initial one-year offering of the EBRD. The new instruments allow foreign investors to gain exposure to the Slovak koruna with a higher level of liquidity than can be expected in the local market. According to the NBS, Euro-SKK issuance has attracted additional attention to the Slovak corporate bond market. However, the investor base for Euro-crown issues does not normally overlap with those international investors interested in the Slovak domestic market. The gap between the two markets stems from the fact that the Euro-bonds are only issued by AAA-rated institutions which are absent from the Slovak domestic market. The *Hungarian forint* is not used as a Euro-currency and according to the EBRD it is unlikely that Euro-HUF issues will take place before the end of 1997.

25. CONCLUSION

The Visegrád countries have progressed very fast in establishing the regulatory and institutional framework for efficient bond markets. However, evaluating the situation on the basis of the end of 1996, some deficiencies still have to be overcome. Before summarising these points it has to be emphasised that the speed of the ongoing capital market reforms is fast both on the side of government legislation and on the side of private market participants. Therefore, some of the mentioned problems might already be clearly realised in the process and might already be moving close to a solution or at least a major improvement.

It was shown that while the transparency at the computerised exchanges is high, market *liquidity on secondary bond markets is often not yet satisfactory*. The two reasons are: First, relatively small market segments do not provide the secondary market with sufficient tradable material. Second, high shares of OTC aggravate this problem further. Therefore it can be expected that liquidity will grow on the one hand with the ongoing growth of the bond market. On the other hand further attempts to improve the efficiency of the exchange relative to the OTC trade should aim at improving the share of bonds trade at the official exchange.

The *incomplete term structure* remains a serious drawback of the Visegrád bond markets. Even where long-run maturities exist (above 5 years) these bond segments suffer even more from illiquidity than shorter maturities. Apart from that in the long-run segments straight fixed interest rate bonds rarely exist, often the long-run papers have a floating interest rate or are callable. Therefore, information on long-run market interest rates is not available. This means that an important point of orientation for long-run intertemporal activities such as saving and investment is missing.

The incomplete term structure is a problem where further improvements on the market infrastructure alone do not seem to be sufficient. In addition, progress in the macroeconomic environment seems essential. Only if inflation and inflationary expectations can be reduced into a single-digit area, where the real interest rate becomes predictable at least up to a certain extent, a liquid market for long-run fixed interest rate bonds can develop.

The *absence (with the exception of Hungary) of highly liquid and standardised derivative contracts on interest rate underlyings* at the official exchanges is a further shortcoming in comparison to mature bond markets in the Western capital markets. Of course, the problems of low liquidity and a missing derivative market are interrelated. The existence of a liquid underlying market is an indispensable precondition for a viable derivative market. Therefore, within the reform sequence attempts to further improve on the markets for straight bonds should precede initiatives to create derivative markets.

The synopsis on the relative importance of issuers in the Visegrád bond markets clearly indicates that a high level of government issues leads to a *crowding out of private activity in the bond market.* In Hungary and Poland where the markets have been flooded with treasuries there has not been much room for a corporate bond market to develop. In contrast to that the favourable budgetary position in the Czech Republic has led to a low level of treasury issues and thus has resulted in the development of the most advanced corporate bond market in the region. Crowding out of private bond issuance activities has often been supported by discriminatory taxational measures favouring government bonds relatively to other issuer groups. Central bank obligation to buy certain shares of government bonds has been another way to promote the sale of government bonds. It is obvious that this kind of crowding out is detrimental for the economic development and in particular for the development of the private sector. For the private sector, bond market finance can be a cost saving alternative to bank credits. Positive tax discrimination of government bonds is not compatible with the aim of an efficient capital market. Central bank activities in financing the public debt are not compatible with the aim of both reducing inflation rate and bringing the economic system in these countries in line with the requirements resulting from the EU application.

The crowding out problem has also to be dealt with in a twofold strategy. On the macroeconomic side fiscal prudence which is necessary in many respects will also be useful in regard to a healthy development of a mixed issuer structure in the bond market. On the institutional side of bond markets legislation has to aim at removing taxational discrimination and other regulatory privileges for government bonds. Credible institutional safeguards have to be constructed in order to prevent future central bank activities in government debt finance.

The increasing integration into international capital markets both through the activities of foreigners on domestic bond markets and the presence of Visegrád issuers on Euro bond markets are a very positive development in at least two respects. First, it shows that the capital market development in these countries has reached an advanced level. Second, the international integration puts the domestic bond markets under growing competitive pressure to overcome the remaining deficiencies.

REFERENCES

Books and Articles:

Bank for International Settlement (1993), Seminar on the Establishment of Securities Markets in Countries in Transition; Proceedings of a Conference in May 1993 in Romania. Basle, BIS.

Benzie, Richard (1992), The Development of the International Bond Markets. Basle: BIS (*BIS Economic Papers*, No. 32, January 1992).

Blommstein, Hans J. and Michael G. Spencer (1994), The Role of Financial Institutions in the Transition to a Market Economy, in: Caprio et al., *Building Sound Finance in Emerging Market Economies*, Washington D.C., pp. 139-189.

Bonin, John P. and István R. Székely (eds.) (1994), *The Development and Reform of Financial Systems in Central and Eastern Europe*. Aldershot: Edward Elgar.

Bröker, Günther F. (1993), Strategies for the Development of a Viable and Efficient National Bond Market. In, *Emerging Bond Markets in the Dynamic Asian Economies*, OECD, pp. 9-39.

Caprio, Gerhard/Folkerts-Landua, David/Lane, D. Timothy (1994), Building Sound Finance in Emerging Market Economies, Proceedings of a Conference in Washington D.C. June 1993.

Chuppe, Terry M. and Micheal Atkin (1992), Regulation of Securities Markets. Policy *Research Working Paper 829*. Washington D.C., World Bank.

Cohen, Kalman J. et al. (1986), *The Microstructure of Securities Markets*. Englewood Cliffs, New Jersey.

Dooley, Micheal/Fernandez-Arias, Eduardo/Kletzer, Kenneth (1996), Is the Debt Crisis History? Recent Private Capital Inflows to Developing Countries. *World Bank Economic Review*, Vol. 10, No. 1.

Eichler, Gabriel (1995), The First Corporate Bond Issue out of Eastern Europe. *Treasury Management International*, December, pp. 44-46.

Euromoney (1995), The 1996 Guide to Poland, *Euromoney* Supplement, December.

Euromoney (1996a), Banking Services in Eastern Europe, *Euromoney Supplement*, April.

Euromoney (1996b), The 1996 Guide to Emerging Currencies, *Euromoney Supplement*, June.

Euromoney (1996c), The 1996 Guide to Central and Eastern European Bond Markets, *Euromoney Supplement*, September.

Fabozzi, Frank J.(1993), *Bond Markets; Analysis and Strategies*, London, Prentice-Hall.

Fanelli, José María and Gary McMahon (1996), Economic Lessons for Eastern Europe from Latin America. In, G. McMahon (ed.), *Lessons in Economic Policy for Eastern Europe from Latin America*, London, Macmillan, pp. 1-42.

Feldmann, Robert A./Kumar, S. Manmohan (1995), Emerging Equity Markets: Growth, Benefits, and Policy Concerns. *World Bank Research Observer*, vol. 10, no. 2, pp. 181-200.

Greenwald, B. and J. C. Stein (1988), The Task Force Report: The Reasoning Behind the Recommendations, *Journal of Economic Perspectives*, Summer, pp. 3-23.

Griffith-Jones, Stephany/Drábek, Zdanek (eds.) (1995), *Financial Reform in Central and Eastern Europe*, New York, St Martin's Press.

Haiss, Peter R. (1995), Handlungsalternativen für die (Re-)Strukturierung der Finanzmärkte in den Reformstaaten Zentraleuropas, *Österreichisches Bank Archiv*, No. 2, pp. 100-112.

Hausner, Jerzy, Bob Jessop, Klaus Nielsen (eds.) (1995), *Strategic Choice and Path Dependency in Post-Socialism; Institutional Dynamics in the Transformation Process*. Aldershot, Edward Elgar.

Hein, Manfred (ed.) (1994), *Bankensysteme in Ostmitteleuropa*, Berlin, Spitz.

Institut pro podporu Rozvoje financnhího thru, *The Capital Market in the Czech Republic 1993-94*, Prague, Magnet Press 1994.

Kaser, Michael (1996), Integration and Homogeneity in the Transition Economies. In: J. Hölscher, A Jacobsen, H. Tomann, H. Weisfeld (eds.), *Conditions of Economic Development in Central and Eastern Europe, Vol. 5, Economic Policy and Development Strategies in Central and Eastern Europe*. Marburg, Metropolis-Verlag, pp. 207-228.

Kemme, David M., Banking in Central Europe during the Protomarket Period: Developments and Emerging Issues, in: Bonin and Székely, 1994, pp. 41-60.

Kern, Holger, *Bankensysteme in Osteuropa*, Wien: Orac Verlag 1996 (Bankwissenschaftliche Schriftenreihe, Bd. 83).

Lorinc, Marek, Investing in Financial Markets of East and Central Europe, Columbia *Journal of World Business*, No. 30 (1), Spring 1995, pp. 88-111.

Lucas, Henry C. and Robert A. Schwartz (1989), *The Challenge of Information Technology for the Securities Markets*. Homewood, Illinois.

Madhavan, Amanth (1992), Trading Mechanisms in Securities Markets. *Journal of Finance*, vol. 47, No. 2, pp. 607-641.

Miller, Jonathan (1994), *The Czech Capital Market.* London, ODA.

Montias, John Michael (1994), Financial and Fiscal Aspects of Systems Change in Eastern Europe, in: Bonin/Székely (eds.), pp. 9-40.

Moody's (1996), European Territorial-Community Finance: An Outlook for the Late 1990s. Moody's Special Comment. November.

Neubauer, Peter and Otmar Stöcker (1995), Der neue Pfandbrief in der Tschechischen Republik, *Der langfristige Credit*, No. 12.

Nickerson, David, Governance and Efficiency in Emerging Financial Markets, *Journal of International Trade and Economic Development*, No. 4/3 (November 1995), pp. 261-281.

Niggle, C., The Role of the Financial Sector in the Socialist Economies, *Review of Social Economy*, No. 53 (3), Fall 1995, pp. 311-31.

Pardy, Robert (1992), Institutional Reform in Emerging Securities Markets, *World Bank Policy Research Papers 907*, May.

Pohl, Gerhard, Gregory Jedrzejczak and Robert Anderson (1995), Creating Capital Markets in Central and Eastern Europe, *World Bank Technical Paper No. 295.*

Schwartz, Robert A. (1991), *Reshaping the Equity Markets -- A Guide for the 1990s.* Harpers Business.

Szabadföldi, Istvan (1996), Financial Centers -- A Regional Chance for Budapest. *Society & Economy in Central and Eastern Europe*, No. 1, pp. 66-97.

Sylla, Richard (1995), The Rise of Securities Markets; What Can Governments Do? *World Bank Research Working Paper*, No. 1539, November.

Verbeek, Giel A. W. (1996), Financial Sector Reform in Central and Eastern Europe. *Society and Economy in Central and Eastern Europe No. 1*, pp. 111-141.

Vos, Rob (1995), Financial Liberalisation, Growth and Adjustment: Some Lessons from Developing Countries. In S. Griffith-Jones and Z. Drábek (eds.), *Financial Reform in Central and Eastern Europe*, New York: St. Martin's Press, pp. 179-220.

Bank Publications:

Bank Austria, Investment Focus. August - December 1996.

Bank Handlowy W Warszawie SA (1995), Rules governing mandated operations connected with the issue of and secondary market trading in Bony Handlowe.

Bank Handlowy W Warszawie SA (1996a), Market Report September.

Bank Handlowy W Warszawie SA (1996b), The Polish Capital Market, Proceedings of a Conference in Geneva, October.

BV - Bayerische Vereinsbank (1995), The Czech Bond Market, February 1995.

BV - Bayerische Vereinsbank (1995), Emerging Markets Eastern Europe, November 1995.

BV - Bayerische Vereinsbank (1996), Monthly Reports of the Treasury Emerging Markets, September - November.

Central European Securities House Bratislava (1996), The Capital Market in the Slovak Republic, May.

CS First Boston (1997), Research, On-line.

Dresdner Bank (1994), Aufstrebende Rentenmärkte in den Reformländer Europas, Trends, Mai.

Hypo-Bank (1996), East European Perspectives, September.

ING Barings (1996), Emerging Europe Strategy, September.

Raiffeisen Zentralbank Österreich (1995a), Der Polnische Kapitalmarkt, February.

Raiffeisen Zentralbank Österreich (1995b), Der Slowakische Kapitalmarkt, February.

Raiffeisen Zentralbank Österreich (1995c), Der Ungarische Kapitalmarkt, March.

Raiffeisen Zentralbank Österreich (1995d), Der Tschechische Kapitalmarkt, November.

Raiffeisen Zentralbank Österreich (1996a), Capital Markets Central Europe, March.

Raiffeisen Zentralbank Österreich (1996b), Capital Markets Central Europe, September.

Raiffeisen Zentralbank Österreich (1996c), Capital Markets Central Europe, December.

VUB (Vseobecná úverová banka s.a.) Bratislava (1996a), Investment Analysis, January 1996.

VUB (Vseobecná úverová banka s.a.) Bratislava (1996b), Investment Analysis; Spring 1996.

VUB (Vseobecná úverová banka s.a.) Bratislava (1997a), Investment Analysis, Winter 1996, January.

VUB (Vseobecná úverová banka s.a.) Bratislava (1997b), Investment Analysis, January 1997.

Official Publications:

AKK - Hungarian State Treasury, Government Debt Management Agency (1996a): Business Conditions for Government Bond Auctions, April.

AKK - Hungarian State Treasury, Government Debt Management Agency (1996b): Business Conditions for 1, 3, 6, and 12-Month Discount Treasury Bill Auctions, July.

AKK - Hungarian State Treasury, Government Debt Management Agency (1996c), Government Securities Market Hungary, Third Quarter.

BIS - Bank for International Settlement (1996), International Banking and Financial Market Developments, August.

BSE- Budapest Stock Exchange (1995a), Annual Report.

BSE- Budapest Stock Exchange (1995b), Five Years of the Budapest Stock Exchange, June.

BSE- Budapest Stock Exchange (1996a), The Handbook of Futures Trading 1996.

BSE- Budapest Stock Exchange (1996b), Monthly Report September.

BSE- Budapest Stock Exchange (1996c), Facts and Prospects. September.

BSE- Budapest Stock Exchange (1997), Annual Report for 1996, January.

BSSE - Bratislava Stock Exchange (1995), Annual Report 1995.

BSSE - Bratislava Stock Exchange (1996a), Trading Results, First Half of 1996.

BSSE - Bratislava Stock Exchange (1996b), Monthly Statistics, July - September.

CNB - Czech National Bank (1995), Annual Report 1995.

CNB - Czech National Bank (1996a), Report on the Monetary Development in the Czech Republic for the First Quarter.

CNB - Czech National Bank (1996b), Quarterly Economic and Fiscal Bulletin of the CR, No. 8.

EBRD - European Bank for Reconstruction and Development (1995), Transition Report.

EBRD - European Bank for Reconstruction and Development (1996), Transition Report.

European Commission (1996), European Economy, Supplement C, Economic Reform Monitor, No. 3 October.

KELER - Central Clearing House and Depository Budapest (1995), Annual Report 1995.

KELER - Central Clearing House and Depository Budapest (1996),Quarterly Information, August.

MoF Poland - Ministry of Finance of the Republic of Poland (1995), Public Debt Quarterly Review, December.

MoF Poland - Ministry of Finance of the Republic of Poland (1996a), Investor Guide to the Domestic Treasury Securities Market, June.

MoF Poland - Ministry of Finance of the Republic of Poland (1996b), Poland's Treasury Securities Characteristics, Second Quarter, June.

MoF Poland - Ministry of Finance of the Republic of Poland (1996c), Public Debt Quarterly Review, No. 2, June.

MoF Poland - Ministry of Finance of the Republic of Poland (1996d), Public Debt Quarterly Review, No., October.

NBH - National Bank of Hungary (1995), Annual Report 1995.

NBH - National Bank of Hungary (1996), Monthly Report, August.

NBP - National Bank of Poland (1995), Annual Report 1995.

NBP - National Bank of Poland 1996), Information Bulletin, Monthly Report, June.

NBS - National Bank of Slovakia (1995), Annual Report.

NBS - National Bank of Slovakia (1996), Monthly Reports, January - October.

OECD (1993), Emerging Bond Markets in the Dynamic Asian Economies.

OECD (1994a): Prospects for Capital Flows to Emerging Markets, OECD Financial Market Trends, No. 75, pp. 13-25.

OECD (1994b): Trends in Government Debt Management and Government Securities Markets, OECD Financial Market Trends, No. 75, pp. 27-33.

OECD (1995): Securitisation; An International Perspective, OECD Financial Market Trends, No. 61, pp. 33-62.

PSC - Polish Securities Commission (1993), Annual Report.

PSE - Prague Stock Exchange (1995a), Annual Report 1995.

PSE - Prague Stock Exchange (1995b), Fact Book 1995.

PSE - Prague Stock Exchange (1995b), Summary 1995.

PSE - Prague Stock Exchange (1996a), Basic Information.

PSE - Prague Stock Exchange (1996b), Quarterly Trading Results, No. 1 - 3.

PSE - Prague Stock Exchange (1996c); Monthly Reports, October.

PSE - Prague Stock Exchange (1996d), Types of Trades Offered at the Prague Stock Exchange.

RM-System Slovakia (1996a), Trading Rules.

RM-System Slovakia (1996b), Statistics on bond trading.

WSE - Warsaw Stock Exchange (1994): Annual Report.

WSE - Warsaw Stock Exchange (1995a), Annual Report.

WSE - Warsaw Stock Exchange (1995b), Organisation and Operation, July.

WSE - Warsaw Stock Exchange (1996a), Quarterly Bulletins, No. 1 - 2.

WSE - Warsaw Stock Exchange (1996b), Monthly Bulletins, July - September.

Newspapers, Journals, and On-line Sources:

Aspekt Financial Information, http://www.infox.eunet.cz/aspekt/
Blick durch die Wirtschaft
Bloomberg Financial News, http://www.bloomberg.com
BSE Online, http://www.formax.hu/fmon/
Business Central Europe
Central Europe Online, http://www.centraleurope.com
CzechInvest Factsheets, http://www.czech.cz/infosrc/czinv/
The Economist
Euromoney
Financial Times

Financial Times, Finance East Europe
Frankfurter Allgemeine Zeitung
Handelsblatt
The Institutional Investor
Komero Bonds and Derivative Research, http://www.anet.cz/komero/obligace.htm
PSE Online, http://www.vol.cz/BURZA, http://www.sati.cz/
Ticker, ÖTOB Vienna
Trend, Slovak Economy and Business Weekly On-line, http://www.savba.sk/logos/news/trend/
The Warsaw Voice, Poland and Central Europe Review, http://www.contact.waw.pl/Pl-iso/voice
WSE Online, http://www.yogi.ippt.gov.pl/gielda/

We are grateful for the co-operation and the supply of information of the following bodies

Bank Handlowy w Warszawie S.A. Capital Market Centre; Bayerische Vereinsbank, Treasury; Bratislava Stock Exchange, International Relations Department; Budapest Resident Office of the European Bank for Reconstruction and Development; Budapest Stock Exchange, Information Centre; Creditanstalt Securities S.A., Fixed Income Department; Czech National Bank, Institute of Economics; Daiwa Europe; EBRD, Treasury; Hungarian State Treasury, Government Debt Management Agency; Hypo Bank CZ a.s.; KELER, Securities Settlement; Komercni Banka a.s.; Ministry of Finance of the Republic of Poland, Public Debt Department; National Bank of Hungary, International Capital Markets Department; National Bank of Poland, Monetary and Credit Policy Department, Foreign Department; National Bank of Slovakia, Banking Transactions Department; Polish Securities Commission; Prague Stock Exchange, Public Relations; Raiffeisen Capital Investment Polska S.A.; RM-System Slovakia; Vseobecna uverova banka, Capital Investment Department; Warsaw Stock Exchange, Market Data and International Relations Department; ZEW Co-operation Partners

Chapter 9

MARKET STRUCTURE, RETURN DYNAMICS AND EFFICIENCY OF THE VISEGRAD STOCK MARKETS*

Jürgen Kähler
Universität Erlangen-Nürnberg

* I wish to thank the members of the ACE project 'Financial Innovation and Deregulation for Economies in Transition' and Oskar Kurer for helpful comments on an earlier draft of this paper.

1. INTRODUCTION

In the process of economic transformation from a centrally planned economy to a market economy, the establishment of a stock market takes a pivotal role. After the political revolutions in Central and Eastern Europe (CEE) in the late 80s and early 90s, stock exchanges were introduced at an early stage of the transformation process. But the development and structure of stock markets in CEE countries varies considerably. This paper studies the stock markets of the four Visegrad countries (Czech Republic, Hungary, Poland and Slovakia) and addresses two related questions: First, to what extent and why do the four stock markets differ? Secondly, to what extent do the four stock markets still lag behind the development of a mature, efficient and well-established stock market? The benchmark for comparisons is the U.K. stock market.

2. MARKET STRUCTURE

The first CEE country to open a stock exchange after the demise of socialism was Hungary on 21 June, 1990. However, the history of the Budapest Stock Exchange (BSE) can be traced back to the 1870s. Since its re-opening the exchange has often been at the forefront of development.

R. MacDonald and R. Cross (eds.), Central Europe Towards Monetary Union: Macroeconomic Underpinnings and Financial Reputation, 247–276.

For instance, the BSE was the first Visegrad exchange to introduce derivatives (in April 1995). Currently, it trades futures on short-term interest rates, treasury bills, currencies, three shares, and the stock market index BUX, although the volume in some contracts is rather low. On the cash market, equity trading constitutes about half of the total turnover. The other half is trading of government and corporate bonds, treasury bills, investment funds, and compensation notes. Over the years, trading volume has increased continuously, with the exception of 1994 when it decreased slightly.

The stock markets in the Visegrad countries, like in many other countries, are segmented into sub-markets, usually a main market and a second-tier (parallel) market with lower listing requirements. The purpose of second-tier markets is to attract young and dynamic companies to a listing on the stock market when their potential is apparent but not fully developed. The equity market of the BSE is actually segmented into three categories with different listing requirements.

Table 1 shows the listing requirements of the main market (category A) and the secondary market (Category B) for the BSE and the other three Visegrad markets. It is apparent that the listing requirements are relatively strict in Budapest. For Category-A trading, the equity series to be listed must have a minimum market value of 10 billion Hungarian forint (HUF). At the end-of-1999 exchange rate of 252.7 HUF to the US dollar this translates into a value of shares of $ 39.6 million. This is substantially higher than in Bratislava or in Warsaw. To ensure sufficient liquidity, the minimum public holding ratio, i.e. the proportion of all shares that are available to the public (owners holding less than 5 per cent), is 25 per cent and the minimum public offering is $ 15.8 million. If the public holding ratio is below 25 per cent, then the public offering has to be at least $ 39.6 million. In addition, there must be at least one thousand shareholders and the company must have a track record of three audited years and must have had a profit in the last year.

The second-tier market puts less emphasis on liquidity and investor protection and has laxer minimum listing requirements. To list its shares in Category B, a company must have been in business and audited for three years, as in Category A, but it does not have to show a profit history. The Category C market is a largely free market with the following minimum listing requirements: value of shares of $ 4.0 million, 25 shareholders and one completed and audited year of business. Of the three sub-markets, the Category A market is by far the most important in term of turnover. Although only 20 of the 69 listed companies have Category A status (as of April 1999), their trading constitutes 97.5 per cent of total turnover. The second-tier segment trades more than twice as many stocks but its share of turnover is only 2.4 per cent while the 7 stocks of Category C make up a mere 0.1 per cent. Therefore, liquidity for stocks of Category B and C is very limited.

Table 1. Minimum Listing Requirements

	Budapest	Prague	Bratislava	Warsaw
Main market				
Value of shares [$ million]	39.6		11.8	9.7
Public offering [$ million]	15.8	5.6	2.4	7.7
Public holding ratio [%]	25	20		25
Period in business [years]	3	2	3	3
Shareholders	1,000			500
Secondary market				
Value of shares [$ million]	4.0			3.4
Public offering [$ million]	2.0	2.8		2.7
Public holding ratio [%]	10	15		10
Period in business [years]	3	2		2
Shareholders	100			300

The Warsaw Stock Exchange (WSE) began trading in April 1991. Similar to the Hungarian case, the history of stock exchanges in Poland goes back to the 19th century. In fact, seven stock exchanges existed in Poland before the outbreak of World War II. In 1991, the WSE opened for trade on Tuesdays only. Gradually, the number of trading days per week was increased but it was not before October 1994 that trading took place on all five working days.

The shares trading at the WSE is subdivided into three markets. The Main Market has 117 companies listed on it (as of the end of 1998) and contributes 90 per cent to total turnover. The listing requirements on the Main Market are not as strict as for Category A shares of the BSE. The value of shares to be admitted to trading has to be at least Zloty 40 million, which is equivalent to $ 9.7 million at the $-Zloty exchange rate at the end of 1999. There must be financial reports and combined profits of at least $ 3.9 million in the last three financial years. For further details see Table 1 and WSE (1999).

The Parallel Market and the Free Market have less restrictive listing rules. To list on the Free Market, a market capitalisation of $ 1 million is sufficient and there are no requirements for minimum public offerings, a public holding ratio or profits in the past. However, liquidity on these two markets is low. Although 51 companies are listed on the Parallel Market and 15 on the Free Market they contribute only 9 per cent and 1 per cent of the total turnover of the WSE, respectively.

Trading on the Prague Stock Exchange (PSE) and the Bratislava Stock Exchange (BSSE) started after Czechoslovakia separated into the

Czech Republic and Slovakia at the beginning of 1993 but trading on both exchanges commenced on the same day, 6 April 1993. For a long time, both exchanges had the reputation of insufficient transparency, liquidity and regulation. As a consequence, confidence of investors, especially foreign investors, in these markets was low. However, the PSE has done much to restore investor confidence and efficiency in recent years. The PSE has three market segments: The Main Market, the Secondary Market and the Free Market. Although only 10 of the 304 companies listed on the PSE were listed on the Main Market (as of the end of 1998), this market segment produced 72 per cent of the total turnover. On the other hand, the Free Market with 198 companies had only 9 per cent of total turnover. Recently, the PSE launched the New Market to attract the type of enterprise that has been so popular with investors around the world in recent years: the young, dynamic, high-tech company.

Listing requirements on the PSE do not seem to be very comprehensive. For instance, there are no requirements for a history of profits or for a minimum number of shareholders. The omission of the latter from the listing rules, however, does not appear to be a problem since voucher privatisation produced very widespread share-ownership. On the other hand, there is a liquidity constraint for listing on the Main Market that requires an average daily trading volume of at least koruna 1 million ($ 28 thousand). In January 1998, 35 companies were transferred from the Main Market to the Secondary Market because they failed to meet this liquidity requirement.

A lack of liquidity and market depth increases the costs of trading. In the wake of mass privatisation, a large number of stocks were listed on the PSE but many were highly illiquid (see below). Although the PSE has done much to alleviate this problem, trading costs remain high. In a study of 45 developed and emerging stock markets by Elkins/McSherry (E/M), the PSE turned out to have by far the highest total trading costs (see IFC, 1999). In fact, its total trading costs of 161 basis points (bp) were 170 per cent higher than the average trading cost in this sample of 45 markets. The breakdown of the total costs into its three components shows that fees at the PSE are very moderate (1.7 bp) but commissions are very high (62 bp which is nearly twice as high as the sample average) and the estimated market impact is extremely strong (97 bp; sample average of 19 bp). E/M estimate the market impact costs as the difference between the price at which a trade is executed and the average of the stock's high, low, opening, and closing prices during the trade date. The estimate of market impact costs confirms that the PSE still lacks market depth. According to the E/M study, in a typical mature and developed stock market the market impact cost of buy and sell orders is less than 10 basis points. It is also interesting to note that, in this sample, the BSE has the 4th highest total trading costs. Its total trading costs were estimated to be 102 bp, with commissions of 62 bp being the largest component and market impact costs of 35 bp. Unfortunately, Poland and Slovakia are not included in the E/M sample.

Since January 1997, the Bratislava Stock Exchange (BSSE) trades on three markets: the Listed Securities Market (main market), the Registered Securities Market (secondary market) and the Free Market. The quantitative listing requirements for the main market are provided in Table 1. The secondary market does not have quantitative listing requirements but a company on the Registered Securities Market has to submit semi-annual performance reports. In many respects the BSSE is the least developed of the four Visegrad stock markets. Many structural problems remain (see below) and, in general, the Slovakian stock market is not very popular with international investors.

To gain further insights into structures of the Visegrad stock markets, it is instructive to have a look at some market indicators that are summarised in Table 2. The first line reports the number of domestic companies excluding investment companies. It is noteworthy that a relatively large number of companies are listed on the stock markets of the Czech Republic and Slovakia. This, of course, is a direct consequence of the mass privatisation strategy pursued in both countries. For instance, in June 1993 the PSE introduced 622 shares to the market from the first wave of voucher privatisation and in July a further 333 shares listed as a result of the second wave. It was the intention of the voucher privatisation to further widespread share-ownership (Lavigne, 1995). As it turned out, however, investment funds undermined this democratisation of share ownership and effectively controlled a large number of companies (Mervart, 1996 a,b and Milonas, 1995).

Table 2. Market Indicators [end of 1998]

	Budapest	Prague	Bratislava	Warsaw	London
Listed Companies[a]	55	261	837	198	2399
Market Capitalisation[b]	14.0	12.0	1.0	20.5	2,374.3
Average Company Size[c]	255.1	46.1	1.2	103.3	989.7
Turnover Ratio (%)	111.3	38.2	74.3	54.7	53.4
P/E Ratio[d]	17.0	-11.3	-174.2	10.7	20.4
Dividend Yield[d]	1.1	3.2	3.3	1.5	2.5
Settlement Index	38.1	76.7	NA	81.9	NA
Safekeeping Index	83.3	84.2	NA	82.7	NA
Operational Risk Index	56.4	64.0	NA	65.8	NA

Table 2. Market Indicators [end of 1998] (Contd.)

	Budapest	Prague	Bratislava	Warsaw	London
Introduction of IT Law[e]	1994	1992	1992	1991	1980
1st Enforcement of IT Law	1995	1993	–	1993	1981

(a) Number of domestic companies excluding investment companies; (b) US$ billion; (c) market capitalisation / number of listed companies, in US$ million; (d) price/earnings ratios for the IFCG indices, see IFC (1999); (e) insider-trading law.
Source: IFC (1999)

According to IFC statistics (IFC, 1999), in 1995 the number of listed companies reached more than 1,600 on the Prague stock exchange. That was more than the combined numbers for France, Germany, Italy and the Netherlands at that time. In 1997, however, the Prague stock exchange reduced the number of listed companies substantially when it removed 1,301 non-liquid shares from its Free Market. With its end-of-1998 figure of 261, the Czech stock market is still comparatively large but it only held rank 30 in the world. In Slovakia, on the other hand, a huge wave of companies listed on the Bratislava stock exchange in 1996. As of 1998, Slovakia had the 11th largest stock market in the world in terms of number of listed companies, ahead of countries like France and Germany.

The more conventional measure of market size is market capitalisation. According to this measure, the Bratislava stock exchange is very small. As a result, the average company size, defined as the ratio of market capitalisation to the number of listed companies, is only US$ 1.2 million in Bratislava. With a figure as low as this, Slovakia has the 6th lowest average company size in the IFC list of 102 countries (IFC, 1999, p.25). The London stock market, being the 3rd largest in the world in 1998 in terms of market capitalisation and in terms of total value traded, dwarfs the Visegrad stock markets in every aspect of size. But the the average company size on the BSE is not much lower than in many developed countries. Indeed Hungary had the 31st largest average company size in the world in 1998.

The liquidity of a market is often measured by the turnover ratio, i.e. the ratio of total value traded to market capitalisation. Although there are many very small companies listed on the Bratislava stock exchange, the overall liquidity does not seem to be negatively affected. In fact, the turnover ratio is higher in Bratislava than in London. Only in Prague is the turnover ratio lower than in London. At first sight, this is a surprising result but it should be remembered that the Visegrad stock markets are small and highly concentrated, i.e. a small number of companies with relatively high capitalisation contributes most of the turnover. For instance, in 1999 the five largest stocks on the PSE had a cumulative share of 48 per cent in terms of market capitalisation but a share of 77 per cent in turnover (PSE, 2000).

What might be at work in this puzzling comparison of turnover ratios between London and the Visegrad exchanges is an effect that is known as Simpson's paradox in statistics. Applied to turnover ratios, the effect would work like this. Imagine there are two groups of shares, call them A and B, and two exchanges, call them XSE and YSE. Assume that turnover of A shares is much higher than turnover of B shares on each exchange. Assume, further that for every category of shares, the turnover ratio is higher on YSE than on XSE. Thus, YSE should be regarded as the more liquid exchange of the two. If, however, XSE trades a much higher proportion of A shares than YSE then, on aggregate, the turnover ratio on XSE can be higher than on YSE. It would be worth researching this conjecture but to do this here would go beyond the scope of this paper.

The price/earnings (P/E) ratio is another popular financial measure and market indicator. In general, a high P/E ratio is regarded as a sign of overvaluation and a low ratio as a sign of undervaluation although this latter interpretation would certainly not apply to negative ratios. In fact, in 1998, the P/E ratios were negative in Prague and Bratislava as measured by the indices of the IFC. The P/E ratio for London is by far the highest of the five stock markets in Table 2. It is not at all clear, however, whether the P/E ratio of 20.4 for London is an indicator of overvaluation. What seems to bias the comparison of P/E ratios in 1998 is the fact that share prices increased in London but decreased in the Visegrad countries in the wake of the Russian crisis.

Table 2 also compares the dividend yield of the five stock markets. Traditionally, Japan is a country with very low dividend yields and very high P/E ratios. But over recent years, many other countries have moved towards dividend yields and P/E ratios that are similar to the Japanese values. For example, Fama and French (1999) report a dramatic decline in dividend payouts in the USA after 1978. The dividend yields of the Visegrad exchanges do not seem to be very different from the UK benchmark. In fact, dividend yields in Budapest and Warsaw are lower than the 2.5 of London and dividend yields in Prague and Bratislava are higher than the benchmark. The IFC reports a world average dividend yield of 1.6 for 1998 (IFC, 1999). The fact that the two exchanges with negative P/E ratios (Prague and Bratislava) are the ones with the highest dividend yields is somewhat puzzling, however.

The organisational efficiency of a stock market has many different aspects that are often difficult to quantify. Table 3 reports three indices of organisational efficiency that were compiled by GSCS (see IFC, 1999). The settlement index measures the overall costs of failed trades. It incorporates the following variables: the proportion of trades that fail, the length of time for which orders fail to be executed, average trade size and interest rate. An index value of 100 represents optimal settlement efficiency and any values below that benchmark indicate some degree of excess settlement costs. Of the three markets for which settlement performance indices are available, perhaps somewhat surprisingly, the BSE has the lowest index value. The settlement for share transactions on the BUX is five working days after the trade whereas the delivery-versus-payment systems of the PSE and the WSE settle transactions three days after the trade was agreed. Quite often there is substantial intra-year variation of the GSCS indices. This is also true for the settlement index for the BSE in 1998 which increased from 24.4 in the first quarter of 1998 to 51.7 in the last quarter to produce an annual average of 38.1 which is reported in Table 2. Unfortunately, the GSCS indices are not available for the BSSE.

The safekeeping index measures aspects of efficiency with respect to collection of dividends, reclamation of withholding taxes and the protection of rights in the event of corporate actions. The index is constructed with five factors: average time between payable date and receipt of payment, total returns, rates of withholding tax and reclaim potential, number and type of corporate actions, and interest rate. The withholding tax on dividends is 10 per cent in Hungary, 20 per cent in Poland, and 25 per cent in the Czech Republic whereas Slovakia does not have a withholding tax on dividend payments. The safekeeping indices for Hungary, the Czech Republic and Poland are quite high reflecting good standards in this aspect of organisational efficiency. It is interesting to note that, from 1997 to 1998, the safekeeping index increased by 10 and 8 index points for the Czech Republic and Poland, respectively. This is a clear sign of improvement. Hungary had a high index value of 80.5 in 1997 already.

The operational risk index captures a wide range of factors of organisational efficiency. It incorporates quantitative measures of compliance with the recommendations of the Group of Thirty, the effectiveness of the regulatory and legal structure of the market, and counterparty and 'force majeure' risk. The values of the operational risk indices are quite low for the three markets in Table 2 but all three improved their performance in 1998. Hungary, in particular, was successful in reducing operational risk with an increase of the index by 20 points compared to the previous year. Operational risk does not seem to be higher on those three Visegrad markets than in other emerging markets. In the 19-country GSCS sample, the average index value for operational risk is 56.9 and the value for Budapest is only marginally lower than that.

In a recent paper, Bhattacharya and Daouk (1999) stressed the importance of insider-trading (IT) legislation and, especially, its enforcement as part of the regulatory framework. With their panel data set of 103 countries and a sample period from January 1968 to December 1998 they estimate that the enforcement of IT legislation reduces the annual cost of capital by about 5 per cent on average. Existence and enforcement of IT laws are measured in their study by the date when IT laws were introduced and when the first prosecution, successful or not, took place. The USA were, by a wide margin, the first country to introduce (in 1934) and to enforce (in 1961) IT legislation. The last two rows of Table 2 show the corresponding data for the Visegrad countries and the UK. Not too much should be read into the dates of introduction and enforcement. After all, stock markets in the Visegrad countries were only (re-)opened in the early 1990s. Moreover, the date of first prosecution is a rather crude measure of prosecution. For a long time, the Czech stock market had a reputation of market manipulation and insider trading and this although insider trading was prosecuted as early as 1993. What is more important is the fact that Slovakia is one of the countries without any prosecution.

This demonstrates again that the BSSE still has some organisational inefficiencies. It certainly lags behind the developments in Budapest, Prague and Warsaw. Perhaps the PSE can serve as of role model for the BSSE. Not long ago, the PSE was criticised by many investors for its lack of efficiency. Since 1998, however, the PSE has made enormous progress in its operational and regulatory aspects of its business. To revive the Czech capital market, the Securities Commission was created to supervise and regulate the market, the law on investment funds was amended to increase the transparency of their operations and to restrict their holdings in companies, and a new quote-driven trading system was installed. The PSE also considerably tightened its membership rules and many other regulations. As a result, the number of exchange members dropped from 88 to 71 in 1998. On the other hand, trade volume increased by 38 per cent in 1998 and 80 per cent in 1999. This underlines the new confidence of investors in the PSE.

3. MARKET DYNAMICS AND RETURN STATISTICS

The previous section examined some issues of organisational efficiency of the Visegrad stock markets. Section 4 will analyse some simple aspects of information efficiency at an aggregate level of price dynamics by searching for possible return anomalies of their stock price indices. This section describes the indices and presents some descriptive statistics of their return dynamics.

The BUX is the official share price index of the BSE. It was launched on 2 January, 1991 with a basis of 1,000 points. The number of stocks in the index varies but it is restricted to a maximum of 25. At the end of 1998, the number of stocks was 18. Currently, the four largest stocks represent 60 per cent of the index. The BUX is a total return index, i.e. it includes dividend payments.

The PX-50 was introduced on 5 April, 1994 as the official index of the PSE with a base value of 1,000. As the name indicates, the PX-50 represents the 50 largest (in terms of market capitalisation) and most liquid stocks on the market. Like in the BUX, the stocks are weighted by market capitalisation. The dominant share on the PSE is Cesky Telecom which currently contributes more than 40 per cent to the index. Unlike the BUX, the PX-50 is a price index, i.e. dividends are not included.

The SAX is the official share index of the BSSE and was launched on 14 September, 1993 with an initial value of 100. It is weighted by market capitalisation and includes the 16 most liquid stocks. As a total return index it includes dividends.

The WSE has three official share indices for its Main Market of which the WIG is the most widely quoted. Like the BUX and the SAX it is a total return index. The base date of the WIG is 16 April, 1991 and the base value is 1,000. The WIG includes all stocks listed on the main market. The other two indices are the blue-chip WIG20 and the mid-market MIDWIG. As a benchmark for the four Visegrad indices, the FTSE100, which is a price index, is used.

The development of the five indices is illustrated Figure 1. Note that the vertical axis has a logarithmic scale. With the exception of the FTSE100 and the PX50, the index series start at their base periods. The PX50 series starts in September 1993, seven months before the base period, to show the strong surge in the index in 1993 and early 1994. In the first six months, the PX50 increased by 270 per cent. The base period of the PX50 can be identified as the second intersection of the thick and grey PX50-line with the horizontal 1000-line.

The FTSE index in this sample begins in January 1991 at the base period of the BUX which has the earliest base of the four Visegrad indices. In this paper different sample periods will be used. For some analysis with monthly data, the sample periods of Figure 1 will be used. However, for the analysis with daily data it is important to use data that are equally spaced in terms of trading days (see below). As mentioned above, the WSE began to trading on all working days in October 1994. To facilitate the comparison between the five index series, most analysis will be based on a sample from October 1994 to February 2000.

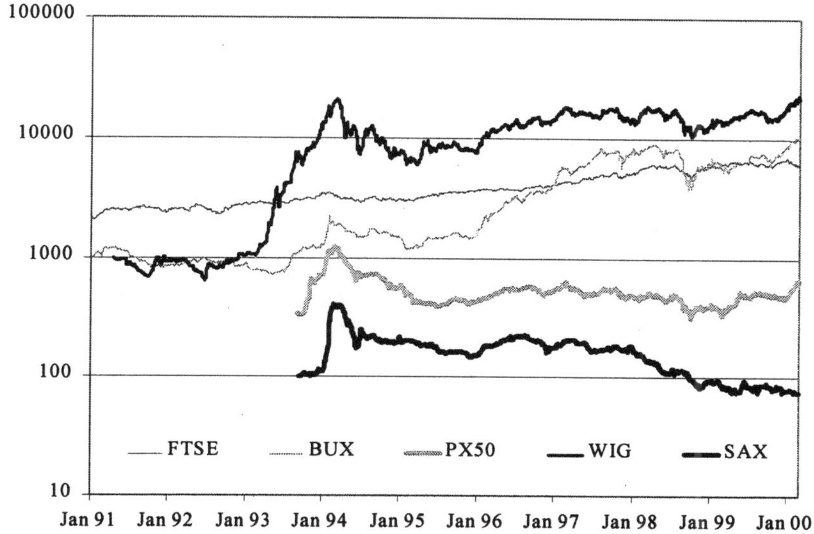

Figure 1. Dynamics of Stock Market Indices

It is quite amazing that even on a logarithmic scale the Visegrad indices show such an explosive increase in 1993 and early 1994. Investors in these markets were subject to a mind-boggling change of fortunes. A quite spectacular episode was the apparent bursting of a speculative bubble in March and April 1994. The WIG crashed from a level of over 20,000 to 9,980.4 (Thursday 14 April) within 12 trading days only to be back at 13,099 a week later and then plummeting back to 11,020 after another week. This sort of roller-coaster ride seems to characterise much of the stock-market dynamics in the Visegrad countries at least until 1994. The experience of the SAX is even more breathtaking. From the first day of trading in 1994 to Wednesday, 23 February the SAX sky-rocketed from 110.11 to its peak of 405.49. On 1 February, the index increased by 32 per cent! By comparison, the FT-SE 100 appears to be very smooth and on a relatively steady upward trend.

Many countries around the world were affected by the emerging-market boom of 1993 and early 1994. But even for the standards of emerging-markets, the four Visegrad indices showed extraordinary volatility in their early years. The IFC (1997) reports that Poland had the largest standard deviation among its 30 price indices of emerging markets for the period from December 1991 to December 1996.

One of the most apparent stylised facts of emerging stock markets is their high volatility of returns. Table 3 shows that this is also true for the Visegrad stock markets. It displays descriptive statistics of continuously compounded returns for the five stock-market indices for a sample period from October 1994 to February 2000. The variances of returns of the BUX, the PX50, the SAX, and the WIG are much higher than the variance of the FTSE100. The BUX has the highest variance which is higher than that of the FTSE100 by a factor of more than 4.5. The variance of the PX50 is much smaller than that of the BUX and the other Visegrad indices but still larger than that of the FTSE100 by about a third.

Table 3. Descriptive Statistics

	BUX	PX50	SAX	WIG	FTSE100
Mean (annualised)	34.263	-1.392	-19.551	15.781	13.212
Variance	4.448	1.301	2.042	4.022	0.970
Skewness	-1.089	-0.207	-0.700	-0.103	-0.112
Excess kurtosis	13.017	3.422	8.832	2.126	1.579
Maximum	-18.034	-7.077	-11.484	-10.286	-3.889
Minimum	13.616	5.820	9.574	7.893	4.345
Observations	1350	1328	1313	1350	1367

However, a high level of volatility is not necessarily equivalent to a high level of risk since, from a global portfolio perspective, it might be possible to reduce some of the risk through international diversification. Indeed, in terms of risk reduction, a high volatility is helpful if the correlation to other markets is negative since this would produce strongly negative covariances. An analysis of this issue is beyond the purview of this paper. But it is interesting to note that the correlation coefficients of the Visegrad markets with the UK stock market seem to indicate that the Czech and Slovak stock markets are the best markets for diversification. Based on monthly returns of the last five years, the correlation coefficients are: 0.46 for the BUX, 0.04 for the PX50, -0.7 for the SAX, and 0.31 for the WIG.

Naturally, investors will also be interested in average returns as estimates of expected returns. Table 3 reports the annualised means of daily returns. Investors would certainly be interested to know that, over a period of nearly ten years, the Hungarian and the Polish stock markets offered very attractive average annual returns of 34 and 16 per cent, respectively. Of course, these are nominal returns and expressed in forints and zloties, respectively. If expressed in US dollars, the average annual return of the WIG is a quite modest 5 per cent and the BUX's return drops to 29 per cent. In the past, the WIG showed highly variable annual returns: whereas the WIG increased by more than 1,000 per cent in 1993, it fell by almost 40 per cent in the following year.

In many empirical studies, stock market returns turn out to have asymmetric distributions. Typically, these distributions are skewed to the left because the occasional stock-market crashes or crashettes, as smaller crashes are sometimes called, produce outliers in the left tails of the distributions. Indeed, the absolute value of the minimum is for all five indices larger than the maximum daily index change. The conventional statistical measure of asymmetry in distribution is the coefficient of skewness which is computed as the third moment of a standardised variable (a variable with a mean of 0 and a variance of 1). As Table 3 shows, all five indices have negative skewnesses in this sample but a formal test indicates that the skewnesses of the WIG and the FTSE100 are not significantly negative.

An especially strong and robust empirical regularity of short-run stock-market returns is the leptokurtosis of return distributions. Kurtosis, as a measure of distributional shape, is computed as the fourth moment of a standardised variable. As a benchmark of distributional shape, a normal (Gaussian) distribution has a value of 3. With reference to the normal distribution, excess kurtosis is defined as kurtosis minus 3. A distribution with positive excess kurtosis is peaked and/or heavy tailed and is said to be leptokurtic. In a formal statistical test (details are omitted to save space) all five indices have highly significant leptokurtosis. It is apparent, however, that the four Visegrad indices (especially the BUX and the SAX) have much higher excess kurtosis than the FTSE100. The economic interpretation is that those indices have more 'outlier' returns and/or numerically (in absolute value) very small returns (in particular zero returns) than the FTSE100. The Markov-switching model that is applied below will be able to capture both the skewness and leptokurtosis of return distributions.

4. CALENDAR ANOMALIES

Organisational efficiency is only one aspect of overall market efficiency. Following the seminal study of Fama (1970), most academic research has concentrated on information efficiency of capital markets instead. A market is said to be informationally efficient if prices fully reflect available information. An equivalent way to define information efficiency is to say that it is not possible to systematically earn (risk-adjusted) excess profits on such a market. Direct tests of information efficiency, however, are relatively rare. Typical direct tests are tests of non-arbitrage conditions such as cash-and-carry relationships between spot and futures markets or covered interest parity.

In most studies of market efficiency, the tests are of an indirect nature. In those studies, market efficiency is tested as a joint hypothesis of efficiency and of a model of price dynamics. The test of the random walk hypothesis is a case in point. If one assumes that expected returns are constant then shares prices should follow a random walk with drift in an informationally efficient market, i.e. returns should not be autocorrelated. The problem with these indirect tests is that it is not clear, when the joint hypothesis is rejected, whether the efficiency hypothesis is false or whether the underlying model of price dynamics is wrong.

A simple way to test information efficiency is to look for potential anomalies in the return series. Meanwhile, a vast literature has emerged that unveils a number of properties of stock returns that are difficult to reconcile with the notion of information efficiency. For a survey of the literature see Dimson (1988) and Thaler (1992). Some of the best documented anomalies are calendar effects, the small-firm effect, and the P/E effect. The available time series for the Visegrad stock markets are too short to examine many of those effects but an analysis of calendar effects is possible.

A puzzling result in the anomalies literature is the day-of-the-week effect. French (1980), for instance, found for the S&P500 in the period from 1953 to 1977, but also for 5-year subperiods, that average Monday returns were significantly negative whereas average returns on all other trading days of the week were positive. It is difficult to find an economic rationale for this effect. The most favoured explanation is that a psychological effect is at work. For some reason, perhaps as a sign of the 'Mondays blues', (mostly individual) investors tend to place sell orders on Mondays when market activity is lower than on other days of the week. An intriguing result is that similar patterns of trading and returns were discovered in experimental markets. Regular trading interruptions produced an effect than was very similar to the effect associated with the weekend.

Usually, the day-of-the-week effect is not strong enough to create direct arbitrage opportunities. Transaction costs tend to be to high to allow systematic arbitrage profits from, for instance, buying on Mondays and selling on Tuesdays. Nevertheless, the smart investor would place buy orders on Mondays instead of Fridays or Tuesdays and sell orders on days other than Mondays to take advantage of this anomaly.

To examine whether the day-of-the-week effect prevails on the Visegrad stock markets, the mean (annualised) returns for each trading day are plotted in Figure 2. It is clear to the naked eye that the Monday returns are not special in Figure 2. Only the PX50 and the SAX have negative mean returns on Mondays but these indices also have negative mean returns on most other days of the week. Somewhat ironically, the WIG has the highest mean return on Mondays. Even the FTSE100, which had a significantly negative Monday effect in the past (Mills and Coutts, 1995), shows a positive mean return on Mondays (19 per cent) that is larger than the overall mean return (13 per cent).

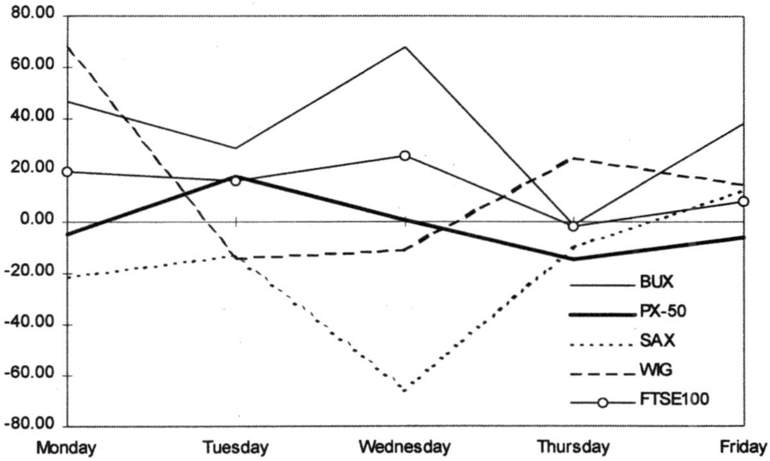

Figure 2. Annualised Returns at Different Weekdays

Formal Analysis-of-Variance (ANOVA) tests confirm that there are no significant day-of-the-week effects in the five indices during the sample period. All F statistics of the ANOVA tests have empirical significance levels in excess of 10 per cent. Details are omitted to save space. However, an interesting detail of the ANOVA tests is that the FTSE100 and the PX50 have much smaller between-group variation than the other three indices. The between-group mean squares for the FTSE100 and the PX50 are 0.487 and 0.612, respectively. The corresponding numbers for the other three indices are all larger than 3. This means that for the FTSE100 and the PX50 the average returns vary far less throughout the week than for the BUX, SAX and WIG. This observation is confirmed by Figure 2. Note that the FTSE and PX50 are also the indices that show the overall smallest variance in Table 2.

Weekend returns are interesting for another reason. Returns on Tuesday, Wednesday, Thursday and Friday (holidays aside) are one-day return whereas the Monday return is a three-day return. If daily returns are independent and identically distributed then the mean and the variance of Monday returns should be three times larger than the mean and the variance of one-day returns, respectively. This is the calendar-time hypothesis. Alternatively, one can argue that it is not calendar time that counts but trading time. When exchanges are closed, no information can be generated from or revealed through trading. Moreover, company news or other relevant macroeconomic news are rarely released throughout weekends. This is the trading-time hypothesis. In essence, the two hypotheses are concerned with the flow of information. If the flow of information to the markets is more or less homogeneous throughout the day and throughout the week then the calendar-time hypothesis applies. If, however, the information flow ebbs off when trading and economic activity come to a halt then the trading-time hypothesis is valid.

It is interesting to examine which of the two hypothesis is true. The trading-time hypothesis is chosen as the null hypothesis. To test this hypothesis, a sub-sample is created that contains only one-day and three-day returns. The results are reported in Table 4. The ANOVA F-statistic is used to test the hypothesis whether one-day and two-day returns have the same means. The test is equivalent to a standard two-sample t-test. Since no significant differences in means can be found in the day-of-the-week comparisons, it is not surprising that the F-statistic is insignificant for all five indices. Therefore, the hypothesis that the means of one-day returns and weekend returns are equal cannot be rejected. However, it could be argued that mean effects are potentially difficult to detect because daily returns are often close to zero. In fact, the overall means of the PX50 and the WIG are not significantly different from zero at the conventional 5 per cent level and the means of the SAX and the FTSE100 are only marginally significant.

Table 4. Weekend Effect

	BUX	PX50	SAX	WIG	FTSE100
ANOVA F statistic	0.590	0.179	0.114	2.663	0.059
Variance of 1-day returns	4.148	1.310	2.111	3.795	0.949
Variance of 3-day returns	5.491	1.284	1.488	4.687	1.022
Variance ratio	1.324	0.981	0.705	1.235	1.077
Levene test (p-value)	0.053	0.983	0.057	0.031	0.575
WMW test (p-value)	0.296	0.574	0.457	0.182	0.708

Table 4 also shows the variances of one-day returns and three-day returns. The calendar-time hypothesis predicts the three-day variance (s_3^2) to be three times larger than the one-day variance (s_1^2) whereas the trading-time hypothesis predicts both variances to be the same. It is obvious from Table 4 that the empirical evidence favours the trading-time hypothesis. The variance ratio s_3^2 / s_1^2 is much closer to 1 than to 3. Indeed, two of the five ratios are smaller than 1. The trading-time hypothesis can formally be tested with Levene's nonparametric test of homogeneity of variances. Table 4 reports the empirical significance levels (p-value) of this test. Applying a notional 5 per cent level, the null hypothesis only marginally fails to be rejected for the BUX and the SAX. The variance ratio of the BUX is larger than 1 but the ratio of the SAX is smaller than 1. The WIG is the only index for which the trading-time hypothesis is rejected with the Levene test. But clearly, this rejection does not imply that the calendar-time hypothesis should be adopted as an alternative to the null hypothesis. Numerically the variance ratio of the WIG is much closer to the value of 1 than to the value of 3.

As a further test of the trading-time hypothesis, the nonparametric Wilcoxon-Mann-Whitney (WMW) test is applied (see e.g. Siegel and Castellan, 1988). The WMW test has the null hypothesis that two independent samples come from the same population. In the context of the trading-time hypothesis this means that the one-day returns and the three-day returns have the same distribution. In a way, the WMW encompassed the equality-of-means test and the homogeneity-of-variances test. The last row of Table 4 shows the empirical significance levels of this test. Since all p-values are well above the 0.05 level, there is no empirical evidence to reject the trading-time hypothesis with this test. In summary, there is no evidence in *favour* of the calendar-time hypothesis or *against* the trading-time hypothesis. A further test of the trading-time hypothesis will be provided below when the extension of the return horizon is analysed.

The results for the weekend effect have an important implication. Due to weekends and holidays, daily return data are not equally spaced in calendar time but equally spaced in trading time. If the calendar-time hypothesis were valid complicated adjustments would be necessary to perform valid time-series analysis with the data. Fortunately, one can regard the daily data as equally spaced because the trading-time hypothesis receives strong empirical support.

Another popular calendar anomaly is the January effect. Numerous studies have shown that returns in January are higher than in other months of the year. Several economic hypotheses were put forward to explain this effect, among others the tax-loss-selling hypothesis and the turn-of-year-liquidity hypothesis. Whatever the merits of these explanations, the smart investor can exploit the January effect with appropriate timing of his or her trades.

Is there a January effect in the Visegrad indices? Figure 3 provides a first answer. It plots the average returns for the twelve months of the year. To maximise the number of observations, the samples are extended to the periods covered by Figure 1. Figure 3 seems to indicate that there is a moderate January effect in the Visegrad indices. For the BUX, the PX50 and the WIG, the average January return is the highest of the 12 means. However, for the SAX the January-average is only the third highest average and for the FTSE100 the January-average is even below the overall average.

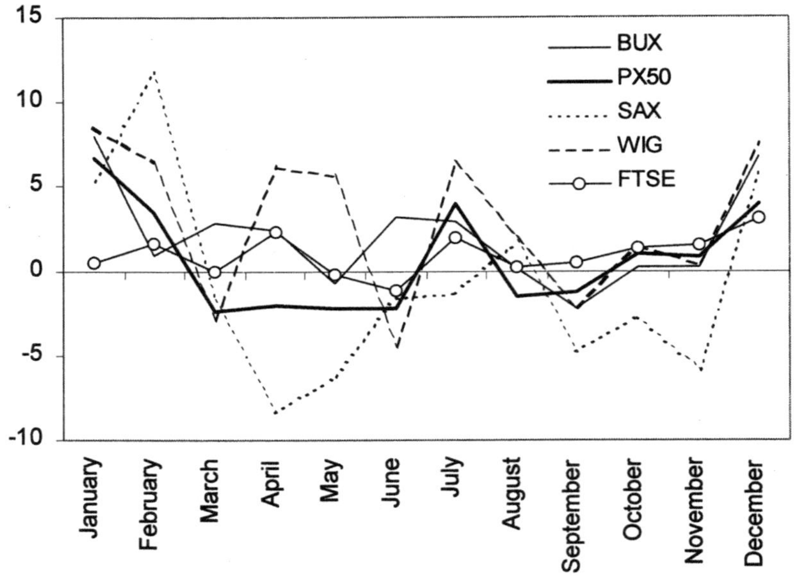

Figure 3. Returns in Different Months

Table 5 provides the results from formal tests of the January effect. The upper panel reports the F-statistics of an ANOVA test that the means of all 12 months are the same. All five test statistics are very low and the empirical significance levels in parentheses indicate that the null hypothesis cannot be rejected for any of the indices. Therefore, the upper panel suggests that there are no month-of-the-year effects.

Table 5. January Effect

	BUX	PX50	SAX	WIG	FTSE100
	All 12 months				
ANOVA F statistic	0.696	0.502	1.383	0.694	0.856
(p-value)	(0.739)	(0.895)	(0.203)	(0.741)	(0.586)
	January vs. all other months				
January	7.995	6.656	5.280	8.537	0.525
All other months	1.515	0.278	−1.012	2.430	1.022
ANOVA F statistic	3.350	2.234	1.439	1.257	0.140
(p-value)	(0.070)	(0.139)	(0.234)	(0.265)	(0.709)

The lower panel of Table 5 shows test results for the specific hypothesis that the average January return is equal to the average of the 11 other monthly returns. On average, January returns are higher than returns in the remaining months of the year on all Visegrad stock markets. For instance, the mean January return for the BUX is close to 8 per cent (not annualised) whereas the other 11 months have an average return of only

1.5 per cent. However, an ANOVA test does not confirm a January effect at the 5 per cent significance level. Even the F-statistic of 3.35 for the BUX has only an empirical significance level of 7 per cent. It is also interesting to note that the FTSE100 does not show any sign of a January effect in this sample from January 1991 to February 2000. Its average January return is only half the mean return of the remaining months.

It is somewhat difficult to judge whether the weak January effects are a consequence of the relatively small sample sizes. For the PX50 and the SAX there are only seven January returns. On the other hand, the samples are certainly not too small for the tests of the day-of-the-week effects and here the results are quite clear. There is no evidence for a Monday effect or any other effect. With respect to calendar effects, therefore, one can conclude that the Visegrad stock exchanges show no signs of information inefficiency. The fact that these calendar effects have also disappeared in the FTSE100 is perhaps a bit surprising. But recently similar disappearances of anomalies have been reported, for instance for the small-company effect. This should not be too surprising. After all, once these anomalies become public there is an incentive for investors to take advantage of the anomalies and that would tend to eliminate the anomalies.

5. MODELLING RETURN DYNAMICS

As explained above, under the assumption of independent and identically distributed returns, the variance of returns is a function of the investment horizon, i.e.

$$\sigma^2(\tau) = \tau\sigma^2(1) \tag{1}$$

where $\sigma^2(1)$ is the variance in a unit time interval (in this case a day) and $\sigma^2(\tau)$ is the variance of returns in an interval of length τ. The analysis in the previous chapter showed that the relevant measure of time is trading time. But what happens when trading time varies? Equation (1) implies that the variance of weekly returns should be approximately five times the variance of daily returns and the variance of τ-day returns should be τ times the variance of daily returns if returns are independent and identically distributed. In other words, the variance ratio VR=$\sigma^2(\tau)/[\tau\sigma^2(1)]$ should be equal to 1 for all τ.[1]

However, Poterba and Summers (1988) find for a wide range of international stock markets that variance ratios tend to have an inverted-u shape, when plotted against τ (this plot is called a 'variogram'), with a peak at one or two years. This result establishes another anomaly which has been called mean reversion. The variogram is just an alternative way

[1] Note that the definition of the variance ratio is slightly different in Table 4.

to represent autocorrelations. The inverted-u shape of VRs implies that short-run returns are positively autocorrelated and that higher-order autocorrelations tend to be negative. The economic interpretation is that, in the short run, return dynamics are self-enforcing. An extreme form of a self-enforcing process would be a bubble but also losses can be self-enforcing. This process produces positive autocorrelation coefficients and an increase in the variance ratio. In the long run, overvaluations or undervaluation are corrected by mean reversion which is reflected in negative high-order autocorrelations and a decrease in the variance ratio. In this way, the variogram can capture overreaction in stock markets (Lo and McKinlay, 1988). It is interesting to examine whether similar effects prevail on the Visegrad stock markets.

Given the relatively short sample period for the Visegrad countries, a horizon for τ of 1 year or more is not advisable (see Lo and MacKinlay (1989)). The variogram in Figure 4 plots the variance ratios for all five indices up to τ =70. A value of 70 corresponds approximately to quarterly returns. Note that the τ-period returns overlap by $\tau - 1$ periods.

The FTSE100 shows a quite different pattern to that of the other four indices. For τ <5, the variance ratios are slightly larger than 1.0 but they are smaller than 1.0 for $\tau \geq 5$. By contrast, variance ratios for the stock indices of the Visegrad countries tend to be larger than one. An extreme case is the PX50. Its variance ratios increase almost monotonically with τ. Therefore, there is no evidence for mean reversion in this index. Quite to the contrary, strong positive autocorrelations even at high-order lags lead to a disproportionate increase in stock-market risk when the return interval increases. A comparison of variance ratios between the Visegrad indices shows that the PX50 and the BUX deviate more strongly from the FTSE100 pattern than the SAX and the WIG.

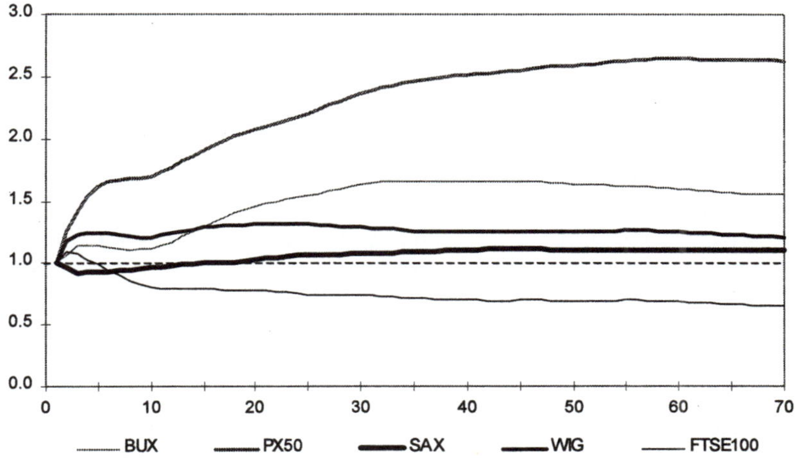

Figure 4. Variogram

To test formally whether the variance ratios of the indices are significantly different from 1, a heteroskedasticity-adjusted test statistic suggested by Lo and MacKinlay (1989) is applied. This test statistic, denoted by $z_2(\tau)$, has asymptotically a standard normal distribution. Table 6 provides values of the variance ratio and the test statistic for selected values of τ. According to the test statistics in Table 6, all variance ratios of the PX50 are significantly larger than 1 whereas the variance ratios of the SAX, the WIG, and the FTSE100 are not significant. The same holds for almost all intermediate values of τ which are not report in Table 6 to save space. Only some low-order variance ratios of the WIG and the FTSE100 are significantly positive.

Table 6. Variance ratios and test statistics

	BUX		PX50		SAX		WIG		FTSE100	
τ	VR	z_2	VR	z_2	VR	z_2	VR	z_2	VR	z_2
10	1.12	0.78	1.70	5.38	0.97	-0.17	1.21	1.73	0.81	-1.58
20	1.46	2.03	2.07	5.68	1.03	0.33	1.32	1.90	0.77	-1.21
30	1.63	2.40	2.36	5.65	1.08	0.59	1.29	1.37	0.74	-1.11
40	1.66	2.26	2.52	5.28	1.11	0.73	1.25	0.99	0.70	-1.10
50	1.64	2.07	2.59	4.75	1.11	0.73	1.25	0.89	0.69	-1.05
60	1.60	1.87	2.65	4.45	1.10	0.72	1.25	0.80	0.69	-0.97
70	1.55	1.67	2.63	4.01	1.10	0.72	1.21	0.60	0.65	-1.00

The variance ratios of the BUX display a somewhat different pattern. Only the variance ratios between $\tau = 20$ and $\tau = 56$ are significantly positive. All other variance ratios are insignificant. Thus the BUX is the only index that shows the inverted-u shape that Poterba and Summers found in other markets.

In summary, the evidence of overreaction and mean reversion is not very strong in the Visegrad indices since October 1994. As indicated by the variance ratios, the PX50 displays overreaction but, apparently, this is not corrected by mean reversion in the relatively short time span of a quarter that is used here. Only the variance ratios of the BUX show the typical inverted-u pattern. Like the FTSE100, the SAX and the WIG have almost no significant variance ratios. Thus overreaction does not seem to be a problem on these markets. This result is somewhat surprising. Is this another case of a disappearing anomaly? Not necessarily. It should be borne in mind that the sample period is relatively short and that return horizons are restricted to three months or less. As mentioned above, the typical peak of variograms occurs at one to two year return intervals. Another problem is that the analysis in this paper is based on daily data which exhibit much short-run noise. But a sample based on monthly data would be too small.

As mentioned in Section 3, the stock markets of the Visegrad countries show enormous price volatility. Figure 1 highlights the roller-coaster nature of these markets as compared with the market in London. It is, of course, no surprise that emerging stock markets are very volatile and risky. Figure 1 also shows that there was quite substantial co-movement in the four Visegrad indices. The Visegrad stock markets benefited greatly from the emerging-stock-market boom of 1993 and the first few months of 1994. The episode of 1993/94 appears very much like a speculative bubble and it was not until 1996 that the stock markets of the Visegrad countries recovered from the crash in early 1994.

Capital flows to and from emerging markets, apparently, follow fads and fashions and stock market prices go through very strong cycles. By comparison, the FTSE100 looks quite smooth in Figure 1. To quantify the observation that the stock markets of the Visegrad countries show cyclical behaviour, a Markov-switching model is applied to the index returns. This model is based on the notion that a time series can be decomposed into 2 (or more) different states. The states can be represented by distributions with different means μ_j and/or different variances σ_j^2. Therefore, the first building block of this model is a mixture of distributions:

$$f(r) = \sum_{j=1}^{J} p_j f_j(r \mid \mu_j, \sigma_j^2) \tag{2}$$

where $f_j(.)$ denotes the density of the return r in state j. Since the objective is to identify and quantify bull markets (or booms) and bear markets (or crashes), the number of states is restricted to $J = 2$. In (2), p_j can be interpreted as the probability of state j. The Markov-switching model is a dynamic version of the mixture model in (2) in that the additional assumption is made that the probabilities to be in state $s_t = j$ follow a time-homogeneous first-order Markov process. Therefore, the transition probabilities between states are:

$$p(s_t = j \mid s_{t-1} = i) = p_{ij}\,. \tag{3}$$

For a Markov-switching model with 2 states, one gets a 2x2 transition matrix of states with 2 independent probabilities p_{11} and p_{22}. Estimation of the model requires that a density function is specified and the normal distribution is a natural choice that is adopted here. The probabilities defined in (3) are conditional on the state in the previous period. The unconditional stationary probability to be in state 1 when there are only 2 states is given by

$$\rho = \frac{1 - p_{22}}{2 - p_{11} - p_{22}} \tag{4}$$

The Markov-switching model for stock return data can also be motivated with the descriptive statistics of Table 3. Most return distributions have significant negative skewness and all five return distributions have highly significant leptokurtosis, i.e. the returns do not follow normal (Gaussian) distributions. Markov-switching models can capture these non-normalities. If the two state densities $f_j(.)$ have different variances then the unconditional distribution is leptokurtic. Moreover, if the two densities have different means and variances then the unconditional distribution will be asymmetric.

Estimates of the model parameters for all five indices are reported in Table 7. State 1 has in all cases a higher mean than state 2 but only for the BUX, the PX-50, and the SAX is the mean of state 2 negative. It follows that the model does not identify booms and crashes for the WIG and the FTSE100 but phases of very strong gains or booms (state 1) and more moderate or normal gains (state 2). It should also be noted that μ_2 is not significantly different from zero for the BUX and the PX50 and, therefore, the same interpretation applies to these indices as to the WIG and the FTSE100. Details of inferential statistics are omitted to save space but the results are available upon request. For the PX50, the SAX and the WIG, μ_1 is not significantly different from zero but this is not surprising since these indices have been on downward trends or increased only slightly since October 1994.

Table 7. Parameter estimates of the Markov-switching model

	BUX	PX50	SAX	WIG	FTSE100
μ_1	0.185	0.023	0.049	0.087	0.069
μ_2	-0.027	-0.037	-0.315	0.007	0.034
σ_1^2	1.249	0.290	0.397	1.911	0.417
σ_2^2	15.248	2.396	5.020	9.074	1.607
p_{11}	0.969	0.953	0.830	0.986	0.996
p_{22}	0.896	0.949	0.683	0.968	0.996
$\mu_1 - \mu_2$	0.213	0.060	0.363	0.080	0.035
σ_2^2/σ_1^2	12.212	8.254	12.637	4.748	3.855
ρ	0.773	0.519	0.651	0.688	0.467

For all indices, the bull market component (state 1) has a lower variance than the bear market component (state 2). For the BUX and the SAX, the variance of state 2 is more than 12 times higher than the variance of state 1. Similarly, the ratio σ_2^2/σ_1^2 is 8.3 for the PX50 and 4.7 for the WIG. It is interesting to note that the state-1 variance of the FTSE100 is not very different from those of the Visegrad indices. In fact, the estimates of σ_1^2 are lower for the PX50 and the SAX than for the FTSE100. What creates the higher overall volatility of the Visegrad indices is the much greater variance in state 2, i.e. in the bear market regime. The FTSE100 has also a much smaller difference between the means of state 1 and state 2 than the Visegrad indices. This underlines that the stock market cycles in the Visegrad country are much more pronounced than on the London stock market. The estimated differences $\mu_1 - \mu_2$ is especially large for the BUX, where the estimated μ_1 is large, and for the SAX, where the estimated μ_2 is very small.

The estimates of the parameters p_{11} and p_{22} indicate that the two states have a large degree of persistence in all five time series. The probability to remain in the current state is especially large for the FTSE where this probability is 0.996 for both states. The stationary probability to be in a boom phase, as measured by the estimate of ρ, is relatively high for the BUX, SAX and WIG. According to the ρ's in Table 7, this probability is 77 per cent for the BUX, and around two thirds for the SAX and the WIG.

The estimated stationary probabilities to be in state 2 are plotted in the Appendix. The probabilities are 'smoothed' in the sense that they use the full sample information. For technical details see Lindgren (1978) or Hamilton (1990). The graphs indicate that the two states are more separated by different volatilities than by different means. Quite a few periods which are associated with state 2 are periods when the stock index increased. Therefore, it is appropriate to associate state 1 with normal or tranquil conditions and state 2 with high volatility and turbulent periods.

All five indices show a marked increase of the unconditional probability of state 2 in 1997 and 1998 when international stock markets were hit by the Asian crisis and the Russian crisis, respectively. It is not all surprising that the Visegrad countries were affected by the Russian crisis but it is interesting to observe that the state of high volatility has dominated in Prague, Bratislava and London since the outbreak of the crises.

The SAX and the FTSE100 are the extremes in terms of persistence of states. As noted above, both states have very high persistence for the FTSE100. This is reflected in the fact that its probability for state 2 was virtually zero for the whole of 1995 and 1996 and for the first half of 1997. The SAX, on the other hand, switches frequently between states of tranquillity and turbulence. It can be conjectured that this is a sign of an relatively immature market and an uneven flow of trading activity.

6. POLICY IMPLICATIONS AND CONCLUSIONS

The development of an efficient stock market should be an integral part of the transition process in Central and Eastern Europe. The analysis in the previous sections has shown that the stock markets in Budapest, Prague and Warsaw have made much progress in recent years in their developments of markets in which trading is regulated sufficiently and organised efficiently. For a long time, the Prague Stock Exchange was criticised for a lack of transparency, market manipulation and insider trading. In recent years, however, the PSE has made great efforts to regain the confidence of investors. It introduced stricter market regulation, improved considerably its trading systems, imposed more restrictive membership rules and removed 1,300 non-liquid shares from its market. It seems that investors have acknowledged these efforts. In the last 12 months (from March 1999 to February 2000), its official share price index rose from 333.4 to 644.8. Also the WSE in Poland and the BSE in Hungary experienced a renew surge of interest in their listed shares and substantial returns in recent months.

The market that was left out in this latest boom is the BSSE in Slovakia. It is not difficult to understand why this is so. The analysis of organisational efficiency of the Visegrad stock exchanges has shown that the BSSE is not up to the standards already achieved by the other exchanges. Initially, the BSSE was in a similar position as the PSE. Its voucher privatisation scheme was meant to lead to a democratisation of share ownership. It is doubtful, however, whether this target has been achieved. Instead, its market is lumbered with hundreds of non-liquid stocks. International investors shy away from the market for the same reasons for which they avoided the PSE in the past. In 1999, the Visegrad exchanges and the Ljubljana Stock Exchange (LSE) agreed to co-operate and to co-ordinate their efforts in the areas of information technology, derivatives, listing and disclosure requirements, marketing and membership. Perhaps this will provide the BSSE with an incentive to catch up.

This paper also examined issues of information efficiency. Simple tests of calendar anomalies and mean reversion were applied but there is not strong evidence of information inefficiency. In fact, calendar effects seem to have disappeared, even in London. There is some overreaction in the BUX and, especially, in the PX50 but the fact that the SAX returns seem to be independent and identically distributed should not be construed to imply that the BSSE is more efficient in the processing and transmission of information than the BSE or PSE. The more convincing explanation would be that investors simply neglect the BSSE to a large extent.

In summary, the stock markets in Budapest, Prague and Warsaw have not yet achieved the depth and sophistication of mature markets like the one in London but, perhaps, they can claim to be mature emerging markets.

REFERENCES

Bhattacharya, U. and H. Daouk (1999), The World Price of Insider Trading, Indiana University, Kelley School of Business, mimeo.

Conover, W.J., M.E. Johnson and M.M. Johnson (1981), A Comparative Study of Tests for Homogeneity of Variances, *Technometrics*, 28, 351-361.

Dimson, E. (1988), *Stock Market Anomalies*, Cambridge: Cambridge University Press.

Fama, E.F. (1970), Efficient Capital Markets: A Review of Theoretical and Empirical Work. *Journal of Finance*, 25, 383-417.

Fama, E.F. and K.R. French (1999), Disappearing Dividends: Changing Firm Characteristics or Lower Propensity to Pay? University of Chicago, Centre for Research in Security Prices Working Paper 509.

French, K.R. (1980), Stock Returns and the Weekend Effect, *Journal of Financial Economics*, 8, 55-69.

Hamilton, J.D. (1990), Analysis of Time Series Subject to Changes in Regime. *Journal of Econometrics*, 45, 39-70.

IFC (1997), *Emerging Stock Markets Factbook 1997*, Washington.

IFC (1999), *Emerging Stock Markets Factbook 1999*, Washington.

Lavigne, M. (1995), *The Economics of Transition*, Basingstoke: Macmillan.

Lindgren, G. (1978), Markov Regime Models for Mixed Distributions and Switching Regressions. *Scandinavian Journal of Statistics*, 5, 81-91.

Lo, A.W. and A.C. MacKinlay (1988), Stock Market Prices do not Follow Random Walks: Evidence from a simple specification test. *Review of Financial Studies*, 1, 41-66.

Lo, A.W. and A.C. MacKinlay (1989), The Size and Power of the Variance Ratio Test in Finite Samples. *Journal of Econometrics*, 40, 203-238.

Mervart, J. (1996a), An Overview of the Czech Voucher Privatization, Czech National Bank, Institute of Economics, mimeo.

Mervart, J. (1996b), Stock Market in CR, Czech National Bank, Institute of Economics, mimeo.

Mills, T.C. and J.A. Coutts (1995), Calendar Effects in the London Stock Exchange FT-SE Indices, *European Journal of Finance*, 1, 79-93.

Milonas, N.T. (1995), Mass Privatization Methods and their Effects on Capital Market Institutions, Agency Relationships and Managerial Monitoring, Katholieke Universiteit Leuven, Leuven Institute for Central and East European Studies, Working Paper 50/1995.

Poterba, J. and L. Summers (1988), Mean Reversion in Stock Returns: Evidence and Implications, *Journal of Financial Economics*, 22, 27-60.

PSE (2000), *Fact Book 2000*, Prague.

Schröder, M. (ed.) (2000), *The New Capital Markets in Central and Eastern Europe*, Mannheim, forthcoming.

Siegel, S. and N.J. Castellan, Jr. (1988) *Nonparametric Statistics for the Behavioral Sciences*, McGraw-Hill.

Thaler, R.H. (1992), *The Winner's Curse: Paradoxes and Anomalies of Economic Life*, Princeton University Press.

WSE (1999), Rules of the Warsaw Stock Exchange, Warsaw (available at http://www.wse.com.pl/gpw/regulen.htm)

Appendix

Estimated probabilities of state 2 in Markov-switching model

a) BUX

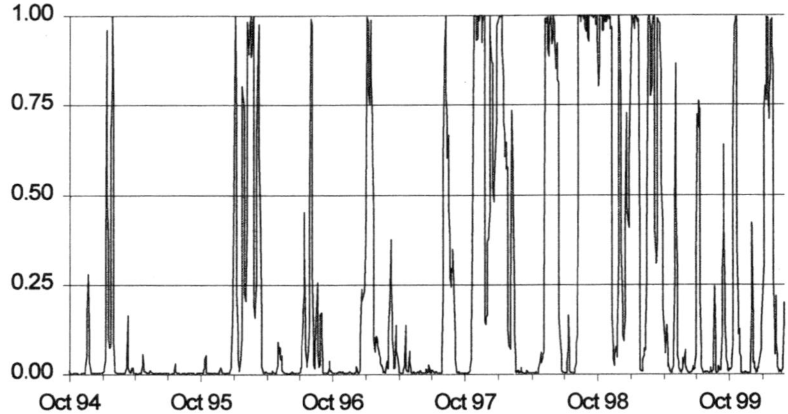

b) PX50

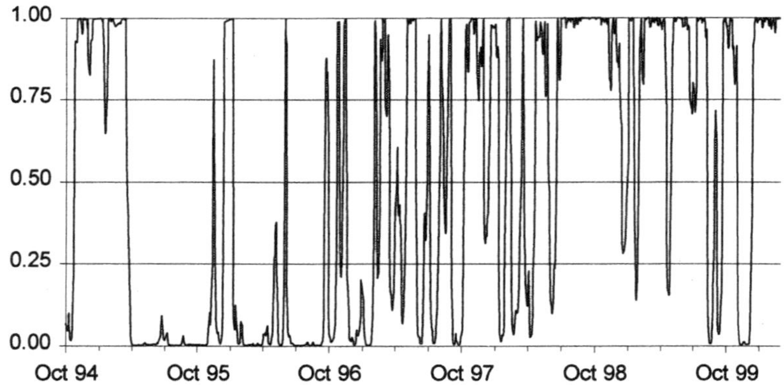

Estimated probabilities of state 2 in Markov-switching model (contd.)

c) SAX

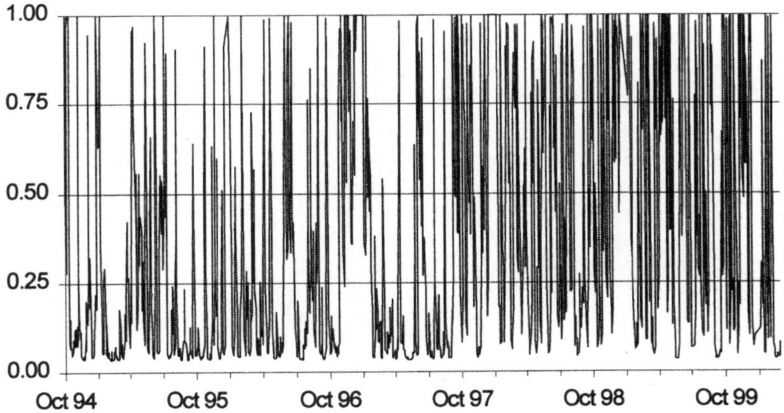

d) WIG

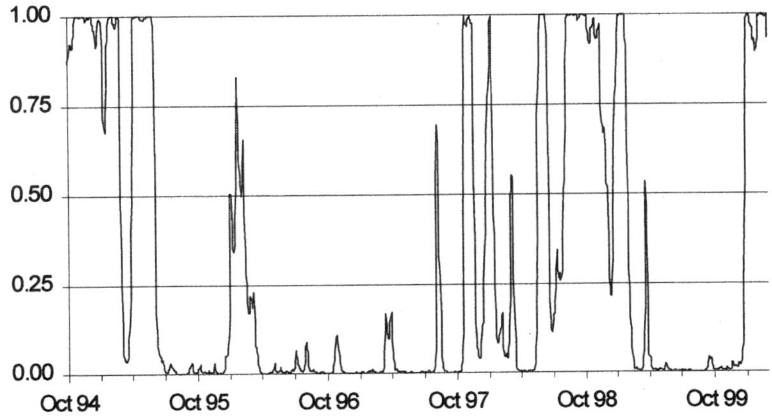

Estimated probabilities of state 2 in Markov-switching model (contd.)

e) FTSE100

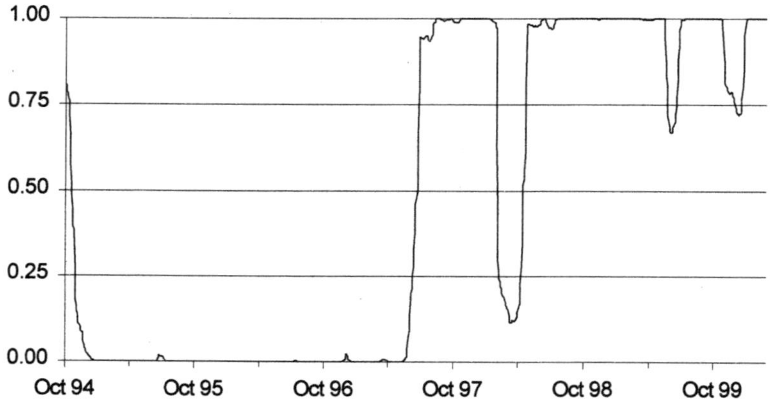

Index

Absorption, 36-39
Accounting system, 90
Anti-inflation policy, 63
Asian crisis, 271
Asset market speculation, 127
Auerbach, 26
Austria, 17
Bad debts/loans, 107, 113, 123 (see also non-performing loans)
Balance of payments equilibrium, 19
Balance of trade disequilibrium, 39
Bank and debt consolidation program, 95
Bank bonds, 166
Bank credit, 166
Bank crisis, 3, 63, 122-123, 225
Bank failure, 91, 121
Bank provisioning and standards, 93, 101, 110
Bank restructuring, 98
Bank runs, 122
Bank's net worth, 125
Banking laws, 91, 94, 127
Banking reforms, 222
Banking regulation, 127
Banking sector problems, 134 - 135
Banking supervision, 98, 127
Bankruptcy Act, 100
Barysch. K, 3, 149
Basle committee, 91
Bauc. J, 4
Benzi. R, 229
Bhattacharya. U, 254
Bi-cameral system, 12
Big-bang reforms, 34
Block trades, 206
Bond issues, 171
Bond law, 170, 173, 174, 184
Bond market, 154-156, 158, 160-165, 168-169, 173-175,177, 184, 186, 190, 201-203, 205, 212-213, 216, 218-220, 222, 227-230, 235, 238
Bond trading, 195, 198, 206, 207, 211, 214, 217
Bond transactions, 188-189, 195
Bond turnover, 205
Bond washing, 192, 222
Bonds, 153-154, 159, 160, 172, 178, 181-182, 183, 192-193, 197-199, 214, 218, 226, 236
Borrower default, 123
Bozzai. R, 4
Brady bonds, 225
Braga de Macedo. J, 2, 8
Branson. W, 2, 8
Bratislava Stock Exchange (BSSE), 185, 188-189, 201-202, 197-198, 206-208, 207, 212, 214, 249
Bretton Woods system of fixed exchange rates, 68
Brokerage houses, 176, 183, 197, 203
Budapest Stock Exchange (BSE), 183-186, 188-189, 196, 201-202, 206-208,212, 216-217, 247, 250, 272
Budget constraint, 23, 166-168
Budget deficit, 8, 25, 26, 81, 101, 159, 161, 165
Budget process, 9, 11, 13-17, 26
Budget surplus, 19,81, 157
Budgetary consolidation, 163
Budgetary targets, 14
Cabinet committees, 15
Calendar effects, 260
Capital account, 72
Capital adequacy, 93,

Capital controls, 125-129, 141-145
Capital flight, 72
Capital flows, 2, 3, 71-85,
Capital market supervision, 186
Capital markets, 22, 34, 166, 169, 180, 190
Capital mobility, 7, 22, 127
Castellan. N.J, 263
Central bank credit, 153, 203
Central bank discount policy, 69
Central bank intervention, 61
Central banks, 68, 76, 101, 159, 161, 238
Central European Economies (CEEs), 2, 24-28, 89-90, 96, 121, 149, 155, 165, 191, 247
Centrally planned economy, 6, 33, 89-90, 247, 179
Chawluk. A, 4
Clearing and Settlement System, 194
Collateral, 174
Commercial banks, 184
Commercial paper, 169, 171, 197
Commodity markets, 39
Communal bonds, 197
Competitiveness, 38, 108
Computerisation of trading systems 187, 201
Consolidation agreements, 106
Consolidation bonds, 106
Constitutional theory, 9
Contagion, 122, 125
Convergence path/trajectory, 8, 28
Convertible bonds, 168-171
Co-ordination failure, 11
Corporate banking market, 111
Corporate bond market, 166, 171
Corporate debt market, 170
Corporate investors, 174
Crawling pegs, 61
Credibility of the transition, 8
Credibility, 126
Credit allocation, 96
Credit creation, 26, 61
Cross. R, 2, 59, 64, 67
Crowding out, 159, 167
Current account convertibility, 34, 81,
Current account objective, 21
Cyprus, 59
Czech bond market, 174
Czech capital market, 255
Czech Investment funds, 185
Czech National Bank, 4, 72-74, 77, 84, 157, 184
Czech Republic, 2, 8, 14-17, 28, 40, 59-60, 69,71-85, 94, 98, 125, 157, 162, 174, 177, 177-179, 185-186, 191, 195, 198, 201, 205-206, 209-210, 212-214, 238, 253-254
Czech Securities Commission, 185
Czech Stock Market, 252, 255, 257
Daouk. H, 254
Darby, J, 67
Day-of-the-week effect, 260
Debt cancellation, 106
Debt dynamics approach, 24
Debt sustainability criteria, 18
Default risk, 124-125
Deficit stabilization, 18
Denmark, 17
Deposit protection schemes, 90
Derivative markets, 3
Direct arbitrage opportunities, 260
Domestic and foreign debt sustainability, 23
Double taxation agreement, 191
EC's First Banking Directive, 91, 101
EC's Second Directive, 91, 101
Economic Monetary Union (EMU), 2, 59-60, 67-68
Efficient bond market, 153
Emerging stock markets, 257

EMU admission criteria, 3, 59-60
Enterprise restructuring, 153, 159
Equilibrium real exchange rate, 22, 32-33, 36, 42
Equity/debt ratios, 110
Estonia, 59
Eurobonds, 85, 231
European Bank of Reconstruction and Development (EBRD), 8, 60
European Monetary System (EMS), 59-60
Exchange rate changes, 137-140
Exchange rate regime, 3, 80- 81, 126
Exchange rate risk, 74, 123- 124, 126
Exchange rate stability, 74, 126
Expectational beliefs, 63
External liberalization, 123
Fama. E.F, 253
Financial crises/turmoil, 122, 129
Financial deregulation, 201, 227
Financial intermediation, 64, 92, 118, 154
Financial market regulation, 125, 184
Financial sector/system, 2, 26, 150, 154, 182, 221
Fiscal consolidation, 25, 161, 230
Fiscal performance, 5, 16, 28
Fiscal policies, 2, 6, 75, 81, 85, 100
Fiscal targets, 5, 16, 28
Fixed exchange rate, 3, 73 –74, 80, 85
Fixed income securities, 161, 166, 195, 196-197, 206
Floating exchange rate monetarism, 61
Foreign credits 74
Foreign debt, 23, 25
Foreign direct investment, 3, 74 - 75, 129, 167, 227
Foreign exchange liberalization, 71
Foreign exchange licenses, 127
Foreign exchange regulation, 190
Foreign exchange reserves, 21, 61, 72, 219, 226, 230, 232-233
Foreign investors, 75, 96, 114, 249, 167, 185, 195, 215, 222, 226-228, 237
Foreign owned banks, 92, 113, 116-117
Foreign portfolio investment, 219, 221-223, 226-227
France, 252
Free repatriation of profits, 222
French Securities Commission, 185
French. K.R, 253
Gaspar. P, 4
Germany, 129, 252
Glasgow, 4
Government budget, 9
Gradualism, 93
Greece, 5
Hagen. J, 2, 3, 11, 12
Hallerberg, 12
Hallwood. P, 2, 31
Hard budget constraint, 34- 35
Heinemann. H, 3, 149
Heterogeneous expectations, 63
Homogenous expectations, 63
Hrncir. M, 3, 71
Hungarian banking act, 102
Hungarian Banking System, 100 -105, 108-110, 113, 116, 118
Hungarian Stock Market, 258
Hungary, 2, 5, 8, 14-17, 28, 31, 59-61, 69, 75, 95, 98, 129, 158-161, 172-174, 176-179, 190, 193, 196, 199, 205, 209, 210, 212, 223, 224-227, 247, 252, 272
Hysteresis effects, 67
Incomplete term structure, 237

Incompleteness in the term structure of interest rate, 3
Independent central bank, 8
Index of Centralization, 13, 16
Index-linked bonds, 156
Industrialized countries, 153, 166, 219
Inefficient pricing, 198
Inflation, 2, 6, 63, 81, 126, 151, 158, 164, 167, 170-171, 230
Information asymmetries, 207
Information efficiency, 255, 259, 272
Insider trading, 255, 271
Insolvency, 93-94
Institutional and regulatory changes, 100
Institutional investors, 160, 171, 174, 195, 200-201, 203, 216, 225, 236
Integration of Central European bond markets, 218-220
Integration with International Capital markets, 3
Inter-bank market, 90, 197, 203, 214
Interest rate ceilings, 123
Interest rate risk, 125
Internal balance, 2, 7, 24-28, 33, 36
International accounting standards, 127
International bond markets, 169, 229, 235
International capital markets, 3, 218-219, 224, 229, 231, 233
International Federation of Stock Exchanges (FIBV), 187
International investors, 128-129, 272, 191, 225, 227, 237
International rating houses/agencies, 181, 235
International Society of Securities Administrators (ISSA), 187
International syndicated loans, 166, 230
Investor confidence, 158
Investor protection, 248, 181
Ireland, J, 67
Issuing methods, 177-179
Italy, 17, 252
January effect, 262-263
Kähler. J, 4, 247
Keynesian perspective, 36
Kominkova. Z, 4
Labour markets, 34, 39
Legal frameworks/systems, 34, 82, 97
Lender of last resort, 123
Liquidity reserve requirements, 101
Liquidity, 3, 198-199, 218-219, 252
Loan and risk exposure, 125
Loan consolidation program/scheme, 94-95, 105-107,
London Stock Exchange, 4, 252, 270
Luxembourg, 229
Maastricht requirements, 59-60
MacDonald. R, 2, 31, 42
MacKinlay. A.C, 266
Macroeconomic equilibrium/balance, 33, 35
Macroeconomic/macro Framework, 24, 26
Managed float, 61
Market based prices, 193
Market capitalisation, 158, 201
Market efficiency, 259, 220
Market liquidity, 156
Market markers, 177, 202-204, 217
Market segmentation, 201, 209-210
Market transparency, 200
Matousek. R, 4
Maturity risk 124-125
Maturity transformation, 74, 194
Mervart. J, 4
Mexican debt crisis, 219, 221, 230

Minimum reserve requirements, 76-78
Ministry of finance, 159, 162, 164, 175-176, 181, 183-186, 195-197, 199, 208, 216, 226, 228, 236
Monetary and credit policy guidelines, 100
Monetary management, 158-159, 164
Monetary neutrality, 60-61
Monetary overhangs, 64
Monetary stability, 80, 157, 159, 162, 164, 227, 229
Money supply targets, 64
Mono-banking system, 3
Monopolistic structure, 154
Monopolized industries, 34
Moral hazard problems, 34
Mortgage bonds, 174-175
Mortgage law, 174
Mortgage markets, 174
Mortgage securities, 158
Muckova. V, 4
Multi-Annual Fiscal Adjustment Strategy (MAFAS), 2, 5, 18, 24-28
Multinational banks, 123, 127-128
Multinational companies, 170-171
Multi-party Coalition, 12
Multi-party democracy, 18
Multiple call options, 169
Municipal bonds, 173, 208, 218
National Bank of Hungary, 186
National Depository of Securities, 197
National Property Fund Bonds, 198
National Property fund, 158, 226
National savings bank, 90
National Stock Exchanges, 200
Natural rate hypothesis (NRH), 65
Neneman. J, 4
Netherlands, 17, 252
Non-arbitrage conditions, 259
Non-bank intermediary system, 118
Non-performing loans, 63, 90, 94, 105
Non-state bond market, 164, 167, 171, 197, 208
Non-traded goods, 34–35
OECD Development Center, 5
OECD economic surveys, 16
OECD, 203, 218, 220, 222, 224, 227
Off-budget funds, 10, 16
Open market operations, 76, 78
Operational risk, 254
Parallel market, 207, 249
Parliamentary stage, 12
Poland, 2, 5, 8, 14-17, 28, 31, 42, 59-61, 69, 75, 96, 98, 129,191, 193, 197, 202, 205, 209, 212, 217, 223, 224-225, 232-234, 254, 257
Policy assignment, 18-20, 23
Policy matrix, 24- 28
Policy mix, 75, 81, 83
Polish Association of Brokerage Houses, 197
Polish banking system, 171
Polish banks, 217
Polish bond market, 228
Polish budget deficit, 165
Polish capital account, 236
Polish capital market, 182, 183, 216
Polish government debt, 236
Polish Securities Commission, 197
Polish Stock Market, 258
Political economy of budgeting, 11
Portfolio capital, 219
Portifolio cleaning, 93
Portugal, 5, 17
Poterba. J, 11, 265

Prague Stock Exchange (PSE), 184-185, 188-189, 195, 196, 201-202, 206-208, 210-211, 216, 249-253, 271-272
Prague, 4, 251-252, 255, 271-272
Pre-announced devaluations, 69
Pre-Pegged Exchange Rate (PPERR), 2, 7, 18, 24 - 28
Price/earnings ratio, 252
Pricing of non-state securities, 155
Primary (budget) deficit, 8, 20, 22, 24
Primary markets, 150, 160, 181, 214
Private savings rates, 153
Private sector bonds, 197
Privatization, 96 –98, 113
Productivity gains, 129
Profit repatriation, 220
Profitability, 92-93, 96, 113-116
Proprietary trading system, 201
Prsuki. J , 4
Prudent bank management, 93
Public debt sustainability, 23
Public deficit financing, 200
Public sector deficit/debt, 6, 23, 25, 152, 176
Quote-driven trading, 255
Raczko. A, 4
Rational expectations, 62-63
Real exchange rate, 21, 31-36
Real interest rates, 22
Regional interdependence, 126
Resource allocation, 2, 31
Restructuring the banking sector, 95
Risk premium, 21, 22
Risk provision, 106
Russia, 3, 75
Russian crisis, 127-129, 271
Secondary market, 150, 159, 193-194 196, 248-249
Second-tier market, 247-248
Securities and exchange commission, 183, 185, 196, 255
Securities law, 195, 197, 198
Segmented banking market, 90, 93
Share price index, 255, 272
Short-term bank credit, 166
Siegel. S, 263
Simpson's paradox, 253
Slovak National Bank, 4
Slovak securities center, 197
Slovakia/Slovak Republic, 2, 5, 8, 14-17, 28, 41-42, 59-61, 69, 126, 185-186, 190,192, 197-199, 205, 209-210, 212-214, 223, 224, 228, 235, 247, 250
Slovakian Stock Market, 251, 258
Social safety nets 67
Social security, 15
Soft budget constraint, 34-35
Solvency ratio, 101
South East Asian crisis 127-129
Spain, 5, 17, 18
Speculative bubbles, 63, 257
State owned banks, 90
Steiger. M, 3, 149
Sterilization, 76- 80
Stock exchange, 197-199, 201, 205, 213, 228, 207-211
Stock market capitalization, 147, 252
Stock market development,1 57, 200
Stop and go reform pattern, 6
Structural adjustment, 18, 28
Summers. L, 265
Supplementary budgets, 12
Syndicated loans, 171
Systematic arbitrage profits, 260
Systemic stability, 182
Tax reform, 8
Term structure of interest rates, 3
Traded goods, 34 –35, 63
Trading time hypothesis, 261
Treasury bills, 78, 248
Turn-of-year-liquidity hypothesis, 263

Two tier banking system, 89, 98-100, 105, 108
UK Stock Market, 247
Uncovered interest rate parity, 22
Undercapitalisation, 69
Undercapitalised banks, 107
Uni-cameral system, 12
Universal banking model, 91, 101
Universal settlement center, 196
Várhegyi. E, 3, 89
Variograms, 268
Verbeck. G.A. W, 221
Viségrad Indices, 255-258, 263, 265, 268, 270
Vos.R, 221
Voting procedure, 16
Voucher privatisation, 96, 272
Warsaw Stock Exchange (WSE), 96, 203, 188-189, 201-202, 206-208, 218 249, 256
Weak regulation, 90
Week-end-effect, 261
Weller. C, 3
Withholding taxes, 254